ON THE THRESHOLD

EDINBURGH CRITICAL STUDIES IN SHAKESPEARE AND PHILOSOPHY
Series Editor: Kevin Curran

Edinburgh Critical Studies in Shakespeare and Philosophy takes seriously the speculative and world-making properties of Shakespeare's art. Maintaining a broad view of 'philosophy' that accommodates first-order questions of metaphysics, ethics, politics and aesthetics, the series also expands our understanding of philosophy to include the unique kinds of theoretical work carried out by performance and poetry itself. These scholarly monographs will reinvigorate Shakespeare studies by opening new interdisciplinary conversations among scholars, artists and students.

Editorial Board Members
Ewan Fernie, Shakespeare Institute, University of Birmingham
James Kearney, University of California, Santa Barbara
Julia Reinhard Lupton, University of California, Irvine
Madhavi Menon, Ashoka University
Simon Palfrey, Oxford University
Tiffany Stern, Shakespeare Institute, University of Birmingham
Henry Turner, Rutgers University
Michael Witmore, The Folger Shakespeare Library
Paul Yachnin, McGill University

Published Titles
Rethinking Shakespeare's Political Philosophy: From Lear to Leviathan
Alex Schulman
Shakespeare in Hindsight: Counterfactual Thinking and Shakespearean Tragedy
Amir Khan
Second Death: Theatricalities of the Soul in Shakespeare's Drama
Donovan Sherman
Shakespeare's Fugitive Politics
Thomas P. Anderson
Is Shylock Jewish?: Citing Scripture and the Moral Agency of Shakespeare's Jews
Sara Coodin
Chaste Value: Economic Crisis, Female Chastity and the Production of Social Difference on Shakespeare's Stage
Katherine Gillen
Shakespearean Melancholy: Philosophy, Form and the Transformation of Comedy
J. F. Bernard
Shakespeare's Moral Compass
Neema Parvini
Shakespeare and the Fall of the Roman Republic: Selfhood, Stoicism and Civil War
Patrick Gray
Revenge Tragedy and Classical Philosophy on the Early Modern Stage
Christopher Crosbie
Shakespeare and the Truth-Teller: Confronting the Cynic Ideal
David Hershinow
Derrida Reads Shakespeare
Chiara Alfano
Conceiving Desire in Lyly and Shakespeare: Metaphor, Cognition and Eros
Gillian Knoll
Immateriality and Early Modern English Literature: Shakespeare, Donne, Herbert
James A. Knapp
Hazarding All: Shakespeare and the Drama of Consciousness
Sanford Budick
Touching at a Distance: Shakespeare's Theatre
Johannes Ungelenk
Shakespeare, the Reformation and the Interpreting Self
Roberta Kwan
On the Threshold: Hospitality in Shakespeare's Drama
Sophie E. Battell

Forthcoming Titles
Making Publics in Shakespeare's Playhouse
Paul Yachnin
The Play and the Thing: A Phenomenology of Shakespearean Theatre
Matthew Wagner
Shakespeare, Levinas and Adaptation
Lisa Starks
Shakespeare's Theatre of Judgment: Seven Keywords
Kevin Curran

For further information please visit our website at: edinburghuniversitypress.com/series/ecsst

ON THE THRESHOLD

Hospitality in Shakespeare's Drama

◆ ◆ ◆

SOPHIE E. BATTELL

EDINBURGH
University Press

Edinburgh University Press is one of the leading university presses in the UK. We publish academic books and journals in our selected subject areas across the humanities and social sciences, combining cutting-edge scholarship with high editorial and production values to produce academic works of lasting importance. For more information visit our website: edinburghuniversitypress.com

© Sophie Battell 2023, 2025 under a Creative Commons Attribution-NonCommercial licence

The open access version of this publication was funded by the Swiss National Science Foundation.

Edinburgh University Press Ltd
13 Infirmary Street
Edinburgh EH1 1LT

First published in hardback by Edinburgh University Press 2023

Typeset in 12/15 Adobe Sabon by
IDSUK (DataConnection) Ltd

A CIP record for this book is available from the British Library

ISBN 978 1 4744 7568 6 (hardback)
ISBN 978 1 4744 7569 3 (paperback)
ISBN 978 1 4744 7570 9 (webready PDF)
ISBN 978 1 4744 7571 6 (epub)

The right of Sophie Battell to be identified as the author of this work has been asserted in accordance with the Copyright, Designs and Patents Act 1988, and the Copyright and Related Rights Regulations 2003 (SI No. 2498).

CONTENTS

Acknowledgements vii
Series Editor's Preface x

    Introduction 1

1. Hospitality and the Supernatural in *The Comedy of Errors* 12
2. Cosmopolitan Soundscapes in *The Merchant of Venice* 58
3. *Troilus and Cressida*: Militarised Encounters 104
4. *Timon of Athens* and Parasitology 134
5. Secretive Hosts in *Pericles* 175

    Afterword 222

Bibliography 225
Index 245

*For Aidan
and in memory of my grandmother*

ACKNOWLEDGEMENTS

This book began as a PhD thesis completed at Cardiff University, and my greatest thanks are due to Martin Coyle for his erudite supervision and intellectual generosity and for supporting me, then and subsequently, in ways too countless to list here. I am grateful to my examiners, Kiernan Ryan and Julia Thomas, for their invaluable comments, and for pushing me to think harder about this topic. In the time it took for this book to be written, I have been fortunate to work alongside many inspiring colleagues at Cardiff and later at the University of Exeter. Particular thanks to medieval and early modern colleagues Derek Dunne, Rob Gossedge, Johann Menon-Gregory, Irene Morra, Carl Phelpstead, Ceri Sullivan and Naya Tsentourou. Jason Baskin personally ensured that I retained access to research materials after I left Penryn, and I cannot thank him enough for his kindness and support. For their friendship and encouragement with the writing process, and much else besides, thanks to Alix Beeston, Megan Leitch, Chris Müller, Varsha Panjwani, Chloe Preedy, Sheri Smith, Mark Truesdale, Alex Watson, Emma West and Rachel Willie. I am glad to acknowledge the support of the Residential Research Library at Durham University, the Centre for Privacy Studies at the University of Copenhagen, and the Herzog August Bibliothek for the award of research fellowships which provided financial assistance as well as time to think and write in idyllic surroundings. Conversations with the following colleagues not only benefited this project, but ensured these trips were a lot of fun: Sara Ayres, Matteo Binasco, Mette Birkedal Bruun, Patrick Gray, Michaël Green, Anni Haahr Henriksen, Adam Horsley, Natacha Klein Käfer, Karly Kehoe, James Kelly, Johannes Ljungberg, Frank Ejby Poulsen, Maj Riis Poulsen, Elizabeth Swann and Toth Zsombor. My thanks to the British Academy and the Council for British Research in the Levant for funding my participation in the Knowledge Frontiers Symposium on 'Belonging'. Alongside the rich scholarly exchanges in Amman, I am glad to have experienced first-hand the wonder that is Jordanian hospitality. *Danke* to my colleagues in the English department at the University of Zurich for the warm welcome and for helping me integrate into a lively and vibrant research culture, especially Antoinina Bevan Zlatar, Elisabeth Bronfen, Stella Castelli, Michael Frank, Isabel Karremann, Thomas Keller, Anne-Claire Michoux, Beatrice Montedoro, Martin Mühlheim, Barbara Straumann and Shane Walshe. Emigrating while completing a book on immigration is a decisive experience. Alice Ragueneau in the international office kindly answered a million questions. For their assistance when it came to finding my own home in Switzerland, endless thanks to Johannes Le Blanc, Malin Stomeo, Nina Suter and Katherine Williams. I am grateful to the upper-level undergraduate and postgraduate students at Zurich who took my lecture course on 'Migrants, Guests, Strangers: Hospitality in Shakespeare'. Our classroom discussions came late in the book-writing process but reinvigorated my thinking on many of the plays and concepts explored in the following pages. Special thanks to Julia Reinhard Lupton for giving a guest lecture on this module over Zoom (at an ungodly time of the morning in California!), as well as her continuing support of me and this project over many years. At Edinburgh University Press, I am indebted to Michelle Houston for her astute editorship and advice, and the two anonymous readers for the Press whose constructive comments improved the manuscript. It is a better book for their involvement. Sincere gratitude to Kevin Curran for his belief in this project, thoughtful feedback and clear editorial vision. I am proud to be part of a series which takes seriously the 'world-making dimensions of Shakespeare's work'. Thank you to Susannah Butler, Fiona Conn, Elizabeth Fraser, Emily Sharp and all the staff at Edinburgh University Press for their guidance throughout the publication process.

Some material has already been published elsewhere. A subsection of Chapter 1 appeared in *Textual Practice* as 'Shakespeare and the Economics of the Death Penalty'. Part of Chapter 3 was published in *Études Épistémè* as '"[L]ike a fountain stirred": Impure Hospitality in *Troilus and Cressida*'. Small sections from Chapter 4 were included in '"Thou weep'st to make them drink": Hospitality and Mourning in *Timon of Athens*', in *The Routledge Companion to Shakespeare and Philosophy*, ed. Craig Bourne and Emily Caddick Bourne. Part of Chapter 5 was published in *Shakespeare* as '*Pericles* and the Secret'. I am grateful for the permission to reproduce the earlier work here. I am pleased to recognize the generous support of the Swiss National Science Foundation for funding to publish the book Gold Open Access, and many thanks to Amy Brown, who first drew this grant to my attention and suggested that I might apply.

My late grandmother, Margaret Knaggs, loved words: books, cryptic crossword puzzles, word wheels, Scrabble, and she always had the *Oxford English Dictionary* within reach. I dedicate *these words* to her with love and gratitude. I would also like to thank my father, John Battell, for being supportive of me and for taking an interest in my work. Finally, it is hard to put into words the appreciation which I feel for my partner, Aidan Tynan. Suffice to say that books are a long time in the making, and he has been there from the beginning.

SERIES EDITOR'S PREFACE

Picture Macbeth alone on stage, staring intently into empty space. 'Is this a dagger which I see before me?' he asks, grasping decisively at the air. On one hand, this is a quintessentially theatrical question. At once an object and a vector, the dagger describes the possibility of knowledge ('Is this a dagger') in specifically visual and spatial terms ('which I see before me'). At the same time, Macbeth is posing a quintessentially philosophical question, one that assumes knowledge to be both conditional and experiential, and that probes the relationship between certainty and perception as well as intention and action. It is from this shared ground of art and inquiry, of theatre and theory, that this series advances its basic premise: Shakespeare is philosophical.

It seems like a simple enough claim. But what does it mean exactly, beyond the parameters of this specific moment in *Macbeth*? Does it mean that Shakespeare had something we could think of as his own philosophy? Does it mean that he was influenced by particular philosophical schools, texts and thinkers? Does it mean, conversely, that modern philosophers have been influenced by him, that Shakespeare's plays and poems have been, and continue to be, resources for philosophical thought and speculation?

The answer is yes all around. These are all useful ways of conceiving a philosophical Shakespeare and all point to lines of inquiry that this series welcomes. But Shakespeare is philosophical in a much more fundamental way as well. Shakespeare is philosophical because the plays and poems actively create new worlds of knowledge and new scenes of ethical encounter. They ask big questions, make bold arguments and develop new vocabularies in order to think what might otherwise be unthinkable. Through both their scenarios and their imagery, the plays and poems engage the qualities of consciousness, the consequences of human action, the phenomenology of motive and attention, the conditions of personhood and the relationship among different orders of reality and experience. This is writing and dramaturgy, moreover, that consistently experiments with a broad range of conceptual crossings, between love and subjectivity, nature and politics, and temporality and form.

Edinburgh Critical Studies in Shakespeare and Philosophy takes seriously these speculative and world-making dimensions of Shakespeare's work. The series proceeds from a core conviction that art's capacity to think – to formulate, not just reflect, ideas – is what makes it urgent and valuable. Art matters because unlike other human activities it establishes its own frame of reference, reminding us that all acts of creation – biological, political, intellectual and amorous – are grounded in imagination. This is a far cry from business-as-usual in Shakespeare studies. Because historicism remains the methodological gold standard of the field, far more energy has been invested in exploring what Shakespeare once meant than in thinking rigorously about what Shakespeare continues to make possible. In response, Edinburgh Critical Studies in Shakespeare and Philosophy pushes back against the critical orthodoxies of historicism and cultural studies to clear a space for scholarship that confronts aspects of literature that can neither be reduced to nor adequately explained by particular historical contexts.

Shakespeare's creations are not just inheritances of a past culture, frozen artefacts whose original settings must be expertly reconstructed in order to be understood. The plays and poems are also living art, vital thought-worlds that struggle, across time, with foundational questions of metaphysics, ethics, politics and aesthetics. With this orientation in mind, Edinburgh Critical Studies in Shakespeare and Philosophy offers a series of scholarly monographs that will reinvigorate Shakespeare studies by opening new interdisciplinary conversations among scholars, artists and students.

Kevin Curran

INTRODUCTION

> Nor sleep nor sanctuary,
> Being naked, sick, nor fane nor Capitol,
> The prayers of priests, nor times of sacrifice –
> Embargements all of fury – shall lift up
> Their rotten privilege and custom 'gainst
> My hate to Martius. Where I find him, were it
> At home upon my brother's guard, even there,
> Against the hospitable canon, would I
> Wash my fierce hand in's heart.[1]

Contradictory as it may appear, when we start thinking about hospitality in Shakespeare, what likely comes to mind first are some of the ways in which this relationship can go spectacularly wrong. Readers of the plays will encounter murderous hosts, a cannibal cook, and all manner of devious or untrustworthy guests. Tarquin, Titus Andronicus, the Macbeths, and a cast of other characters who commit acts of violence under the pretext of offering or receiving welcome knowingly violate what Aufidius in *Coriolanus* refers to above as 'the hospitable canon'. Found across nearly every world culture, these are the unwritten laws meant to safeguard guests and hosts from harm. Self-consciously styling himself as a revenger whose 'fury' knows no bounds, Aufidius claims that his hatred for

Caius Martius, and resolve to be revenged upon him, is so great that he will show no mercy even if they should meet in a setting which is held to be sacred. By visualising himself committing murder inside a space of 'sanctuary', or 'home upon my brother's guard', Aufidius equates hospitality with other mystical and quasi-religious experiences.

This is a book about the relationship between guests and hosts in Shakespeare's theatre. *Coriolanus* attests to the fact that hospitality is not without risk or danger. Yet within the discourses of theology and anthropology, the sacred stranger tradition claims that unexpected guests should be welcomed lest they turn out to be angels in disguise. In this book, we will come across extraordinary gestures of welcome and meet individuals who are determined to forge intimate connections with one another against all odds and sometimes in strange circumstances. Alongside treacherous guests and hosts, *On the Threshold* explores the miraculous nature of hospitality, revealing how, in the right hands, the welcome of strangers can assume a healing, messianic and life-restoring power. As I will show, hospitality not only informs the legal, economic and political landscapes of the plays, but also offers a searching analysis of their values and ethics as these are enacted on stage. More than simple salutations, hospitality relates to a set of *contested thresholds* fashioned by lively interactions between inside and outside, belonging and non-belonging, citizen and alien. These exchanges are crucial to encounters which are moving and life-affirming, but my investigation is also deeply invested in the situations of xenophobia, intolerance and exclusion from the centre which tend to occur when hospitality fails or turns to violence. We must therefore consider questions of ethics, politics and philosophy in far-reaching ways that range from the individual body to the state.

Critical work over the last three decades has shone light on some of the complexities which surround this seemingly mundane relationship. Jacques Derrida's *Of Hospitality* seminars and related writings have been extremely influential in this regard. Derrida studied the conditions which prevent hospitality from being given unreservedly, inviting consideration of the demands that hosts place upon their guests and vice versa, and the ways in which this creates an economy of debt and obligation. Another legacy of this body of work is a greater appreciation for how hospitality is predisposed to violence. Yet while justly credited with bringing about a theoretical revival in the scholarship on hospitality, Derrida was hardly the only Francophone thinker to speak to this topic in the 1990s. *Le Livre de l'hospitalité* by French-Egyptian writer Edmond Jabès was published in 1991, and award-winning Moroccan novelist Tahar Ben Jelloun's *French Hospitality: Racism and North African Immigrants* appeared in print eight years later. These two texts have further enriched our understanding of the way hospitality dovetails with and is intersected by the larger political environment. Space prevents me from tracing the many directions that the field has gone in since then, but I think it is worth noting the impact of this revival on postcolonial criticism. Mireille Rosello's *Postcolonial Hospitality: The Immigrant as Guest* deepens our knowledge of what it means to conceptualise immigration in terms of guest and host behaviours, arguing that 'hospitality as metaphor blurs the distinction between a discourse of rights and a discourse of generosity, the language of social contracts and the language of excess and gift-giving'.[2] Rosello's comment is pertinent to the wider argument of this book, because much of the ensuing discussion is focused not simply on individual actors, but on government policy and the responsibility of host nations in granting or denying the admission of strangers.

At this point, it is worth pausing to explain how I will be using the term 'hospitality' in the chapters which follow. According to the *Oxford English Dictionary*, to be 'hospitable' means 'affording welcome and entertainment to strangers; extending a generous hospitality to guests and visitors'.[3] But the same entry adds that the word can be used in a more intangible sense as well, either to denote 'things, feelings, qualities' or to mean 'open and generous in mind or disposition'.[4] In this book, I move freely between these separate emphases, considering gifts, banquets and the shelter or accommodation of strangers alongside the senses and emotions and the role of intentionality or temperament. I frequently return to the etymology of hospitality to inform the analysis. In his *Dictionary of Indo-European Concepts and Society*, Émile Benveniste notes that the 'classical meaning "enemy"' is contained within the Latin *hostis* (which translates as 'guest').[5] As he puts it, '"stranger, enemy, guest" are global notions of a somewhat vague character'.[6] Numerous world languages share an etymological bridge between guest and enemy, a fact which did not go unnoticed by Jacques Derrida, who coined the expression 'hostipitality' in order to articulate the affinity of hospitality and hostility. In addition, Benveniste points out that the Latin word *hospes* 'is an ancient compound', of which '[t]he second component alternates with *pot-*, which signifies "master," so that the literal sense of *hospes* is "the guest-master"'.[7] This complex etymology has implications for my reading of the plays and, in particular, their concern with violence and mastery.

The word 'hospitality' occurs only twice in Shakespeare's vocabulary: in the poem *The Rape of Lucrece* and in *As You Like It*.[8] Far more widespread are examples of 'welcome' and its many variants, which appear almost four hundred times. In conjunction with the reception of strangers, the plays and poems often allude to doorways, windows, entranceways and other architectural features of the built environment. Accordingly, the title to this book, *On the Threshold*, serves two purposes. It gestures towards the spatial imaginary of hospitality in the early modern theatre. As we will see, however, borders or boundary lines are as often as not *immaterial*, for these texts are filled with unseen obstacles to hospitality. Moreover, the title seeks to convey the transformative nature of this relationship. For the persons involved, accepting (or declining) an invitation can be a defining moment or turning point. Anthropologists and ethnographers who analyse social behaviours are familiar with this phenomenon. Arnold van Gennep has charted the ceremonies by which an individual moves between different social groups. Following van Gennep, Julian Pitt-Rivers notes how, through contests or trials of strength, outsiders can either be incorporated into communities or rejected by them.[9]

Thresholds are an impediment to strangers, yet they offer the means for their inclusion and assimilation. Doorways and other entrances are charged spaces, synonymous in Shakespeare with heightened emotion. Consider, for example, the scene where Coriolanus enters Aufidius' home uninvited. Recognising the unexpected visitor, Aufidius says:

> Know thou first,
> I loved the maid I married; never man
> Sighed truer breath. But that I see thee here,
> Thou noble thing, more dances my rapt heart
> Than when I first my wedded mistress saw
> Bestride my threshold.
> (4.5.115–20)

These lines capture the eroticism and danger of the threshold encounter. James Heffernan makes a related observation in *Hospitality and Treachery in Western Literature*, when comparing hospitality to the headlong sensation of falling in love:

> Yet if hospitality can occasionally furnish something like the pleasures of love, it also resembles love in exposing all of its parties to the perils of intimacy. To fall in love is to give someone the power to break your heart. To ask one or more people into your home, whether to dine at your table, sleep under your roof, or simply converse, is to give them the power to complicate your life right up to the act of taking it.[10]

Hospitality's capacity to foster pleasure and intimacy is reflected in the cover image to this book, *Two Women at a Window* by seventeenth-century Seville painter Bartolomé Esteban Murillo. In the painting, two women look out at the spectator from a window. One of the women is partly concealed behind a wooden shutter, and then again by her headscarf, which she holds up to her mouth. Her younger companion stares directly at us, smiling and visibly amused. *Two Women at a Window* is an enigmatic work, which has led art historians to speculate on whether the subjects are prostitutes, soliciting street custom from their window. Murillo's composition invites continued contemplation of who these two women are and what they find so entertaining. Framed by the window, on a threshold which is architectural, and maybe economic or class based as well, they seem on the cusp of offering us welcome.

Within early modern studies, hospitality has emerged as a serious category of study in its own right. Important cultural histories by Felicity Heal and Daryl Palmer appeared in the 1990s and have done much to increase our awareness of the material practices of welcoming guests in early modern England.[11] Since then, another major strand of literary scholarship has both responded to and reinforced the revival of hospitality in French philosophy. Influential scholars including Julia Reinhard Lupton, David Goldstein, Kevin Curran, Paul Kottman and David Ruiter have conducted theoretically informed readings of hospitality in Shakespeare. The 2016 publication of a volume of essays on *Shakespeare and Hospitality*, co-edited by Lupton and Goldstein, confirmed this as a vibrant topic of academic concern.[12] Developing the insightful work of these critics, *On the Threshold* seeks to intervene in the field of theoretical literary studies. Despite a growing interest in the topic, there is currently no detailed or full-scale inquiry into how Shakespeare's theatre represents hospitality as a matter of ethical, philosophical and political importance. As well as filling this gap, the book makes several other interventions in the critical landscape. To begin with, it provides a comprehensive reassessment of the guest and host dynamic in Shakespeare, proposing a new way of approaching the subject. In contrast to earlier books on this topic by Heal and Palmer, as well as Lupton's 2018 monograph, *Shakespeare Dwelling: Designs for the Theatre of Life*, all of which are aligned with the material culture of early modern domesticity, the methodology advanced in *On the Threshold* is at once larger and smaller in scale.[13] Larger for two reasons. First, I consider the nation state to be a significant player in the hospitality relationship, which, in places, leads the discussion into political territory, particularly issues related to immigration and asylum. As I argue in the first two chapters on *The Comedy of Errors* and *The Merchant of Venice*, inhospitality can become an official part of diplomatic relations, creating for outsiders a hostile environment. Second, my critical method extends beyond the household, for I examine how hospitality reflects the ethical or moral universe of the drama. In other words, I see hospitality as integral to the larger framing of the plays and not merely one of their themes. Conversely, my approach is, at times, microscopic in scale because I pay attention to some of the ways in which hospitality is experienced at the level of the body, the senses and the emotions. Troilus' dizzy sensation of being whirled around with excitement while he waits on the threshold to meet Cressida alone for the first time is just one example of how scenes of welcome are performed through quickened heartrates, blushing faces, and in every particle or atom of the encounters that they enact. Informed by the groundbreaking research agenda of Patricia Parker and Molly Mahood, *On the Threshold* sets out to uncover the marginal, the unnoticed or what has previously been overlooked.[14] I read, then, for a poetics of hospitality, analysing how it is interwoven into the language, senses and rich texture of these plays.

From this overview, it will be clear that another of the book's contributions is its contention that we should separate our notion of hospitality from the household. As we will discover, hospitality takes place in all manner of surprising settings, from the warzone to the courtroom, in the woods or on the beach. Ultimately, the goal of this monograph is to add complexity to the literary study of hospitality by uncovering a fuller picture of what it means to welcome outsiders. In so doing, I construct an interdisciplinary framework which draws on fields like philosophy, postcolonial studies, economic theory, anthropology and ecocriticism to expand our understanding of this key term. Finally, a few brief qualifications on scope and limitations, or what this book does *not* try to do. Given the subject matter, I am indebted to the existing work on stranger relations, especially Leslie Fieldler's classic investigation of *The Stranger in Shakespeare* and Marianne Novy's *Shakespeare and Outsiders*.[15] Yet this book is and is not about strangers. Indeed, they are everywhere in the pages which follow – along with tourists, travellers, refugees and other people on the move – but where this study diverges from its critical predecessors is that it is not concerned with cataloguing the different types of outsider in Shakespeare, however rigidly (Fieldler) or with greater fluidity (Novy). I am rather interested in exploring the guest and host interaction in the drama and what pressures shape it. Following Derrida, I seek to better understand what holds hospitality back from being granted unconditionally, asking how and why it ends up becoming so provisional and qualified. It is not my intention to recreate the everyday life of the early modern household, nor does this monograph attempt to provide a material reconstruction of hospitality in Shakespeare's England, fascinating though such work undoubtedly is. Lastly, *On the Threshold* is not about what today is commonly referred to as the 'hospitality industry', and which, in the early modern period, we can recognise as the growing commercialisation of inns and taverns. Even though it would be intriguing to conduct, for example, a survey of tavern scenes in the history plays, these profit-driven settings leave little margin for ambiguity in terms of guest and host conduct, and are therefore less relevant to my purposes.

This book appears at a time when governments the world over are closing their borders, building walls, and passing punitive immigration legislation, all of which is designed to keep strangers out. We are witnessing a surge in the criminalisation of migrants and the establishment of ever more hostile environments. In the chapters to come, I present close readings of the poetics of Shakespearean hospitality, in terms of the language and the anxieties that shape it, and in its unexpected form and shapes, its diverse being and manifestations. But it is hoped that *On the Threshold* will have broader applications beyond the literature of the early modern period. In foregrounding hospitality, the book aims to encourage critical reflection about what it means to be a welcoming person, place or nation state, as well as the ongoing socio-political and moral implications of rejecting outsiders. Alongside its intended readership of Shakespeare students and literary scholars, I hope that this study may be useful to readers interested in pressing questions of home and belonging, citizenship and exclusion, immigration and asylum. The stories told here of welcome offered or denied in the theatre space convey not only the tensions and concerns informing this relationship, but also the cultural resonances and implications for human action.

Notes

1. William Shakespeare, *Coriolanus*, ed. Peter Holland (London: Bloomsbury, 2013), 1.10.19–27. Further references are to this edition and given parenthetically in the text.
2. Mireille Rosello, *Postcolonial Hospitality: The Immigrant as Guest* (Stanford: Stanford University Press, 2001), p. 9.

3. 'Hospitable, adj.', *OED Online*.
4. 'Hospitable, adj.', *OED Online*.
5. Émile Benveniste, *Dictionary of Indo-European Concepts and Society*, trans. Elizabeth Palmer (Chicago: HAU Books, 2016), p. 61.
6. Benveniste, *Dictionary of Indo-European Concepts*, p. 66.
7. Benveniste, *Dictionary of Indo-European Concepts*, p. 62.
8. William Shakespeare, *The Rape of Lucrece*, in *Shakespeare's Poems*, ed. Katherine Duncan-Jones and H. R. Woudhuysen (London: Bloomsbury, 2007), l. 575, and William Shakespeare, *As You Like It*, ed. Juliet Dusinberre (London: Bloomsbury, 2006), 2.4.81.
9. Arnold van Gennep, *The Rites of Passage*, trans. Monika B. Yizedom and Gabrielle L. Caffee (Chicago: University of Chicago Press, 1960), and Julian Pitt-Rivers, 'The Law of Hospitality', in *From Hospitality to Grace: A Julian Pitt-Rivers Omnibus*, ed. Giovanni da Col and Andrew Shryock (Chicago: HAU Books, 2017), pp. 163–84.
10. James A. W. Heffernan, *Hospitality and Treachery in Western Literature* (New Haven and London: Yale University Press, 2014), p. 1.
11. Felicity Heal, *Hospitality in Early Modern England* (Oxford: Oxford University Press, 1990), and Daryl Palmer, *Hospitable Performances: Dramatic Genre and Cultural Practices in Early Modern England* (West Lafayette: Purdue University Press, 1992).
12. Julia Reinhard Lupton, 'Making Room, Affording Hospitality: Environments of Entertainment in *Romeo and Juliet*', *Journal of Medieval and Early Modern Studies*, 43:1 (2013), 145–72; *Shakespeare and Hospitality: Ethics, Politics, and Exchange*, ed. David B. Goldstein and Julia Reinhard Lupton (London and New York: Routledge, 2016); Kevin Curran, 'Hospitable Justice: Law and Selfhood in Shakespeare's Sonnets', *Law, Culture and the Humanities*, 9:2 (2013), 295–310; Paul Kottman, 'Hospitality in the Interval: *Macbeth*'s Door', *Oxford Literary Review*, 18:1 (1996), 87–115; David Ruiter, 'Shakespeare and Hospitality: Opening *The Winter's Tale*', *Mediterranean Studies*, 16 (2007), 157–77.

13. Julia Reinhard Lupton, *Shakespeare Dwelling: Designs for the Theatre of Life* (Chicago: University of Chicago Press, 2018).
14. Patricia Parker, *Shakespeare from the Margins: Language, Culture, Context* (Chicago: University of Chicago Press, 1996); Molly Mahood, *Bit Parts in Shakespeare's Plays* (Cambridge: Cambridge University Press, 1992).
15. Leslie Fiedler, *The Stranger in Shakespeare* (New York: Stein and Day, 1973); Marianne Novy, *Shakespeare and Outsiders* (Oxford: Oxford University Press, 2013).

CHAPTER 1

HOSPITALITY AND THE SUPERNATURAL IN *THE COMEDY OF ERRORS*

Newly arrived in Ephesus and unable to understand why the locals not only seem to know his name, but are insistent that he and his master join them for dinner, Dromio of Syracuse says to himself:

> O, for my beads! I cross me [*crossing himself*] for a sinner.
> This is the fairy land; O, spite of spites,
> We talk with goblins, owls and sprites!
> If we obey them not, this will ensue:
> They'll suck our breath or pinch us black and blue.[1]

Alluding to the town's longstanding reputation for black magic and the occult, Dromio of Syracuse predicts a future of violent subjugation by the inhabitants of this 'fairy land'.[2] Wishing he had his rosary beads to guide him through prayers for spiritual protection, Dromio settles for visibly making the sign of the cross over his body. If it seems incongruous for him to use the practices of the Christian Church to fight supernatural threats like 'goblins, owls and sprites', then the reality for people in the late medieval and early modern period was more complex. As Eamon Duffy has shown, 'the dividing line between prayer and magic is not always clear'.[3]

Hospitality and the Supernatural in *The Comedy of Errors*

Magic and the supernatural occupy an ambivalent place in *The Comedy of Errors*. On the one hand, the existence of the two pairs of identical twins provides a rational justification for the 'one-day's error' (5.1.397) which would appear to negate the otherworldly explanations sought by so many of the characters, including Dromio of Syracuse above. And yet, the supernatural retains a compelling hold over the drama. Kent Cartwright notes that 'the play concedes residual power to the idea of magic'.[4] Jan Frans van Dijkhuizen has drawn attention to the sharp rise in the number of recorded cases of individuals being possessed by demons throughout the 1580s and 1590s, meaning that *The Comedy of Errors* was 'performed when the interest in demonic possession in England was at its peak'.[5] Almost certainly intended to capitalise on the contemporary popularity of accounts of demonic possession – many of which ran to the remarkable or lurid – *The Comedy of Errors* includes two exorcisms, as well as numerous other references to the conjuring of spirits and uses of apotropaic magic.

This chapter considers the supernatural environment of *The Comedy of Errors*, using it as a way of articulating the play's wider interest in how strangers are welcomed or excluded. In what follows, I suggest that the supposed presence of the occult in Ephesus usefully directs our attention onto those individuals who, for different reasons, find themselves on the fringes of the dominant culture: the enslaved twin brothers, Dromio and Dromio, or Egeon, the refugee from Syracuse, for instance.[6] Refugees and asylum seekers, like ghosts, are visitors who appear unannounced and without invitation. In asking for our hospitality, they proceed to make an ethical claim on us. 'The whole essence', Avery F. Gordon notes, 'if you can use that word, of a ghost is that it has a real presence and demands its due, your attention.'[7]

Across academic disciplines the figure of the outsider has long been associated with a disconcerting opacity. In 'The

Law of Hospitality', the anthropologist and ethnographer Julian Pitt-Rivers argues that '[t]he essence of the stranger is, tautologically enough, that he is unknown. He remains potentially anything: valiant or worthless, well-born, well-connected, wealthy or the contrary, and since his assertions regarding himself cannot be checked, he is above all not to be trusted.'[8] Similarly, in *Strangers at Our Door*, Polish sociologist Zygmunt Bauman shows how '[s]trangers tend to cause anxiety precisely because of being "strange" – and so, fearsomely unpredictable, unlike the people with whom we interact daily and from whom we believe we know what to expect.'[9] The unknowability of the stranger and, above all, their motivations towards us poses an interpretative challenge which is accentuated in situations where the newcomer is believed to be a supernatural being. Shakespeare's famous example of ghostly indeterminacy is *Hamlet*. Once Hamlet encounters the ghost bearing a striking resemblance to his dead father, he resolves to speak to it even though he realises that he cannot know for sure whether it is a good or evil spirit:

> Angels and ministers of grace defend us!
> Be thou a spirit of health or goblin damned,
> Bring with thee airs from heaven or blasts from hell,
> Be thy intentions wicked or charitable,
> Thou com'st in such a questionable shape
> That I will speak to thee.[10]

Throughout this passage, the juxtaposition of good and evil stresses the ghost's ontological indeterminacy, which becomes a more pressing concern after it asks Hamlet to take revenge for his murder by killing Claudius. While Hamlet delays, it is on the grounds that the spirit might be a devil come to tempt him to damn himself by committing a mortal sin. Although *The Comedy of Errors* is a farce, not a tragedy, the supernatural context creates a similar diagnostic predicament, as the figures on stage repeatedly (and incorrectly) label one another as witches, sorcerers or demoniacs. As we will see in this book, regardless of genre, issues of moral obscurity, trust and risk are characteristic of the hospitality relationship in Shakespeare, and not only applicable to encounters with the paranormal.

In sociology and postcolonial studies, the ghost has emerged as a way of theorising social marginality and exclusion from the centre. Gordon suggests that '[t]he ghost is not simply a dead or a missing person, but a social figure', which is why '[h]aunting is a frightening experience. It always registers the harm inflicted or the loss sustained by a social violence done in the past or in the present.'[11] Homi Bhabha has taken up 'the uncanny structure of cultural difference' to argue that the *unheimlich* or 'the "unhomely" is a paradigmatic postcolonial experience'.[12] Recently, spectral imagery has become intertwined with the global migrant crisis and its racialised injustices. Discussing how British politicians consciously stoke unease about asylum seekers entering the country illegally, Sara Ahmed explains how '[t]he figure of the bogus asylum seeker may evoke the figure of the "bogeyman," a figure who stalks the nation and haunts its capacity to secure its borders. The bogeyman could be anywhere and anyone, as a ghostlike figure in the present, who gives us nightmares about the future, as an anticipated future of injury.'[13] This ghostly bogeyman is calculated to play on our most instinctual fears about the danger posed by the anonymous stranger, at the same time justifying ever tighter immigration protocols. The French anthropologist Michel Agier uses comparable imagery in his ethnography of the refugee camp, concluding that there is 'a partition between two great world categories that are increasingly reified: on the one hand, a clean, healthy and visible world; on the other, the world's residual "remnants", dark, diseased and invisible'.[14] Reflecting back over his many years of employment in the service of Antipholus of Ephesus in Act 4 of *The Comedy of Errors*, Dromio of Ephesus says:

> I have served him from the hour of my nativity to this instant and have nothing at his hands for my service but blows. When I am cold, he heats me with beating; when I am warm, he cools me with beating. I am waked with it when I sleep, raised with it when I sit, driven out of doors with it when I go from home, welcomed home with it when I return. Nay, I bear it on my shoulders as a beggar wont her brat, and I think that when he hath lamed me, I shall beg with it from door to door.
> (4.4.31–40)

Compared with his twin brother's prediction of violent servitude to the malevolent fairies, the circumstances which Dromio of Ephesus outlines are depressingly mundane. He envisages how the beatings have 'lamed' him, so that when he begs 'from door to door', he carries the weight of a disability on his back 'as a beggar wont her brat'. In this speculative future, Dromio of Ephesus imagines himself as a ghostly presence on the margins of Ephesian society, or, to use Agier's phrase, he has become 'dark, diseased and invisible'.

One of the aims behind the approach taken in this chapter is that, by attending to the supernatural world in *The Comedy of Errors* through the lens of theoretical work on hospitality, we encourage an overdue reconsideration of stranger relations in the play. With this goal in mind, I read scenes of apotropaic magic and the expelling of demons alongside far more ordinary examples of unwanted visitation like the 'lock-out' scene or the harsh immigration policy of Ephesus. Another advantage of reading hospitality and the supernatural together is it restores to the text a thematic and structural cohesion which has often been found lacking. A problem for critics of *The Comedy of Errors* is how to reconcile the serious humanitarian disaster of the opening scene with the ensuing laughter and knockabout farce. By foregrounding the figure of the intruder (both earthly and supernatural), however, the refugee tale that bookends the action no longer seems awkwardly tacked on to *The Comedy of Errors*, but rather integral to the text as a whole. As I argue, the play stages a sophisticated meditation on the theme of social exclusion.

The chapter begins with a discussion of the refugee detention scene in Act 1, in which I examine how government bureaucracy and the legal system produce an asylum experience hostile to outsiders. Extending the unwanted guest theme in new directions, I then look in the second section at Doctor Pinch's exorcism of the demon thought to be inhabiting the body of Antipholus of Ephesus. The third section ('Circe's Cup') investigates how gender shapes cultural attitudes towards hospitality, as I consider the seductive figure of the witch-hostess. The fourth and final section addresses the implications of the supernatural and, in particular, what it means for our understanding of hospitality in *The Comedy of Errors*. On the one hand, the ghostly doppelgänger disrupts the fantasy that the stranger can be safely contained; on the other, the supernatural is not always a cause for disquiet. Drawing on the sacred stranger tradition in religion and anthropology, this last section suggests how the play's otherworldly context presents the prospect of a more inclusive citizenship predicated on the unconditional welcome of guests and ghosts.

Economies of the Death Penalty

As *The Comedy of Errors* opens, Solinus, the Duke of Ephesus, is explaining to Egeon, a new arrival from Syracuse, that by coming here he has flouted the reciprocal sanctions on travel between the two towns:

> It hath in solemn synods been decreed,
> Both by the Syracusans and ourselves,
> To admit no traffic to our adverse towns.
> Nay, more: if any born at Ephesus
> Be seen at Syracusan marts and fairs;
> Again, if any Syracusan born
> Come to the Bay of Ephesus, he dies,
> His goods confiscate to the Duke's dispose,
> Unless a thousand marks be levied
> To quit the penalty and ransom him.
> Thy substance, valued at the highest rate,
> Cannot amount unto a hundred marks:
> Therefore, by law thou art condemned to die.
> (1.1.13–25)

Shakespeare straightaway plunges us into a discourse of illegality, questioning what happens to the values of hospitality and international asylum when the entry of particular people is judged to be unlawful.[15] Solinus also informs Egeon that he will soon be executed unless he can find 'a thousand marks' to purchase his acquittal. By making Ephesian hospitality contingent on the economy, the play scripts a humanitarian emergency where an innocent civilian is sentenced to death for no other crime beyond that of arriving on foreign soil. Immanuel Kant defined hospitality as 'the right of a stranger not to be treated in a hostile manner by another upon his arrival on the other's territory'.[16] In Ephesus, however, the Kantian understanding of hospitality as a fundamental human right to arrive safely anywhere on the surface of the globe has been abandoned.

This state-mandated criminalisation of hospitality which we notice at the start of *The Comedy of Errors* is an issue that Derrida has considered in relation to the 'sans-papiers', or undocumented persons, in modern France:

> I remember a bad day last year: It just about took my breath away, it sickened me when I heard the expression for the

first time, barely understanding it, the expression *crime of hospitality* [délit d'hospitalité]. In fact, I am not sure that I heard it, because I wonder how anyone could ever have pronounced it, taken it on his palate, this venomous expression; no, I did not hear it, and I can barely repeat it; I read it voicelessly in an official text. It concerned a law permitting the prosecution, and even the imprisonment, of those who take in and help foreigners whose status is held to be illegal. This 'crime of hospitality' (I still wonder who dared to put these words together) is punishable by imprisonment.[17]

In a parody of the nourishing meal, the words 'crime of hospitality' are said to be poisonous in the speaker's mouth and harmful to the listener as well since, as Derrida recalls, 'it sickened me when I heard the expression for the first time'. Shakespeare includes one such 'crime of hospitality' early on in *The Comedy of Errors*, when Antipholus of Syracuse is advised by a merchant to conceal his country of origin:

Therefore, give out you are of Epidamium,
Lest that your goods too soon be confiscate.
This very day a Syracusan merchant
Is apprehended for arrival here
    (1.2.1–4)

Not unlike the Good Samaritans whom Derrida describes as those 'who take in and help foreigners whose status is held to be illegal', the merchant recommends that Antipholus of Syracuse keep his national identity a secret and to pretend that he has travelled from Greece, lest he, too, suffer Egeon's fate and be 'apprehended for arrival'.

The merchant's display of sympathy for the plight of an illegal alien would appear to contradict the cruel treatment of Antipholus' father, Egeon. However, the blend of emotion and political diplomacy in *The Comedy of Errors* is more complicated. In his first speech, Solinus acknowledges the grim human rights record of his Syracusan counterpart, reminding Egeon that:

> The enmity and discord which of late
> Sprang from the rancorous outrage of your duke
> To merchants, our well-dealing countrymen,
> Who, wanting guilders to redeem their lives,
> Have sealed his rigorous statutes with their bloods,
> Excludes all pity from our threatening looks
>   (1.1.5–10)

By stressing how he is merely responding to Syracuse's earlier execution of the merchants of Ephesus, it is plain that Solinus harbours no resentment towards the detainee personally. On the contrary, he later confesses to Egeon that he has much empathy for his guest's unfortunate situation and 'were it not against our laws / Against my crown, my oath, my dignity' then '[m]y soul should sue as advocate for thee' (1.1.142–4). Despite the emotive language used throughout Solinus' speech above, this diplomatic incident is, in reality, as coldly impersonal as the economic transactions between the two towns. Just as the 'guilders' demanded from visitors to Syracuse are duplicated in the 'thousand marks' (1.1.21) monetary fine imposed on Egeon, Ephesus also emulates the 'enmity and discord' of its neighbour until their mutual hatred has become its own form of circulating currency. Contending that there is an 'economic model of emotions' at work in political discourse, Ahmed suggests that 'hate does not reside in a given subject or object. Hate is economic; it circulates between signifiers in relationships of difference and displacement.'[18] This is surely the case in *The Comedy of Errors* where the social transmission of emotion gives us a different perspective on the economic imagery that floods the play.[19] Shakespeare shows how international relations can be governed by ill feeling and how innocent civilians like Egeon are then caught in the crossfire. His incarceration and death sentence can be read as an example of hostage diplomacy, in which the immoral confinement of foreign nationals operates as a form of diplomatic leverage.

Strangers are dealt with dispassionately by the government of Ephesus. If the new arrival is from Syracuse, their financial capital is the only criteria that matters and will determine whether they are welcomed as a guest or detained as an illegal immigrant. That this cruelty has passed into official state policy is clear from Solinus' description of the Ephesian merchants executed by Syracuse, whose deaths '[h]ave sealed his rigorous statutes with their bloods' (1.1.9). In this gruesome metaphor, the spilt blood of the massacred visitors is put to prosaic use as the red sealing wax used on the paperwork encoding inhospitality into formal government bureaucracy. Hostage diplomacy condones these and other international abuses of hospitality, as foreigners become pawns who can be imprisoned or executed for political advantage. Even Egeon seems to have internalised the bureaucratic rhetoric since, when asked to explain why he came to the town in defiance of the travel ban, he relates how a storm at sea issued to those passengers on board his ship '[a] doubtful warrant of immediate death' (1.1.68). He uses the same word again later while speaking of his lost relatives when he says, 'happy were I in my timely death / Could all my travels warrant me they live' (1.1.138–9). Egeon's 'warrant' – with its administrative connotations – encapsulates his welcome reception in Ephesus. By ratifying violence towards foreigners into state paperwork, *The Comedy of Errors* reveals how inhospitality can be legalised on a global stage.

Bureaucracy not only reduces the length of Egeon's natural life, but also alters his experience of time, leaving him in a state of limbo while he waits for the death sentence to be carried out. Unable to pay the fine, his last lines before he leaves the stage in the jailer's custody are: '[h]opeless and helpless doth Egeon wend / But to procrastinate his lifeless end' (1.1.157–8). Egeon's world-weariness is reminiscent of the preceding delays and setbacks on his journey (see, especially, 1.1.74–132). Furthering his association with time being drawn out, in Act 5, Egeon comments on his old age:

> O Time's extremity,
> Hast thou so cracked and splitted my poor tongue
> In seven short years that here my only son
> Knows not my feeble key of untuned cares?
> Though now this grained face of mine be hid
> In sap-consuming winter's drizzled snow,
> And all the conduits of my blood froze up,
> Yet hath my night of life some memory,
> My wasting lamps some fading glimmer left
> (5.1.307–15)

Making a conventional comparison between winter and old age, Egeon uses the icy landscape to convey the physical and mental changes brought about by the ageing process. His hair and beard have turned as white as 'winter's drizzled snow', while his 'wasting lamps' (or fading eyesight) recall the darkness of a December 'night'. The symbolism of the cold season also shows the impact of time on the humoral composition of the body. In old age, the humours were thought to become colder and more sluggish; winter's frost is 'sap-consuming', which is why 'all the conduits of my blood froze up'. Egeon alludes to comparable imagery of the natural world in Act 1 when, contemplating his execution, he observes that his 'woes end likewise with the evening sun' (1.1.27). However, the diurnal rhythm of the seasons is in conflict with Egeon's fraught experience of time as a bureaucratic process.

Obstructions, hold-ups, adjournments and other delays are a notorious part of official bureaucracy but have a unique impact on refugees and asylum seekers who often endure

Hospitality and the Supernatural in *The Comedy of Errors*

lengthy periods of waiting. In *Postcolonial Asylum: Seeking Sanctuary before the Law*, David Farrier notes that:

> Where it is granted, asylum is designed to confer on individuals the capacity to remake their lives free from threat and limitation. To seek asylum, however, refers to their induction into a condition of waiting, uncertainty and dependency that frustrates any chance for self-creation; it is a period of especially fraught relations with the host nation, and with the law.[20]

In Shakespeare's theatre, what we find time and again is that the host (whether an individual or a host nation) has the capacity to keep guests waiting or to refuse them entry altogether. During the 'lock-out' scene in Act 3, Antipholus of Ephesus with Dromio and guests are kept waiting at the door, while Dromio of Syracuse prevents anybody from entering:

Dromio of Ephesus	What patch is made our porter? – My master stays in the street.
Dromio of Syracuse [*within*]	Let him walk from whence he came, lest he catch cold on's feet.

(3.1.36–7)

This short extract shows the humiliation of being forced to linger in the public street, aside from the physical discomfort of hunger and cold while waiting around in the fresh air. As Ephesian Dromio quips, '[y]our cake is warm within; you stand here in the cold' (3.1.71). Egeon's apathy and Antipholus of Ephesus' rage (he quickly threatens violence against both house and inhabitants) are differing responses to the same phenomenon of being kept waiting by a host who is disinclined to be hospitable. Waiting is, after all, a demonstration of the unequal power dynamic between prospective guest and host authority. Egeon's complaint – not about the immediacy of his death, but about the delay before the sentence of execution will be carried out – hints at the cruelty of unpunctuality within a bureaucratic system. As Yasmine Shamma notes, '[b]ureaucracy is a forceful waiting. The word itself contains within it "cracy," from the Greek "kratos" which translates to power, and the violence that comes with it.'[21]

By making hospitality in Ephesus contingent on bureaucracy, economics and the law, *The Comedy of Errors* does nothing to negate the hostility directed at outsiders, although this aggression takes different forms, some of which are subtler than incarceration or the death penalty. One instance of the covert violence of the opening scene is when Solinus asks Egeon to give his life story:

Solinus   Well, Syracusan, say in brief the cause
             Why thou departed'st from thy native home,
             And for what cause thou cam'st to Ephesus.
Egeon   A heavier task could not have been imposed
             Than I to speak my griefs unspeakable.
             (1.1.28–32)

As Egeon's response makes clear, Solinus' question is distressing because it requires the speaker publicly to relive episodes from a painful past. In requiring a guest to reproduce their trauma, the lines evoke Sophocles' *Oedipus at Colonus*, where the Chorus demands to hear from Oedipus the story of his anguish:

Chorus   A terrible thing, my friend,
            to wake an old grief, laid to rest so long . . .
            nevertheless I long to learn –
Oedipus   What now?
Chorus   The dreadful agony you faced – no recovery,
            no way out – that agony you lived through.

> Oedipus   No!
> For the sake of kindness toward a guest,
> don't lay bare the cruelty I suffered![22]

Derrida analyses this passage, although with a different translation of Oedipus' last line: 'In the name of your hospitality (*xenias*), don't ruthlessly open up what I suffered.'[23] 'The question of hospitality' is, therefore, for Derrida, 'the question of the question'.[24] He asks: 'Shouldn't we also submit to a sort of holding back of the temptation to ask the other who he is, what her name is, where he comes from, etc.?'[25] Questions vocalise the mechanisms of authority by probing the secrets and vulnerabilities of the addressee since the host (or the person in charge) gets to pose questions, whereas the newcomer – subject to their interrogation – is put at a disadvantage. *Hamlet* opens with an equivalent power struggle over who has the right to ask the first question:

> *Barnardo*   Who's there?
> *Francisco*   Nay, answer me. Stand and unfold yourself.
> *Barnardo*   Long live the King.
> *Francisco*   Barnardo?
> *Barnardo*   He.
>   (1.1.1–3)

As the night sentinels cross-examine one another in the darkness of the pre-dawn hours, the use of passwords ('Long live the King') and conjecture ('Barnardo?') contributes to the play's atmosphere of distrust of the stranger.

Often tense occasions, the interrogation of guest by host authority assumes a special intensity in the case of refugees and asylum seekers where a great deal is riding on the answers given. On the role of storytelling in informing the outcome of asylum hearings, Farrier writes that:

'Refugee determinations', as Jenni Millbank rightly points out, 'involve the most intensely narrative mode of legal adjudication.' Refugee status depends on the claimant's ability successfully to present herself/himself as subject to a well-founded fear of persecution as defined in the 1951 Refugee Convention. Refugee determinations therefore place significant emphasis on narrative – on the claimant telling a convincing story, often supplemented by country guidance or expert evidence.[26]

Egeon's narrative of the natural disaster which brought him to Ephesus is not just convincing but hypnotic, for Solinus is gripped by this adventure story of storm, shipwreck and global travel. Several times Egeon hesitates and momentarily interrupts his own statement, yet Solinus urges him to continue: 'Nay, forward, old man; do not break off so' (1.1.96), and again later, 'dilate at full / What have befall'n of them and thee till now' (1.1.122–3). Egeon's ordeal can, I suggest, be read as a microcosm of the modern-day immigration system, with its paperwork, the endless waiting times, and the importance placed on narrative. But at least with refugee determinations there is the prospect of a hopeful resolution. In *The Comedy of Errors*, though, the detainee is notified from the beginning that the state 'may pity, though not pardon thee' (1.1.97). Considering Solinus' reluctance to intervene and overturn the death penalty, his morbid curiosity to hear Egeon's 'sad stories' (1.1.120) seems especially cruel.

'Credibility assessment has always been a major issue in refugee determinations,' Millbank argues.[27] Without neighbours, friends or relatives nearby to vouch for them, the stranger's personal history – the story that they tell about themselves – must speak for them and inspire trust and credibility. Just as important is the outsider's *creditworthiness*, both in terms of the money they carry on their person, and their future financial solvency. Recent work in economic criticism and religious studies has noticed the close etymological connection between faith and money, or between credibility and credit. In his *Dictionary of Indo-European Beliefs and Society*, Émile Benveniste considers the 'Latin *credo* and its derivatives', showing how '[f]rom the time of the earliest texts the meaning of "credit" is extended to include the notion "belief"'.[28] Laurent Milesi notes 'the whole economic palette of the French *croire* and *croyance*, in particular their consonance with "credit"'.[29] The *Oxford English Dictionary* preserves both the economic and religious usages in its etymology of the noun 'credit': 'Middle French *credit* (French *crédit*) belief, faith, trust [. . .] reputation, influence, esteem [. . .] money lent or borrowed with an agreement as to repayment [. . .] trust or confidence in a customer's ability and intention to pay at some future time'.[30] Across different languages and world cultures, then, credit is the international currency by which we put our faith in strangers.

In an often-quoted passage from *The Philosophy of Money*, Georg Simmel notes how '[t]he role that the stranger plays within a social group directs him, from the outset, towards relations with the group that are mediated by money, above all because of the transportability and the extensive usefulness of money outside the boundaries of the group.'[31] 'Money', Simmel concludes, was 'originally [. . .] a domain of the stranger.'[32] And yet, if the outsider's connection to the host community is 'mediated by money', then so, too, is the nation state's relationship with its immigrant populations. For governments to conceive of their hospitality in economic terms elicits a weight of expectation that the stranger will pay their way as necessary, while contributing to the local economy. We might reflect, for instance, on the numerous examples of countries that only open their national borders according to a points-based immigration system, which typically includes a minimum salary threshold as well as other financial criteria based on the applicant's current economic prosperity and earning potential in later years. That most (if not all) government administrations prefer skilled over unskilled migrants entering the country and applying for residency is another form of fiscal policymaking.[33]

The Comedy of Errors confirms the decisive importance of cash flow in calculating acts of hospitality. Egeon has only 'a hundred marks' (1.1.24) to his name, but for 'a thousand marks' (1.1.21) he could secure his release from prison and buy hospitality from the Ephesian government. According to Colette Gordon, even though 'Egeon clearly fails to live up to the fantasy of the stranger who is associated with a glamorous and mysterious liquidity, the city expects him to be carrying coin to compensate for his lack of credit'.[34] In contrast, the ideal foreigner is surely Antipholus of Syracuse, who not only arrives in Ephesus with a substantial amount of money in his custody, but is already part of the established credit networks of mercantile trade and exchange.[35] The hospitality extended to outsiders in *The Comedy of Errors* is intimately intwined with economics; it can be bought, sold or bartered. Solinus, echoing the mercantile ethos of Ephesian hospitality, recommends to the prisoner-guest that he should '[t]ry all the friends thou hast in Ephesus / Beg thou or borrow to make up the sum' (1.1.152–3).

Conversely, the hardening of social attitudes towards outsiders and immigrants is often accompanied by an economic vocabulary, as well as apprehensions about impoverishment, unemployment and resource scarcity. Ahmed gives another insightful example of how the political discourse surrounding migrants has a tendency to fuse with other figures of opprobrium, such as the bogeyman. She explains how '[t]he figure of the asylum seeker [. . .] gets aligned with the figure of the burglar. The alignment does important work: it suggests that the asylum seeker is "stealing" something from the nation.'[36] Conceiving of immigration as a form of financial theft is an age-old theme. In the collaborative play *Sir Thomas More*, the citizens' xenophobic attacks on the strangers are couched in economic terms of wage theft and food shortages. The bill that is drawn up for the Spital sermons denouncing London's alien population reads: '*For so it is that aliens and strangers eat the bread from the fatherless children, and take the living from all the artificers, and the intercourse from all merchants, whereby poverty is so much increased that every man bewaileth the misery of other; for craftsmen be brought to beggary, and merchants to neediness.*'[37] By involving local artisans and merchants alike, the bill implies an embezzlement of funds that cuts across class lines.

As we can see from *Sir Thomas More*, it is not only governments who are capable of cynically assessing whether they stand to make a profit or a loss out of welcoming guests. Hospitality between individuals can be every bit as motivated by financial concerns. In *The Comedy of Errors*, we notice this when Antipholus of Syracuse invites a merchant to eat dinner with him:

Antipholus of Syracuse	What, will you walk with me about the town And then go to my inn and dine with me?
1 Merchant	I am invited, sir, to certain merchants, Of whom I hope to make much benefit; I crave your pardon.
	(1.2.22–6)

Commensality in *The Comedy of Errors* is shown to be inseparable from the world of finance and commerce as, politely excusing himself, the merchant tells Antipholus that he expects to accrue some pecuniary 'benefit' from his prior dinner arrangement. A more disturbing example of mercenary hospitality is Egeon's tale of the greedy sailors who rescue him from the ocean and 'knowing whom it was their hap to save / Gave healthful welcome to their shipwrecked guests' (1.1.113–14). Egeon characterises these sailors as opportunists who only offer a warm greeting to their 'shipwrecked guests' because they realise that they will be richly remunerated for their efforts. Relations between friends and strangers are, on each occasion, dictated by an expectancy of monetary advantage. Of course, reckonings such as these undermine the principle of hospitality by making economics the driving force behind acts of generosity.

Amid the wealth of economic criticism on *The Comedy of Errors*, the death penalty has so far escaped scholarly attention, yet it is the definitive example of an unethical calculation involving foreigners. Over the course of two volumes of seminars on *The Death Penalty*, Derrida persuasively shows how state execution operates along the same lines as capitalism. Its economic logic ('the capital of capital punishment') is centred on an understanding of state-sanctioned murder as the prisoner's repayment of a pre-existing debt to society, as well as an underlying trust in the credit system:

> The origin of the legal subject, and notably of penal law, is commercial law; it is the law of commerce, debt, the market, the exchange between things, bodies, and monetary signs, with their general equivalent and their surplus value, their interest. This would mean, in sum, that what *makes us believe*, credulous as we are, what makes us believe in an equivalence between crime and punishment, at bottom, is belief itself; it is the fiduciary phenomenon of credit or faith (*Glauben*).[38]

In Egeon's situation, the resemblances which Derrida identifies between a proto-capitalist marketplace and calculations in a court of law are heightened through Shakespeare's inclusion of the monetary fine. The death penalty in *The Comedy of*

Errors – which governs neighbourly relations between Ephesus and Syracuse but can be paid off – shares the mercantile ethos of the credit system.

The penal code's dependence on an economic symbolism of debt and repayment aside, by assigning an arbitrary monetary value to a stranger's life, *The Comedy of Errors* exemplifies how the death penalty performs 'the calculation of the incalculable'.[39] Derrida wonders, '[w]hat then is the price of life? What gives life value? It is harder than ever to avoid these questions when speaking of the death penalty, that is, when one must, as they say, "pay with one's life" or "make someone pay with his life."'[40] Once it has been decided by representatives of the justice system that a sentence of execution will be carried out, the implementation of the death penalty now calls for a *second* incalculable calculation, impossible because '[i]f there is one thing that it is not given to us to know, and thus to calculate with absolute precision, it is the given moment of my death'.[41] As Derrida puts it, the death penalty is 'the only example of a death whose instant is calculable by a machine, by machines (not by someone, finally, as in a murder, but by all sorts of machines: the law, the penal code, the anonymous third party, the calendar, the clock, the guillotine or another apparatus).'[42] Contrary to Egeon's ecological metaphors of growing older in tandem with the change of the seasons, capital punishment mechanises the exact time of death.

I have argued so far that *The Comedy of Errors* opens in a world where strangers are dealt with according to an impersonal and calculating logic. Ephesian hospitality is dictated by the same kinds of automated techniques, including fiscal policy and bureaucracy, as those which ensure the smooth functioning of the legal system as well as the apparatus of the death penalty. The hostage diplomacy to which Egeon is subjected is only part of a broader credit-driven society based on the principles of international trade and exchange. As a result, any undesirable visitors from Syracuse who arrive in the town must either pay the financial penalty or be sentenced to receive the death penalty. As soon as the main action of *The Comedy of Errors* gets under way, however, the text immediately goes on to problematise and challenge these neat 'stranger equations'. In the remainder of this chapter, I consider how the supernatural environment of Shakespeare's Ephesus makes it increasingly difficult to determine the extent of the stranger's welcome according to bureaucratic, legal and economic criteria.

Pinch's Exorcism

In Act 4 of *The Comedy of Errors*, the ridiculous Doctor Pinch, a schoolmaster and conjuror, performs an exorcism on a highly irritated Antipholus of Ephesus:

> I charge thee, Satan, housed within this man,
> To yield possession to my holy prayers,
> And to thy state of darkness hie thee straight;
> I conjure thee by all the saints in heaven.
> (4.4.55–8)

Since Antipholus is *not* possessed by Satan, merely enraged at the rude conduct of his wife and neighbours, the scene is one of many amusing episodes in the play. Yet while we are clearly invited to laugh at Pinch, the perception that the Devil and other diabolical spirits could invade the human form and take up residence was a widely held belief throughout the early modern period. The evil spirit was thought to be literally inside the body of the possessed person, as was seemingly evidenced by the fact that demoniacs tended to lose control of their corporeal faculties. Part of the reason why Antipholus of Ephesus is misdiagnosed as a possession case is on account of his altered physical appearance: his 'fiery and sharp' demeanour, and the way that he 'trembles in his ecstasy' (4.4.51–2).[43] After entering the body, the intruder wrested control of its functions away from the host organism. In early modern England, to be possessed by demons was therefore to participate in a spiritually perilous form of hospitality.

Reinforcing the comparison of demon to trespasser is the conventional analogy between body and house, explicit in Pinch's direct address to the malevolent spirit 'housed within this man' (4.4.55), and a recurring feature of early modern possession narratives, which drew on household imagery in order to present the occupying spirit as an illegal tenant who refuses to vacate the host's premises. From here, authors experimented with more creative similes of non-human dwelling spaces. Hence, in *The Anatomy of Melancholy* (1621), Robert Burton makes a creaturely comparison when he says of unclean spirits that 'they goe in and out of our bodies, as Bees doe in a Hive'.[44] Boyd Brogan cites another interesting usage of architectural imagery from Nicholas Remy: 'Very often he [the devil] has his dwelling in those parts which, like the bilge of a ship, receive the filth and excrements of the body.'[45] This latter example relates to ongoing theological disputes which sought to accurately pinpoint the location within the human body where the Devil would reside (with some reasoning that it would naturally choose for its habitation the bowels and the digestive tract).[46]

Early modern narratives of demonic possession were framed as a contest over dwelling space, as the spirit intruder competed against the host for control of the interior architecture of the body. Household metaphors were brought to life through the belief in this period that houses as well as people were susceptible to attack from malign interference and could also be exorcised. James I wrote of witches that they 'can make spirites either to follow and trouble persones, or haunt certaine houses, and affraie oftentimes the inhabitants'.⁴⁷ Contemporary fears that the home could be besieged by supernatural forces are alluded to during the 'lock-out' scene in Act 3 of *The Comedy of Errors* when, through a case of mistaken identity, Antipholus and Dromio of Ephesus are barred from entering their house. Dromio of Ephesus, locked out along with his master, shouts for the domestic servants to let them inside: 'Maud, Bridget, Marian, Cic'ly, Gillian, Ginn!' (3.1.31), to which Dromio of Syracuse quips, '[d]ost thou conjure for wenches, that thou call'st for such store?' (3.1.34). Although sarcastic, the reference to incantatory black magic and the summoning of spirits attests to the belief that neither homes nor people were safe from demonic possession.

Exorcism, then, can be understood as the culmination of this struggle over dwelling, as the demon is banished from the body and returned to its own loathsome habitation. During the ritual, an exorcist would habitually remind the possessing spirit that its proper abode was elsewhere. One of the prayers for exorcism reads: 'Therefore now depart, seducer depart. Your abode is the wilderness. Your habitation is the serpent.'⁴⁸ In *The Comedy of Errors*, Pinch likewise orders the Devil to leave Antipholus' body and return 'to thy state of darkness' (4.4.57). Hilaire Kallendorf notes that the malign presence was sometimes expelled by being driven into a small, confined area such as 'a single hair, a toe, or some other extremity'.⁴⁹ Here, an exorcism was a mode of imprisonment. Prospero in *The Tempest* remembers how the witch Sycorax confined Ariel, an airy spirit, within a 'cloven pine':

> Refusing her grand hests, she did confine thee,
> By help of her more potent ministers
> And in her most unmitigable rage,
> Into a cloven pine, within which rift
> Imprisoned thou didst painfully remain

> A dozen years; within which space she died
> And left thee there, where thou didst vent thy groans
> As fast as mill-wheels strike.⁵⁰

While not usually read as an exorcism scene, Prospero's description of an unwanted spirit being expelled and, in the process, incarcerated offers intriguing parallels to the conjuring of demons.

The Tempest, with its allusion to Ariel's endless 'groans', conveys how the expulsion of a spirit could be a painful procedure. 'One Dutch priest claimed in 1650 that the Devil could tear a person into a thousand pieces during an exorcism,' Brian Levack notes, before commenting that exorcists 'compounded this alleged demonic violence by taking forceful physical action against the possessed person on the presumption that they were struggling with the demon, not its human host'.⁵¹ Towards the end of *The Comedy of Errors*, these rough treatments are reversed when Pinch the exorcist is abused by the demoniacs, as a messenger reports:

> Whose beard they have singed off with brands of fire,
> And ever as it blazed, they threw on him
> Great pails of puddled mire to quench the hair.
> My master preaches patience to him, and the while
> His man with scissors nicks him like a fool;
> And sure, unless you send some present help,
> Between them they will kill the conjuror.
> (5.1.171–7)

In a carnivalesque inversion, the physical violence which was, at times, deemed a necessary part of the exorcism ritual across early modern Europe is directed against the exorcist by the escaped demoniacs. Antipholus and Dromio of Ephesus throw 'pails of puddled mire' over Pinch's face in a parody of the church baptismal ceremony which was, as Duffy has observed, 'explicitly concerned with the expulsion of the Devil'.⁵²

From the hostile immigration legislation of Ephesus to the expulsion of demonic spirits, *The Comedy of Errors* presents a sustained engagement with the theme of the unwanted intruder. As in the dark ceremonies of exorcism, unexpected guests in this play are routinely subjected to verbal threats, physical violence and are liable to exclusion or imprisonment.

'Circe's cup'

Already disconcerted by their weird experiences in Ephesus, in Act 4 of *The Comedy of Errors*, Antipholus and Dromio of Syracuse encounter the Courtesan. In response to her friendly greeting (she presumes the pair to be their Ephesian twins), they call her a devil and then, in the second of the play's exorcism scenes, attempt to banish her:

Antipholus of Syracuse	Satan, avoid! I charge thee, tempt me not!
Dromio of Syracuse	Master, is this Mistress Satan?
Antipholus of Syracuse	It is the devil.
Dromio of Syracuse	Nay, she is worse, she is the devil's dam, and here she comes in the habit of a light wench, and thereof comes that the wenches say, 'God damn me' – that's as much to say, 'God make me a light wench'. It is written they appear to men like angels of light; light is an effect of fire, and fire will burn: *ergo*, light wenches will burn. Come not near her.

(4.3.49–59)

Antipholus and Dromio regard the Courtesan's salutation as the lure of 'Satan', who has come to 'tempt' them to eternal damnation. It is likely, from Dromio's comments, that she is provocatively dressed. Cartwright speculates that '[s]he may wear distinctive clothing in flame colours or red, since her *habit* is associated with fire'.[53] Red had a range of cultural associations in the medieval and early modern period. Owing to Judas Iscariot's red hair and beard, the colour was connected with betrayal, but could equally denote lust, as hinted at here in Dromio's reference to fire, evoking both the flames of hell and the burning sensation of venereal disease. In her study of the court records of witch hunts in early modern Germany, Lyndal Roper notes the presence of vibrant colours in female defendants' reports of how the Devil first appeared to them: 'Often the Devil wore vivacious colour combinations: red clothes with a black hat, or as another woman described him, "he was a beautiful young man with a black beard, red clothing, green stockings and black hat, with a red feather upon it."'[54] Early modern witchcraft was a gendered crime, whose suspected perpetrators were, in the majority of cases, women.[55] In claiming that women were predisposed to the worship of demons, sixteenth- and seventeenth-century authors referred to biblical precedent. 'As Eve's gender exposed her to Satan's temptations,' Frances Dolan explains, 'so women's especially defenceless, fluid, penetrable, and manipulable "natures" made them vulnerable to demonic seduction.'[56] Dolan's final comment about 'seduction' is significant because there was often an eroticised dimension to witchcraft accusations.[57]

On account of their excessive sexual desire, women were sometimes believed to be complicit in their possession by demons, confirmed by reports of witches having sex with the Devil.[58] In *The Trial of Witchcraft* (1616), John Cotta touches on the nature of consent in relation to the supernatural when he differentiates between the demoniac and the witch. As he sees it, '[t]he possessed and the witch, are both the habitacles of devils; with this only difference, that the witch doth willingly entertain them.'[59] I noted earlier the prevalence of imagery of dwelling in early modern writings on demonic possession, yet here the connection to hospitality is given further prominence through Cotta's intimation that, unlike the demoniac, 'the witch doth willingly entertain' her spirit visitors. Entertaining guests at home was, of course, an indispensable component of the female householder's role. Joseph Candido has shown how a wife's identity 'was linked in some measure to her success at entertaining'.[60] But in the passage from Cotta, women's skill at household management is perverted into an image of the demoniac voluntarily welcoming malevolent spirits. William Perkins makes a similar rhetorical manoeuvre in *A Discourse of the Damned Art of Witchcraft* (1610), when he argues that, ever since Eve succumbed to temptation, women have been the Devil's preferred target '[f]or where he findeth easiest entrance, and best entertainement, thither will he oftlnest resert'.[61] As well as implying an affinity between women's domestic economy and the diabolical, 'to entertain' had unmistakable sexual connotations in the early modern period. In *Measure for Measure*, for example, Claudio complains of his lover's pregnancy that 'our most mutual entertainment / With character too gross is writ on Juliet'.[62] By drawing on a vocabulary of hospitality and the reception of visitors at home, authors including Cotta and Perkins can bolster their argument that women are the favoured sites of demonic possession, even deriving sexual pleasure from their encounter with the supernatural world.

Representations of women willingly hosting spirit intruders are part of a long tradition of dangerous female hostesses in western literature. In Homer's *The Odyssey*, Odysseus and his men land their ship on Circe's island, where the sorceress treats them to her extravagant table fare, which comprises 'a dish of cheese and barley-meal, of yellow honey and Pramnian wine, all together'.[63] In another eroticised description, Odysseus later recalls how his hostess 'made me sit in a bath and bathed me with water from the cauldron, tempering hot and cold to my mind and pouring it over my head and shoulders until she had banished from my limbs the weariness that sapped my spirit'.[64] Circe's sensual hospitality is famously short-lived, however, since she uses her magic to transform the crew into swine before shutting them in the pig shed. When she invites Odysseus to come to her 'sumptuous bed', he declines on the grounds that 'when I lie naked there you may rob me of courage and of manhood'.[65] *The Odyssey* captures an underlying sense of unease surrounding female hospitality. Circe is, after all, the archetypal sorceress-hostess, capable of leaving her male guests sexually emasculated.

The Comedy of Errors evokes the Classics with allusions surely intended to remind us of the dangers of being a guest. In Act 5, Solinus says to the assembled crowd, 'I think you have all drunk of Circe's cup' (5.1.271), implying those present have been drugged like Odysseus' crew. In another classical reference, the tavern where the Syracusan strangers are lodging is called 'the Centaur' (1.2.9), named after the mythological creature that had the upper body of a man and the lower body and legs of a horse. Whereas Circe had a reputation for being a treacherous hostess, the centaurs were known for being disruptive *guests*. Book 12 of Ovid's *Metamorphoses* recounts how the wedding feast of Pirithous and Hippodamia is interrupted by one of the centaurs attempting to abduct the bride:

> For Eurytus, the fiercest of the fierce
> Centaurs, was fired by wine and by the sight
> Of that fair girl, and drink was in command,
> Doubled by lust. Tables were overturned,
> The banquet in confusion, and the bride,
> Held by her hair, was seized and carried off.[66]

Drunk and lascivious, the centaur Eurytus initiates what quickly descends into a bloodthirsty battle between the guests and members of the wedding party. During the fight, the tableware from the banquet is repurposed for weaponry as 'goblets went flying and fragile jars / And bowls and dishes meant for banqueting / Now turned to war and carnage'.[67] Ovid goes into plenty of detail about how the unruly guests misappropriate the paraphernalia of the wedding feast, first attacking one another with the glassware and crockery, before picking up candlesticks, table legs and even some ornamental antlers which, in a memorable line, are used to gouge out Gryneus' eyes. Shakespeare's engagement with the classical tradition, most notably through references to the Centaur inn and Circe's cup, arouses a comparable anxiety about table fellowship in *The Comedy of Errors*.

Nervousness at the prospect of dining in the company of strangers pervades the encounter between Antipholus and Dromio of Syracuse and the Courtesan:

Dromio of Syracuse	Master, if you do, expect spoon-meat, or bespeak a long spoon.
Antipholus of Syracuse	Why, Dromio?
Dromio of Syracuse	Marry, he must have a long spoon that must eat with the devil.
	(4.3.62–6)

Superstition had it demonic spirits could gain access to the body through the mouth, which meant ordinary actions like eating, drinking or yawning could have spiritual repercussions. Sari Katajala-Peltomaa notes there was a well-known story where 'a hungry nun devoured a lettuce without making the sign of the cross and happened to swallow a demon simultaneously'.[68] It was thus sensible to take religious precautions to defend the body in its vulnerable moments, such as saying a blessing before the meal or if somebody sneezed.[69] Similarly, hospitality has long relied on folkloric customs in order to protect home and hearth, many of which offer guidance on table etiquette and the safe consumption of food and beverages. At least since Judas knocked over a salt cellar at the Last Supper, for example, it has been considered unlucky to spill salt, and if you leave discarded eggshells intact after a meal, then witches might use them for tiny boats.[70] Dromio of Syracuse's recommendation that his master bring a 'long spoon' to dine with the Courtesan is another piece of superstitious wisdom about the need to exercise caution at mealtimes. A long spoon allows the eater to maintain a careful distance from any dangerous dinner table companions. Dromio's second suggestion, that Antipholus consume only 'spoon-meat', means that he should stick to pulped food, meant for babies or the infirm, which can slip down the throat without difficulty. Because there is no need to open the mouth wide for biting or chewing solid food, this option would mitigate the risk of a demon entering the body in the act of reception.

Commensality and the exchange of gifts should strengthen social bonds between friends and neighbours in Ephesus, but the Courtesan's generosity is greeted with suspicion by the Syracusan newcomers. The same thing happens when she requests that Antipholus either return her jewellery or give her the gift which he promised her. Dromio says, '[s]ome devils ask but the parings of one's nail, a rush, a hair, a drop of blood, a pin, a nut, a cherry-stone; but she, more covetous, would have a chain' (4.3.73–6). In *Macbeth*, the refusal of a gift is the justification given by the first witch for her intention to punish the sea captain:

> A sailor's wife had chestnuts in her lap,
> And mounch'd and mounch'd, and mounch'd: 'Give me',
>   quoth I: –
> 'Aroynt thee, witch!' the rump-fed ronyon cries.[71]

Witches were known to use personal belongings stolen or coerced from prospective victims in their spells, with effluvia and other waste products from the body, like those which Dromio of Syracuse lists above, favoured ingredients. 'Bodily excretions and excrescences, household objects, and worn items of clothing', Dolan writes, 'were considered so many parts of the self that witchcraft belief construed them as avenues of entry, fragile thresholds of vulnerability.'[72] Nuts, stones, pips and other edible ephemera were ideal for occult magic because they were thought to retain some lingering impression of the eater.

As noted earlier, the economy of the death penalty relies on clear demarcations between foreign national and native citizen, or between Syracusan and Ephesian. On the other hand, when Dromio of Syracuse envisages the Courtesan trading in bodily effluvia, he presents her as a threat to that economy. Mary Douglas notes that matter emanating from the body is 'marginal stuff of the most obvious kind. Spittle, blood, milk, urine, faeces or tears by simply issuing forth have traversed the boundary of the body. So also have bodily parings, skin, nail, hair clippings and sweat.'[73] Gail Kern Paster takes this idea further, arguing that the body's discharge of effluvia and other fluids is 'a crucial problematic in the social formations of capitalism'.[74] Indeed, in the proto-capitalist society of Shakespeare's Ephesus, an economy of this nature – female, magical and centred on corporeal waste products usually discarded – is transgressive. The occult exchanges associated with the Courtesan blur the boundary between self and world in a manner that is entirely antithetical to the neat calculations made about strangers at the beginning of the play.

'A living dead man'

The Comedy of Errors is a play about the precautions we take to defend ourselves against outsiders. Antipholus of

Syracuse's uneasiness over whether his money is safe at the Centaur makes him the archetypal traveller, suspicious of the locals, while Dromio of Syracuse's faith in apotropaic magic and folkloric wisdom offers another means of keeping the supernatural world at bay. And yet, these and other safeguards are discovered to be illusory, because the outsider can never be completely eradicated, nor kept at a safe distance. Shakespeare's play rather supports Jean-Luc Nancy's conjecture that 'the stranger insists and intrudes'.[75]

The chaos created by the two sets of identical twins in *The Comedy of Errors* does much to disrupt the fantasy that the stranger can be safely contained. Throughout Acts 4 and 5, the repeated confinement of Antipholus and Dromio, followed by their ostensibly miraculous escapes (of course, the appearance of the other set of twins) leads even the locals to believe that magical forces must be at work in Ephesus. Believing that her husband and servant have gone mad, Adriana and her neighbours tie the pair up and leave them confined to the cellar at the Phoenix, only for them seemingly to break their bonds and reappear moments later. Soon afterwards, Adriana then watches her husband enter the sanctuary only mysteriously to resurface outside:

> Ay me, it is my husband! Witness you
> That he is borne about invisible:
> Even now we housed him in the abbey here,
> And now he's there, past thought of human reason.
>   (5.1.186–9)

Resembling airy spirits, Antipholus and Dromio seem to have acquired supernatural powers of speed and invisibility which enable them to be in two places at once.

In Act 5, the threat of the supernatural deepens when the twins appear together on stage for the first time. Seeking to explain the inexplicable, the Ephesians turn to pagan ideas about ghosts and spirit apparitions in order to make sense of this strange vision. Once Solinus notices the two Antipholus brothers, he wonders 'which is the natural man / And which the spirit?' (5.1.343–4). Recognising his father, Antipholus of Syracuse says, 'Egeon, art thou not? Or else his ghost' (5.1.337). Both guest and ghost, Egeon the Syracusan refugee returns from his temporary exile on the margins of the text to haunt the present.[76] Doctor Pinch is compared to a reanimated corpse:

> They brought one Pinch, a hungry, lean-faced villain,
> A mere anatomy, a mountebank,
> A threadbare juggler and a fortune-teller,
> A needy, hollow-eyed, sharp-looking wretch,
> A living dead man.
>   (5.1.238–42)

In this unnerving description, Antipholus notes Pinch's emaciated appearance ('hungry', 'lean-faced', 'hollow-eyed', 'sharp-looking'), concluding that he is the 'living dead'. The uncanny atmosphere, embodied in the skeletal figure of Doctor Pinch, is intensified through Antipholus of Ephesus' account of how he was treated by his wife and neighbours:

>   Then all together
> They fell upon me, bound me, bore me thence,
> And in a dark and dankish vault at home
> There left me and my man, both bound together
>   (5.1.246–9)[77]

Antipholus and Dromio are presumably confined to an underground cellar or storeroom, where the darkness and damp elicits a sensation of being buried underground.

    For Freud, the *unheimlich* is the opposite of what is homely. He argues that 'the uncanny is that class of the frightening which leads back to what is known of old and long familiar', adding that, for some people, 'the idea of being buried alive by mistake is the most uncanny thing of all'.[78] The figure of the intruder is significant for Freud's theories of psychoanalysis. Julia Kristeva notes that 'Freud does not speak of foreigners: he teaches us how to detect foreignness in ourselves.'[79] In an essay on repression, for instance, Freud uses a hospitality metaphor to illustrate how the mind must work hard to counteract intrusive thoughts: 'it amounts to much the same thing as the difference between my ordering an undesirable guest out of my drawing-room (or out of my front hall), and my refusing, after recognizing him, to let him cross my threshold at all.'[80] Repression requires vigilance because the intruder is intent on gaining admittance. As Freud sees it, 'I must set a permanent guard over the door which I have forbidden this guest to enter, since he would otherwise burst it open.'[81] This conveys something important about the nature of foreignness. Freud's intruder (the surfacing of unwanted thoughts or memories) will not cease in their attempts to get entrance to the interior, which means that guest and host remain caught in a struggle. Intrusion is theorised as disproportionate and relentless.

With its image clusters of ghosts, revenants and reanimated corpses, not to mention the uncanny confinement and reappearance of the two sets of identical twins, *The Comedy of Errors* captures the intruder's persistence. The refugee detention scene in Act 1 sets in motion a powerful fantasy that the unwanted intruder can be securely incarcerated, even eradicated altogether. However, the supernatural context in the remainder of the play undermines this comforting illusion, presenting us with spectres who are aggressive in their attempts to gain access.

The Sacred Stranger

Be not forgetful to entertain strangers: for thereby some have entertained angels unawares.

Hebrews 13:2

The promise that the stranger might be an angel in disguise or some other manifestation of the divine is part of a vast mythological tradition of gods disguised as mortals. Ovid's *Metamorphoses* tells the story of Jupiter and Mercury who conceal their true identities to see what kind of a response they get from humankind. Countless doors remain closed on them, but when they reach the tiny, thatched cottage of Philemon and Baucis, they are given a generous reception in spite of the old couple's poverty. In Book 8 of the *Metamorphoses*, hospitality thus becomes a means of assessing the moral values of the community. Only Philemon and Baucis pass the test and are spared from the flood which the gods send to drown their neighbours' homes.

Ethnographers and anthropologists have observed how, in archaic societies, the stranger is imbued with magical qualities. Arnold van Gennep notes that '[f]or a great many peoples a stranger is sacred, endowed with magico-religious powers, and supernaturally benevolent or malevolent'.[82] According to Pitt-Rivers, '[t]he stranger belongs to the "extra-ordinary" world, and the mystery surrounding him allies him to the sacred and makes him a suitable vehicle for the apparition of the God, the revelation of a mystery.'[83] Within the sacred stranger tradition, the host's generosity is indexed by their ability to mitigate the stranger's fatigue, as well as any bodily discomforts caused by their journeying. Ghosts on temporary release from the afterlife, for example, are often said to be hungry and malnourished. In *Hamlet*, the ghost claims that it has come from purgatory where it has been 'confined to fast in fires / Till the foul crimes done in my days of nature / Are burnt and purged away' (1.5.11–13). For this reason, gifts of food and drink comprise an important part of hospitality to ghosts, as seen in modern-day world religions which celebrate the hungry ghost festival. Patrice Ladwig gives an account of a Lao Buddhist festival where the living are encouraged to extend their hospitality to the dead:

> The following day the ritual starts around 4 a.m., when the temple bell is struck. Continuing for over an hour, this signifies the opening of the doors of hell and the coming of the *peta*, or *phiphed*, the hungry ghosts who fear light and can only appear on new moon. Laypeople flock to the temple and deposit the small packets on the temple grounds, make a short offering prayer, and light candles. These parcels 'decorate the earth' – hence the name of the ritual – and are eagerly looked for by the hungry ghosts and consumed by absorbing the vapour (*aay*) of the food offerings. In some temples in Vientiane, the whole compound is converted into a huge table of food offerings. The word for receiving guests and hospitality (*dtoonhab*), or other words referring explicitly to hospitality, might occasionally be used by Lao to describe this reception of ghosts.[84]

By prioritising the material needs of the ghost visitors, who are offered a wide selection of culinary delicacies alongside paper gifts of money and clothes before they continue on their way, these customs serve as exemplars of hospitality.

In French philosophy, the ghost has emerged as a useful category of thought in relation to hospitality, acting as a cypher of what this relationship can achieve. Derrida uses the welcoming of ghosts to characterise a more expansive definition of hospitality that does not seek to impose limits, conditions or expectations on the newcomer:

> Let us say yes to who or what turns up, before any determination, before any anticipation, before any identification, whether or not it has to do with a foreigner, an immigrant, an invited guest, or an unexpected visitor, whether or not the new arrival is the citizen of another country, a human, animal, or divine creature, a living or dead thing.[85]

The supernatural world can teach us an important ethical lesson about how to be more welcoming because the ontological unknowability of the ghost forces us to accept this stranger on their own terms, whatever they are ('divine creature, a living or dead thing'), and whenever they might choose to arrive.

Following so many attempts to control the stranger's welcome, the concluding scene of *The Comedy of Errors* enables us to glimpse a lessening of these limitations. At the end of the play, Egeon is reunited with his lost family members and incorporated into the community of Ephesus. The refugee and 'ghost' (5.1.337) is welcomed to 'a gossips' feast' (5.1.405) hosted by his wife, Emilia. He is pardoned by Solinus, and his monetary debt to the government of Ephesus is absolved. Disrupting the earlier calculations associated with the death penalty, Egeon's pardon in Act 5 is an exemption to the legal system. It is not a subtraction or any other form of arithmetic. Giorgio Agamben reminds us that '[t]he exception does not subtract itself from the rule; rather, the rule, suspending itself, gives rise to the exception.'[86] In *The Death Penalty* seminars, Derrida notes that a pardon is, by its very nature, 'always outside the law, always heterogeneous to order, to norm, to rule, or to calculation, to the rule of calculation, to economic as well as juridical calculation'.[87] Egeon's reprieve from the death sentence, together with the annulment of his unpaid debt, and his honoured place at the gossips' feast, speaks to a more inclusive hospitality that extends a welcome to ghosts, refugees and other revenants.

The ghost tests our capacity of who or what we are prepared to welcome. To foreground the supernatural environment in a play which is also about the refugee crisis is, therefore, to challenge some of our assumptions regarding the hospitality relationship. *The Comedy of Errors*, with its uneasy representation of selfhood and identity, proves that the newcomer could be anybody or anything, alive or dead. Yet while this opacity may, at times, be cause for concern, we have seen across the classical and scriptural traditions that the stranger is a figure allied with the sacred and with religious mysteries. Welcoming the other in advance of any prior calculation is to leave the door open for the coming of the sacred stranger and is an essential part of the ethics of hospitality. In this sense, the weird or uncanny mood of *The Comedy of Errors* reflects hospitality's transformative potential.

Notes

1. William Shakespeare, *The Comedy of Errors*, ed. Kent Cartwright (London: Bloomsbury, 2016), 2.2.194–8. All further references are to this edition and given parenthetically in the text.
2. Cartwright discusses Ephesus' magical reputation in his 'Introduction' to *The Comedy of Errors*, pp. 1–132; see pp. 28–32. Ironically, the scenario which Dromio of Syracuse imagines is not dissimilar to his daily life as servant to Antipholus of Syracuse, by whom he is frequently beaten. For a reading of the two servant brothers as racially 'bruised bodies', see Patricia Akhimie, *Shakespeare and the Cultivation of Difference: Race and Conduct in the Early Modern World* (New York: Routledge, 2018), p. 87.
3. Eamon Duffy, *The Stripping of the Altars: Traditional Religion in England, 1400–1580* (New Haven and London: Yale University Press, 1992), p. 269. Duffy goes on to suggest that 'in any case, it would be a mistake to see even these "magical" prayers as standing altogether outside the framework of the official worship and teaching of the Church. The world-view they enshrined, in which humanity was beleaguered by hostile troops of devils seeking the destruction of body and soul, and to which the appropriate and guaranteed antidote was the incantatory or manual invocation of the cross or names of Christ, is not a construct of the folk imagination. Such ideas were built into the very structure of the liturgy, and formed the focus for some of its most solemn and popularly accessible moments' (p. 279).
4. Cartwright, 'Introduction', p. 29.

5. Jan Franz van Dijkhuizen, *Devil Theatre: Demonic Possession and Exorcism in English Renaissance Drama, 1558–1642* (Woodbridge: D. S. Brewer, 2007), p. 31.
6. I am not the first to consider Egeon a refugee. Geraldo U. de Sousa describes the play's 'wandering refugees' in his essay 'Home and Abroad: Crossing the Mediterranean in Shakespeare's *The Comedy of Errors*', *Mediterranean Studies*, 26:2 (2018), 145–58, p. 156. For Colby Gordon, Egeon is 'a person of limited means, a victim of natural disaster and family separation, and an illegal resident in a hostile city' who exists in 'a state of impaired personhood'; see 'Two Doors: Personhood and Housebreaking in *Semayne's Case* and *The Comedy of Errors*', in *Renaissance Personhood: Materiality, Taxonomy, Process*, ed. Kevin Curran (Edinburgh: Edinburgh University Press, 2020), pp. 62–84, p. 69.
7. Avery F. Gordon, *Ghostly Matters: Haunting and the Sociological Imagination* (Minneapolis: University of Minnesota Press, 2008), p. xvi.
8. Julian Pitt-Rivers, 'The Law of Hospitality', in *From Hospitality to Grace: A Julian Pitt-Rivers Omnibus*, ed. Giovanni da Col and Andrew Shryock (Chicago: HAU Books, 2017), pp. 16–384, pp. 166–7.
9. Zygmunt Bauman, *Strangers at Our Door* (Cambridge: Polity Press, 2016), p. 9.
10. William Shakespeare, *Hamlet*, ed. Ann Thompson and Neil Taylor (London: Bloomsbury, 2016), 1.4.39–44. All subsequent references are to this edition and are given parenthetically in the text.
11. Gordon, *Ghostly Matters*, p. xvi.
12. Homi Bhabha, 'The World and the Home', *Social Text*, 31/32 (1992), 141–53, p. 142.
13. Sara Ahmed, 'Affective Economies', *Social Text*, 22:2 (2004), 117–39, p. 123.
14. Michel Agier, *Managing the Undesirables: Refugee Camps and Humanitarian Government* (Cambridge: Polity Press, 2011), p. 4.

15. For continued discussion of the play's legal themes, see Eric Heinze, '"Were it not against our laws": Oppression and Resistance in Shakespeare's *Comedy of Errors*', *Legal Studies*, 29:2 (2009), 230–63.
16. Immanuel Kant, 'Toward Perpetual Peace: A Philosophical Sketch', in *Toward Perpetual Peace and Other Writings on Politics, Peace, and History*, ed. Pauline Kleingeld, trans. David L. Colclasure (Binghamton: Yale University Press, 2006), pp. 67–109, p. 82.
17. Jacques Derrida, 'Derelictions of the Right to Justice', in *Negotiations: Interventions and Interviews, 1971–2001*, ed. and trans. Elizabeth Rottenberg (Stanford: Stanford University Press, 2002), pp. 133–46, p. 133.
18. Ahmed, 'Affective Economies', p. 119.
19. Plenty has been written about money in *The Comedy of Errors*: Shankar Raman, 'Marking Time: Memory and Market in *The Comedy of Errors*', *Shakespeare Quarterly*, 56:2 (2005), 176–205; Rui Carvalho Homem, 'Offshore Desires: Mobility, Liquidity and History in Shakespeare's Mediterranean', *Critical Survey*, 30:3 (2018), 36–56; Barbara Freedman, 'Egeon's Debt: Self-Division and Self-Redemption in *The Comedy of Errors*', *English Literary Renaissance*, 10:3 (1980), 360–83; Colette Gordon, 'Crediting Errors: Credit, Liquidity, Performance and *The Comedy of Errors*', *Shakespeare*, 6:2 (2010), 165–84; Thomas Cosgrove, 'The Commodity of Errors: Shakespeare and the Magic of the Value-Form', *Shakespeare*, 14:2 (2018), 14–56; Curtis Perry, 'Commerce, Community, and Nostalgia in *The Comedy of Errors*', in *Money in the Age of Shakespeare: Essays in New Economic Criticism*, ed. Linda Woodbridge (Basingstoke and New York: Palgrave, 2003), pp. 39–51.
20. David Farrier, *Postcolonial Asylum: Seeking Sanctuary before the Law* (Liverpool: Liverpool University Press, 2011), p. 6.
21. https://www.emptymirrorbooks.com/personal-essay/on-waiting [accessed September 2021].
22. Sophocles, *Oedipus at Colonus*, in *The Three Theban Plays: Antigone, Oedipus the King, Oedipus at Colonus*, trans. Robert Fagles (London: Penguin, 1984), pp. 577–82.

23. Jacques Derrida, *Of Hospitality: Anne Dufourmantelle invites Jacques Derrida to respond*, trans. Rachel Bowlby (Stanford: Stanford University Press, 2000), p. 41.
24. Derrida, *Of Hospitality*, p. 29.
25. Derrida, *Of Hospitality*, p. 135. Following Farès, in 'The Law of Hospitality', Pitt-Rivers notes that 'ancient Arab custom forbade asking the guest who he was, where he came from or where he was going' (p. 166n).
26. Farrier, *Postcolonial Asylum*, p. 156.
27. Jenni Millbank, '"The Ring of Truth": A Case Study of Credibility Assessment in Particular Social Group Refugee Determinations', *International Journal of Refugee Law*, 21:1 (2009), 1–33, p. 2.
28. Émile Benveniste, *Dictionary of Indo-European Beliefs and Society*, trans. Elizabeth Palmer (Chicago: HAU Books, 2016), p. 133.
29. Laurent Milesi, 'Believing in Deconstruction', in *Credo Credit Crisis: Speculations on Faith and Money*, ed. Laurent Milesi, Christopher John Müller and Aidan Tynan (London and New York: Rowman & Littlefield International, 2017), pp. 271–99, p. 271.
30. 'Credit, n.', *OED Online*.
31. Georg Simmel, *The Philosophy of Money*, ed. David Frisby, trans. Tom Bottomore and David Frisby (London and New York: Routledge, 2005), p. 224.
32. Simmel, *The Philosophy of Money*, p. 227.
33. Imtiaz Habib discusses '[t]he practice of employing foreigners with specialist skills' in 'The Black Alien in *Othello*: Beyond the European Immigrant', in *Shakespeare and Immigration*, ed. Ruben Espinosa and David Ruiter (Farnham: Ashgate, 2014), pp. 135–58, p. 136.
34. Gordon, 'Crediting Errors', p. 179.
35. Gordon makes a similar observation, finding that 'Antipholus of Syracuse does live up to the fantasy', 'Crediting Errors', p. 179.
36. Ahmed, 'Affective Economies', p. 123.
37. Anthony Munday, Henry Chettle, Thomas Dekker, Thomas Heywood and William Shakespeare, *Sir Thomas More*, ed. John Jowett (London: Bloomsbury, 2011), 1.123–9.

38. Jacques Derrida, *The Death Penalty*, vol. 1, ed. Geoffrey Bennington, Marc Crépon and Thomas Dutoit, trans. Peggy Kamuf (Chicago and London: University of Chicago Press, 2014), p. 262, p. 152.
39. Derrida, *The Death Penalty*, vol. 1, p. 166.
40. Jacques Derrida, *The Death Penalty*, vol. 2, ed. Geoffrey Bennington and Marc Crépon, trans. Elizabeth Rottenberg (Chicago and London: University of Chicago Press, 2017), p. 83.
41. Derrida, *The Death Penalty*, vol. 2, p. 4.
42. Derrida, *The Death Penalty*, vol. 1, p. 257.
43. Other common symptoms included vomiting unusual objects, distended body parts, and sudden changes in voice and behaviour. As James Sharpe notes in *Instruments of Darkness: Witchcraft in England, 1550–1750* (London: Penguin, 1997) 'in studying possession cases, we are looking at very stereotyped patterns of behaviour' (p. 195).
44. Robert Burton, *The Anatomy of Melancholy*, vol. 1, ed. Thomas C. Faulkner, Nicholas K. Kiessling and Rhonda, L. Blair (Oxford: Oxford University Press, 2012), Subsection 2, l. 6.
45. Quoted by Boyd Brogan in 'His Belly, Her Seed: Gender and Medicine in Early Modern Demonic Possession', *Representations*, 147 (2019), 1–25, p. 7.
46. For detailed analysis of these debates in the Middle Ages, see Nancy Caciola, *Discerning Spirits: Divine and Demonic Possession in the Middle Ages* (Ithaca and London: Cornell University Press, 2003), pp. 179–207.
47. James I, *Daemonologie*, in *King James VI and I: Selected Writings*, ed. Neil Rhodes, Jennifer Richards and Joseph Marshall (London and New York: Routledge, 2016), Book 2, Chapter 5, p. 178.
48. Cited by Stuart Clark in *Thinking with Demons: The Idea of Witchcraft in Early Modern Europe* (Oxford: Oxford University Press, 2005), p. 401.
49. Hilaire Kallendorf, *Exorcism and Its Texts: Subjectivity in Early Modern Literature of England and Spain* (Toronto: University of Toronto Press, 2003), p. 23.
50. William Shakespeare, *The Tempest*, ed. Stephen Orgel (Oxford: Oxford University Press, 2008), 1.2.274–81.

51. Brian P. Levack, *The Devil Within: Possession and Exorcism in the Christian West* (London and New Haven: Yale University Press, 2013), p. 81. In particular, see the discussion of 'Physical Force', pp. 103–5.
52. Duffy, *Stripping of the Altars*, p. 280.
53. *The Comedy of Errors*, 4.3.45n.
54. Lyndal Roper, *Witch Craze: Terror and Fantasy in Baroque Germany* (New Haven: Yale University Press, 2004), p. 87.
55. For a revisionist view, see Charlotte-Rose Millar, 'Diabolical Men: Reintegrating Male Witches into English Witchcraft', *The Seventeenth Century* (2020), 1–21.
56. Frances Dolan, *Dangerous Familiars: Representations of Domestic Crime in England, 1550–1700* (Ithaca: Cornell University Press, 1994), p. 190.
57. See Julia M. Garrett, 'Witchcraft and Sexual Knowledge in Early Modern England', *The Journal for Early Modern Cultural Studies*, 13:1 (2013), 32–72.
58. For further reading, see Sari Katajala-Peltomaa, *Demonic Possession and Lived Religion in Later Medieval Europe* (Oxford: Oxford University Press, 2020), and Roper, *Witch Craze*, especially the chapter on 'Sex with the Devil', pp. 82–103.
59. John Cotta, *The Trial of Witchcraft*, in *The Major Works of John Cotta: The Short Discovery (1612) and The Trial of Witchcraft (1616)*, ed. Todd H. J. Pettigrew, Stephanie M. Pettigrew and Jacques A. Bailly (Leiden: Brill, 2018), Chapter 12, p. 372.
60. Joseph Candido, 'Dining out in Ephesus: Food in *The Comedy of Errors*', *Studies in English Literature, 1500–1900*, 30:2 (1990), 217–41, p. 225.
61. William Perkins, *A Discourse of the Damned Art of Witchcraft* (London, 1610), p. 169.
62. William Shakespeare, *Measure for Measure*, ed. J. W. Lever (London: Thomson Learning, 2006), 1.2.143–4.
63. Homer, *The Odyssey*, trans. Walter Shewring (Oxford: Oxford University Press, 2008), Book 10, p. 118.
64. Homer, *The Odyssey*, Book 10, p. 122.
65. Homer, *The Odyssey*, Book 10, pp. 121–2. For further reading, see James A. W. Heffernan, *Hospitality and Treachery in*

Western Literature (New Haven and London: Yale University Press, 2014), especially the chapter on 'Classical Hospitality', pp. 13–40.

66. Ovid, *Metamorphoses*, trans. A. D. Melville (Oxford: Oxford University Press, 2008), Book 12, p. 280.
67. Ovid, *Metamorphoses*, Book 12, p. 281.
68. Katajala-Peltomaa, *Demonic Possession and Lived Religion*, p. 35. In *Devil Within*, Levack provides numerous examples of demoniacs whose possession by demons took place via the mouth, while adding that the Devil could also enter the body through its other orifices: the 'nostrils, ears, wounds, the anus, and so on' (p. 20).
69. Of the term 'bless you!', Richard Sugg writes in *The Smoke of the Soul: Medicine, Physiology and Religion in Early Modern England* (Basingstoke: Palgrave, 2013) that 'for many people in past centuries the phrase would probably have been a much more dramatic magical safeguard. It reflected the belief that a sneeze could temporarily eject the soul, leaving the body especially vulnerable to demonic attack or possession until its return' (p. 47). For further reading, see Laura Seymour, 'The Feasting Table as the Gateway to Hell on the Early Modern Stage and Page', *Renaissance Studies*, 34:3 (2020), 392–411.
70. Ebenezer Cobham Brewer, *Dictionary of Phrase and Fable* (Cambridge: Cambridge University Press, 2014). Brewer notes that '[i]n Leonardo da Vinci's famous picture of the Lord's Supper, Judas Iscariot is known by the saltcellar knocked over accidentally by his arm' (p. 782). See, too, Margaret Visser, *The Rituals of Dinner: The Origins, Evolution, Eccentricities, and Meaning of Table Manners* (London: Penguin, 1992). Reginald Scot wrote of witches in *The Discoverie of Witchcraft* (London, 1584) that they can 'sail in an Egge-shel, a Cockle or Muscel-shel, through and under the tempestuous Seas' (Chapter 4, p. 6).
71. William Shakespeare, *Macbeth*, ed. Kenneth Muir (London: Methuen & Co. Ltd., 2006), 1.3.4–6.
72. Dolan, *Dangerous Familiars*, p. 183.
73. Mary Douglas, *Purity and Danger: An Analysis of Concepts of Pollution and Taboo* (London: Routledge, 2002), p. 150.

74. Gail Kern Paster, *The Body Embarrassed: Drama and the Disciplines of Shame in Early Modern England* (Ithaca: Cornell University Press, 1993), p. 25.
75. Jean-Luc Nancy, *Corpus*, trans. Richard A. Rand (New York: Fordham University Press, 2008), p. 162.
76. Several scholars have called Egeon's disappearance from the play ghostly. In 'Following Hapless Egeon: Casting the Wanderers in *The Comedy of Errors*', *POMPA: Publications of the Mississippi Philological Association* (2006), 19–23, John R. Ford notes that 'Egeon will remain absent from the play, like a ghost, until well into the final scene' (p. 19). Heinze finds that he 'becomes more a forgotten spectre than a looming one', in 'Were it not against our laws' (p. 236). Furthering the uncanny atmosphere, Cartwright speculates on how Egeon's part was likely doubled with Doctor Pinch and that both roles were played by John Sinklo, see, 'Language, Magic, the Dromios, and *The Comedy of Errors*', *Studies in English Literature 1500–1900*, 47:2 (2007), 331–54.
77. For more on this, see: G. R. Elliott, 'Weirdness in *The Comedy of Errors*', *University of Toronto Quarterly*, 9:1 (1939), 95–106; Barbara Freedman, 'Reading Errantly: Misrecognition and the Uncanny in *The Comedy of Errors*', in *The Comedy of Errors: Critical Essays*, ed. Robert S. Miola (London: Routledge, 2012), pp. 261–97.
78. Sigmund Freud, 'The Uncanny', in *The Standard Edition of the Complete Psychological Works of Sigmund Freud*, vol. 17, trans. James Strachey (London: The Hogarth Press, 1981), pp. 217–56, pp. 220–46.
79. Julia Kristeva, *Strangers to Ourselves*, trans. Leon S. Roudiez (New York: Columbia University Press, 1991), p. 191.
80. Sigmund Freud, 'Repression', in *The Standard Edition of the Complete Psychological Works of Sigmund Freud*, vol. 14, trans. James Strachey (London: The Hogarth Press, 1981), pp. 141–58, p. 153.
81. Freud, 'Repression', p. 153*n*.
82. Arnold van Gennep, *The Rites of Passage*, trans. Monika B. Yizedom and Gabrielle L. Caffee (Chicago: University of Chicago Press, 1960), p. 26.

83. Pitt-Rivers, 'The Law of Hospitality', p. 172. For other anthropological perspectives on the sacred stranger tradition, see: A. M. Hocart, *The Life-giving Myth and Other Essays*, ed. Lord Raglan (London: Methuen, 1952); Marshall Sahlins, 'The Stranger-King or, Elementary Forms of the Politics of Life', *Indonesia and the Malay World*, 36:105 (2009), 177–99.
84. Patrice Ladwig, 'Visitors from Hell: Transformative Hospitality to Ghosts in a Lao Buddhist Festival', *Journal of the Royal Anthropological Institute*, 18 (2012), 90–102, pp. 91–2. See, too, Dan Waters and Tim Ko, 'The Hungry Ghosts Festival in Aberdeen Street, Hong Kong', *Journal of the Royal Asiatic Society Hong Kong Branch*, 44 (2004), 41–55.
85. Derrida, *Of Hospitality*, p. 77.
86. Giorgio Agamben, *Homo Sacer: Sovereign Power and Bare Life*, trans. Daniel Heller-Roazen (Stanford: Stanford University Press, 1998), p. 18.
87. Derrida, *The Death Penalty*, vol. 1, p. 47.

CHAPTER 2

COSMOPOLITAN SOUNDSCAPES IN *THE MERCHANT OF VENICE*

> Hath not a Jew eyes? Hath not a Jew hands, organs, dimensions, senses, affections, passions?
> Shakespeare, *The Merchant of Venice*

Somehow the senses have got detached from the stranger question in critical work on *The Merchant of Venice*, even though Shylock's urgent appeal to the universality of the senses and emotions is at the heart of this play. The present chapter reads hospitality in *The Merchant of Venice* as a sensory experience. Hospitality entails the movement of bodies coming into contact with one another and with their environment; it is a moment rich in corporeal and emotional possibilities. Given hospitality's affinity with food and eating, it might seem intuitive to begin an analysis with the senses of smell and taste. After all, as Mikhail Bakhtin notes, '[t]he encounter of man with the world, which takes place inside the open, biting, rending, chewing mouth, is one of the most ancient, and most important objects of human thought and imagery.'[1] Certainly, much excellent scholarship on *The Merchant of Venice* has focused on negative portrayals of eating and the failure of table fellowship.[2]

Religious prohibitions on consuming certain foods and other differences in dietary cuisine reinforce the tensions and divisions between the Jewish and Christian characters. In response to Bassanio's dinner invitation, Shylock says:

> Yes, to smell pork, to eat of the habitation which your prophet the Nazarite conjured the devil into. I will buy with you, sell with you, talk with you, walk with you and so following. But I will not eat with you, drink with you nor pray with you.[3]

Culinary allusions in the play are used to indicate the extent to which social relations have deteriorated. Early on, Shylock consents to lend Antonio three thousand ducats (to subsidise Bassanio's wooing expedition to Belmont) on the condition that, if Antonio defaults on the terms of the bond and does not repay the loan within a three-month period, then Shylock can cut off a pound of flesh. Shylock approaches the bond in gastronomic terms, remarking that he will 'feed fat the ancient grudge' (1.3.43) he bears the Christian. When pressed on the impracticality of the bond's main clause, he says later that Antonio's mutilated flesh will 'bait fish withal; if it will feed nothing else, it will feed my revenge' (3.1.48–9). All the way through *The Merchant of Venice*, the gustatory and olfactory pleasures of a meal shared with friends and neighbours are replaced with signifiers of empty nourishment.

By contrast, this chapter takes a different approach from the above. It centres on the sense of hearing, which has been somewhat neglected in the existing scholarship even though *The Merchant of Venice* is one of Shakespeare's more musical plays. In particular, it is the *ethical* importance of listening to the language and practices of hospitality which informs the thematic direction of the argument. I am interested in the ethics of listening and argue that to give someone your time and attention is a form of hospitality related to cognate ideas of openness, receptivity and care. Welcoming societies tend to encourage a polyphony of voices. On the other hand, selective deafness and a refusal to listen to other people is usually synonymous with intolerant ethics. As we will see, in *The Merchant of Venice*, music can bring people together, but there are risks to being overheard by one's neighbours, and the play correspondingly includes more sinister representations of eavesdropping and other intrusive modes of listening. Acoustics in *The Merchant of Venice*, then, can either inform or undermine acts of hospitality. Attending to the Shakespearean soundscape can thus enable us to reconsider how ethical dilemmas connect to hospitality, as well as some of the ways in which the reception of outsiders is a sensory event. In *The Merchant of Venice*, relations among friends and strangers are characterised by acts of listening, by choices *not* to listen and by active silencing. It is not simply a matter of recognising the rich and seductive cosmopolitan soundscapes of Shakespeare's Venice but of conceptualising how selective listening, unspoken rules and unheard voices are central to the profound ethical questions the drama raises.

The chapter begins with some of the sounds and noises which accompany performances of hospitality in the early modern theatre, before going on to provide a taxonomy of ethical listening in current criticism. I end the first section by drawing a connection between deaf ears and inhospitality in *The Merchant of Venice*. Section two then provides historical context on key discoveries in Renaissance otology, looking at how scientific and religious debates about the anatomy of the ear emerged in tandem with a vocabulary of hospitality. As noted in the introduction to this book, Shakespearean thresholds are liminal spaces, alternately sites of hospitality or expulsion. Our ears, too, are bony little thresholds that have become adept at filtering out unwanted noises. Listening and welcoming guests are ethical choices, dependent on a selection process designed to exclude particular sounds or people. Indeed, we do not give the same concentration to every noise we hear, nor do we welcome just anybody inside our homes. In the third section, I turn to how this filtering process is staged in Portia's Belmont, while the fourth section examines Jewish auditory experience, comparing public and private soundscapes in *The Merchant of Venice* in order to reveal how Shylock's listening habits are a reflection of his precarious civilian status as a guest resident within the Republic. The fifth section considers the acoustics of the courtroom scene, reading the law court as a counter-space where you go after hospitality has failed. By briefly surveying the philosophical literature, I suggest some of the ways that the law has long been considered a problem for hospitality. Here, the legal framework ensures that hospitality remains only ever conditional and contingent on the continued compliance of the foreigner. Lastly, to read hospitality through the soundscape of *The Merchant of Venice* paradoxically means being alert to silences, pauses, gaps and omissions, things left unsaid, as well as the unspoken laws and customs which control relations between guest and host. The chapter ends with Shylock's silence when he leaves the Venetian courtroom, and how this grows into a more troubling quiet during the play's closing scene in Belmont.

'I know him by his knock'

On a recent visit to Morocco, I was wandering around the old part of the Fez medina with a local guide when he pointed out a house with a curious front door. On the door were two door knockers: one was set in the top right-hand corner of the wooden frame, while the other was lower down and attached to the door itself. As the guide explained, one was meant to be used by neighbours, friends and family, while the other was reserved for strangers. Once rapped by an unseen newcomer, each door knocker would make a distinctive noise, sending its unique acoustic reverberations echoing through the interior spaces of the home. It struck me at the time that this old-fashioned Fez house had found a particularly elegant way to answer the age-old question of who's there.

In early modern drama, visitors are sometimes audibly recognisable from a distance or even when unseen. Ben Jonson's *Volpone*, for example, has Mosca respond to the sound of knocking at the door with, "'Tis Signor Voltore, the advocate / I know him, by his knock.'[4] Voltore's signature door knock is one of several aural markers on the early modern stage that is moreover indicative of the ways in which we listen out for newcomers as well as watching for their arrival. In Shakespeare's plays, characters are often identified by their 'gait' which, according to the *Oxford English Dictionary*, means both a person's '[m]anner of walking or stepping' and one's 'bearing or carriage while moving'.[5] Upon hearing someone coming in *Julius Caesar*, Cassius says, "'Tis Cinna. I do know him by his gait', while in *Othello*, Roderigo comments of Cassio, 'I know his gait', and Ceres in *The Tempest* says, 'Great Juno comes; I know her by her gait.'[6] Shakespeare's interest in characters who have a distinctive style of walking has been taken up by modern scholars working in the field of behavioural biometrics. Conducting research into the degree of accuracy with which we recognise other people based on the sound that they make while walking (apparently nearly 80 per cent under test conditions), Patrick Bours and Adrian Evensen explain how they named their project the Shakespeare Experiment in 'homage to Shakespeare for "initiating" the field of biometric sound-based gait recognition over 400 years ago'.[7] *The Merchant of Venice* proves the theory that the outsider in Shakespeare is recognisable through aural sensations. As they sit together in the garden at Belmont, Jessica interrupts her new husband, Lorenzo, to say: 'But hark, I hear the footing of a man' (5.1.24). Lorenzo then correctly identifies the sound of Portia returning home:

> | | |
> |---|---|
> | *Lorenzo* | That is the voice, |
> | | Or I am much deceived, of Portia. |
> | *Portia* | He knows me as the blind man knows the cuckoo: |
> | | By the bad voice! |
> | *Lorenzo* | Dear lady, welcome home. |
>
> (5.1.110–13)

Not long afterwards, Lorenzo notifies his hostess, '[y]our husband is at hand, I hear his trumpet' (5.1.122). As is clear from these examples, hospitality generates its own acoustics – from the sound of footsteps to music and shouts of salutation. At the noisier end of the spectrum, we might think of Antipholus of Ephesus' attempts to break into his own house, Timon's extravagant dinner parties, or Hal and Falstaff's rowdy antics at the Boar's Head inn. Jacques Derrida discusses the loud clamour of hospitality when he writes that '[w]e are welcomed at the very outset under the sign of a sign of hospitality, at the sign of hospitality, by the witty remark of a hosteller, the questionable words of a host or the bad humour of an innkeeper.'[8] In the current chapter, however, I am less concerned with the sounds of hospitality than with the ethical dimensions of listening.

Within early modern studies, important work by Bruce R. Smith, Wes Folkerth and Jennifer Linhart Wood has enhanced our knowledge of literary and cultural soundscapes. Smith, for instance, makes an interesting distinction between listening and hearing:

> About hearing you have no choice: you can shut off vision by closing your eyes, but from birth to death, in waking and in sleep, the coils of flesh, the tiny bones, the hair cells, the nerve fibres are always at the ready [. . .] To listen, however, is a choice. What's more, you can choose *how* to listen.[9]

Our ears are permanently open but, in spite of this fact, they are *not* universally receptive to the world around us, which is why to choose to give someone your time or attention can be interpreted as an act of welcome, extending our definition of how hospitality works in practice. Discussing James Joyce's *Ulysses*, Derrida picks up on this concept of receptivity:

> There are several modalities or tonalities of the telephonic *yes*, but one of them, without saying anything else, amounts to marking, simply, that one is *there*, present, listening, on the other end of the line, ready to respond but not for the moment responding anything other than the preparation to respond (hello, yes: I'm listening, I can hear that you are there, ready to speak just when I am ready to speak to you).[10]

Even without needing to say anything, a disembodied listener whose presence is merely felt down the telephone line is comforting and signals a future commitment to respond. Silence can be intensely welcoming and again offers another iteration of hospitality that we might not expect. Derrida is surely right to argue that there is 'a series of metonymies that bespeak hospitality, the face, welcome: tending toward the other, attentive intention, intentional attention, *yes* to the other'.[11] At the same time, though, and as I show later in the chapter, silence can indicate exclusion and a rejection of the other.

The scholarly discussion of sound in early modern drama has not touched on these ethical dimensions of listening and acoustics. In *Sounding Otherness in Early Modern Drama and Travel: Uncanny Vibrations in the English Archive*, Jennifer Linhart Wood draws on Freud's theory of the *unheimlich* to read the sonic uncanny. Although not writing about hospitality (the word appears nowhere in the book), Wood notes the way in which acoustic vibrations trouble the separation between self and other, familiar and foreign. Sound, she suggests, 'is a vibrational action that undoes the boundaries between a listening subject and a sound-producing object or other, between sensor and sensation'.[12] The philosophical implications of this are not explored in Wood's work, however. Nevertheless, scholarship in other disciplines suggests the potential for fresh insights into Shakespeare's plays. As the communication theorist Lisbeth Lipari notes, listening 'is essential to the ethical encounter', for it creates 'a *dwelling place* from where we offer our hospitality to the other and the world'.[13] Lipari writes, too, of the ethical response that 'arises from intentionally engaging with what is unfamiliar, strange, and not already understood' and which 'listens to the other's suffering as a kind of hospitality, invitation, a hosting'.[14] In a similar mode, the theologian Krista E. Hughes draws on a vocabulary of civic responsibility and, in particular, neighbourliness, in order to demonstrate that, even though 'listening carries risk', at the same time an 'unwillingness to have our perspective challenged, at the risk that we ourselves might be changed, works in tandem with a refusal to listen well'.[15] In what follows, I draw on insights from communication studies and philosophy to show how this can be used to interrogate hospitality in Shakespeare in interesting new ways.

Of special relevance to my reading of *The Merchant of Venice* is the fact that listening carefully is not simply a private or individual act. It is a civic and public duty that contributes to the creation of community. Listening indicates an openness to change and a willingness to be moved by the harmonies of social life, the appeal of the other, or by the world at large. Furthermore, to be truly welcoming means permitting oneself to be *emotionally* impacted as well as tangibly intruded upon by the coming of the stranger. 'To welcome a stranger', Jean-Luc Nancy writes, 'is necessarily to experience his intrusion.'[16] According to Judith Still, to be hospitable 'implies letting the other in to oneself, to one's own space – it is invasive of the integrity of the self, or the domain of the self. This is why it may be seen as both foundational (to be fully human is to be able to alter, to be altered – as Rousseau suggests) and dangerous.'[17] We might speak here of a *kinetics of hospitality*. Sensory experience is embodied in spaces and things, in the realm of visceral encounter where limits are maintained or breached. But there is also an ethical interleaving of inner and outer in which the external movement of crossing a threshold is replicated in the inner life of the senses and emotions. Other people have a tendency to stir us and get under our skin, moving us in some incomprehensible way. Conversely, a refusal either to listen or be hospitable can dovetail with a wider reluctance to be emotionally swayed by the outside world. As Lorenzo says to Jessica in the play's conclusion, to which I will return later in the chapter:

> The man that hath no music in himself,
> Nor is not moved with concord of sweet sounds,
> Is fit for treasons, stratagems, and spoils;
> The motions of his spirit are dull as night
> And his affections dark as Erebus.
> Let no such man be trusted.
>   (5.1.83–8)

As Lorenzo sees it, the subject who refuses either to listen to music or to let himself be passionately influenced by the pleas of others is deeply troubling and threatening to the whole social edifice. However – and this is a crucial point – by the ending of *The Merchant of Venice*, the superficial achievement of social and domestic harmony is accompanied by discord and the enforced silencing of unwelcome outsiders. Lorenzo says that he distrusts those who are unmoved by music, yet he and many other characters are receptive only to those whose sounds are pleasing to them.

In *The Merchant of Venice*, then, acts of listening enable social harmony but are selective and premised on competing exclusions or silencings. Throughout the play, there is a dynamic of heard and unheard, spoken and unspoken at work in the interactions between the Jewish and Christian characters. Before the courtroom scene, Antonio comes on stage in the jailer's custody and has this curt encounter with Shylock:

> *Antonio*   I pray thee, hear me speak.
> *Jew*   I'll have my bond. I will not hear thee speak.
> (3.3.11–12)

The extent to which words fall on deaf ears in *The Merchant of Venice* is an indication that cosmopolitanism in the Republic has failed. Later, Shylock will attempt to rely on the letter of the law in order to silence moral objections to his bond. What he does not realise, though, is that the justice system and the nuances of legal language in the Republic encode silences and omissions that will eventually lead to the erasure of his Jewishness and his forced conversion to Christianity. In the end, Shylock becomes a victim of what the law implies but leaves unsaid. The ethics of listening in Shakespeare's play thus extend into the legal dimensions by which the community of Venice regulates its openness to strangers.

'These darke laborinths'

Early modern anatomists looking to depict the curiously hidden recesses of the human ear frequently drew on a household topography of winding passages, doors and stairways. One of the most significant achievements in Renaissance otology was made by Italian physician Bartolomeo Eustachi, who did just this. He discovered what would later become known as the Eustachian tube, or the narrow channel connecting the ear and throat. Describing the discovery in *An Epistle on the Organs of Hearing*, Eustachi refers to the pipeline as 'a way', a 'passage' and as 'a very ample pathway'.[18] Equally, of the smaller facial nerve, he writes that it 'slips from the skull by a remarkably twisted exit'.[19] Near the end of the *Epistle*, while praising 'the ingenuity of nature in the construction and protection of the auditory organ', Eustachi notes that the ear contains 'steps' which enable 'the voice to ascend'.[20] The metaphor is of a household interior, with movement from the lower floor to the upper, or from the outer to the inner rooms.

These glimpses of residential building design found in Eustachi's *Epistle* are echoed and expanded upon in Helkiah Crooke's *Microcosmographia* (1616). Crooke introduces new comparisons to domestic space and everyday objects. In the extract below, he explains how the sense of hearing works:

> The Ayre endowed with the quality of a sound is through the auditory passage, which outwardly is always open, first stricken against the most drie and sounding membrane, which is therefore called Tympanum, or the Drumme. The membrane being strucken doth mooue the three littel bones, and in a moment maketh impression of the character of the sound. This sound is presently receiued of the inbred Ayre, which it carryeth through the windowes of the stony bone before described, into the winding burroughs, and so into the Labyrinth, after into the Snail-shell, and lastly into the Auditory Nerue which conueyeth it thence vnto the common Sense as vnto his Censor and Iudge.[21]

The corkscrew parts of the ear are compared to a '[l]abyrinth', a '[s]nail-shell' and, in another chapter of the *Microcosmographia*, 'the windings of these darke laborinths'.[22] Crooke offsets these convoluted, maze-like spatial images with another group of references to ordinary domestic architecture. Thus, sounds are 'carryeth through the windowes of the stony bone'. The *Oxford English Dictionary* cites *Microcosmographia* as the first recorded usage in English of the term 'windows' for the two openings connecting the middle and inner ear (known today as the oval window and the round window).[23] By including these and other comparisons to architectural design, Crooke domesticates for his reader the labyrinthine topography of the human ear. In addition, a comparable effect is achieved through allusions to commonplace objects that one might find lying around the house. One of the ear's membranes is said to be 'translucide and pollished like a Looking-glasse'.[24]

Crooke's imagery is playful and inventive throughout, but it is his analogies of urban architecture which are most compelling. Of another auditory canal, for instance, he writes that '[t]his passage therefore is oblique and winding to breake the vehement appulsion, or rushing in of cold ayre'.[25] Concepts of ventilation, heating and air flow are again known to us from residential building design. In this way, English Renaissance otology builds on the Italian tradition by helping to ingrain scientific models of the ear within a domestic setting.

Before long, early modern writing about acoustic perception evolved past the static references to household architecture noted already. Our sense of hearing is, of course, dependent on movement, friction and impact. Sound is produced through the motion of airy particles coming into contact with their environment and the resulting acoustic vibrations and echoes which are felt along the tympanum, or drum. So as to describe the materiality of sound and the movement of the air, authors drew on a vocabulary of hospitality and other guest behaviours. Sounds from the outside world penetrating 'the air-filled chambers of the listener's ears' could intuitively be compared to visitors being ushered inside the private household.[26] In several places, Eustachi's *Epistle* uses the language of hospitality to illuminate the hidden workings of the ear. While labelling the fifth pair of cerebral nerves, he points out that 'on each side there are two branches of unequal size, of which the larger [acoustic] nerve has a canal [internal acoustic meatus] skilfully hollowed out along its length in the form of a semicircle in which it *hospitably receives and enfolds* the smaller [facial] nerve fleeing from the others' [my emphasis].²⁷ Later, writing about a portion of the Eustachian tube, Eustachi repeatedly directs his reader's attention to the 'strong cartilage' it contains, explaining how 'its substance is cartilaginous and very thick', before continuing:

> At the end of the same passage [pharyngeal orifice] there seems to be a kind of doorway, not rounded in shape but somewhat depressed with two angles; the width of the cavity almost equals that of a reed, but at the end it is double the width of its origin and covered with a thin, mucous-like substance.²⁸

Eustachi's allusion to 'a kind of doorway' is taken up by Crooke in the *Microcosmographia*. In the chapter entitled 'of the Canale out of the Eare into the mouth', he notes how:

> the inward extremity or end of this passage where it respecteth the middle cauity of the nostrilles becommeth a strong gristle bunching or swelling much outward, which is couered with the mucous or slimy coate of the nose, and set as a Porter to keep the end or outlet of the passage.²⁹

Converting Eustachi's doorway into a dynamic reference to a *doorkeeper*, Crooke personifies the tough inner ear cartilage as a 'Porter', whose responsibility is 'to keep the end or outlet of the passage'. In the same way a porter is selective over the admission of guests to the home, the gristly part of the ear is supposed to exercise caution when it comes to admitting foreign entities into the body.

Another literary genre where we notice the hospitable ear metaphor gaining in popularity is in sixteenth-century sermons which instructed their readers on the right way to listen in church.³⁰ In seeking to communicate the spiritual importance of listening carefully, preachers turned to the same language of hospitality found in the anatomy books. The overarching aim of these sermons was to produce congregations of astute listeners, who did not attend to everything they heard indiscriminately, but were attuned only to the spiritual word. Jennifer Rae McDermott notes the contradiction inherent in the fact that early modern preachers praised 'the open pathway of the ear' as the route to religious awakening, yet simultaneously drew on a 'recurring language of locks, thresholds, and doorways' to stress the necessity of 'acoustic vigilance'.[31] Citing from William Harrison's *The Difference of Hearers* (1614), she suggests that 'the door of the ear must be open enough to admit God, but it should also be guarded carefully so that the "Diuell" cannot steal in "to take the worde out of your hearts"'.[32] Similarly, in his *Sermon of hearing or, A jewell for the eare* (1593), Robert Wilkinson reasons that, 'if the ear be the door of the heart', then 'might David say, Lift up your heads, ye gates, and be you open you everlasting doores: and *not every guest*, but the King of glory shal come in' (my emphasis).[33] Sermons like these by Harrison and Wilkinson employ a rhetoric of hospitality in order to emphasise the need for acoustic discretion, encouraging the parishioner to listen to God's teachings, but to turn a deaf ear to the devil and other temptations.

Sensory caution is a recurring theme in Shakespeare's drama as well. Noticing that a 'strange guest' has found their way inside Aufidius' home in *Coriolanus*, a serving man says, '[h]as the porter his eyes in his head that he gives entrance to such companions?'[34] Although *Coriolanus* alludes to sight, acoustic perception is another important defence against unwanted intruders. As numerous literary critics have noted, Shakespeare appears to have been fascinated by the ears' perpetual openness and hence their susceptibility to intrusion.[35] 'Among the associations ears have in the early modern period', Folkerth argues, 'is that they are pregnable, and therefore potential targets of violent attack. This is especially apparent in Shakespeare's work. The ears are specified as sites of extreme vulnerability in almost every one of the major tragedies.'[36] In *Hamlet*, the ghost remembers how, one afternoon, Claudius stole into the orchard while he was sleeping:

> And in the porches of my ears did pour
> The leperous distilment whose effect
> Holds such an enmity with blood of man
> That swift as quicksilver it courses through
> The natural gates and alleys of the body.[37]

The ghost uses architectural imagery of the built environment to convey how his vulnerable ears or 'porches' had no choice but to welcome these poisonous guests.

Across a broad range of sixteenth- and seventeenth-century writings – and in fields as diverse as science, religion and literature – we find listening compared to a form of hospitality or openness to the world at large. Microscopic thresholds constructed of flesh, bone and gristle, our ears are adept at filtering out unwanted sounds, just as a good porter can expertly shield us from unwanted visitors. Of course, for every guest who is welcomed, many others are left out, and neither listening nor being welcoming are neutral activities. In the next section, I examine how this filtering method is staged in *The Merchant of Venice*. For whether we picture them as gates, doors or other threshold spaces, our ears are sites to guard against potential danger or transgression, as well as more complex ethical choices.

Eavesdropping

Over in Belmont, Portia is a reluctant hostess. On account of the casket test planned by her father before his death, she is obliged to accommodate a long line of temporary house guests. 'The will of Portia's father creates a paradox', Geraldo de Sousa notes, because 'he wants his daughter to find a loving Venetian husband and have a secure home; yet the lottery of the caskets turns her house into a lodging house for adventurers and passersby'.[38] Complaining to her companion Nerissa about their unusual living arrangement, Portia says:

> O me, the word 'choose'! I may neither choose who I would, nor refuse who I dislike, so is the will of a living daughter curbed by the will of a dead father. Is it not hard, Nerissa, that I cannot choose one, nor refuse none?
> (1.2.21–5)

The *supposedly* impartial casket test, referred to several times in the play as a 'lottery' (1.2.27, 2.1.15), is intended to eliminate choice from the hospitality relationship.[39] As Portia's comment above makes clear, she has no say in the decision-making process, since any undesirable visitors to Belmont are weeded out through their own poor judgement. Shakespeare does not leave things there, however, on this apparently neutral note. Part of what makes *The Merchant of Venice* so intriguing from an outsider perspective is that it vocalises things often left unsaid when accommodating visitors.

By permitting the audience to eavesdrop on Portia's uncensored opinion of her house guests, the play makes a usually private soundscape audible. In personal conference with Nerissa, Portia confesses that the suitors whom she has met so far have aroused in her a unanimous dislike, to the extent that she cannot wait to be rid of them. Upon hearing that they are all preparing to leave Belmont, she says, 'I am glad this parcel of wooers are so reasonable, for there is not one among them but I dote on his very absence, and I pray God grant them a fair departure' (1.2.103–6). As another suitor, the Prince of Morocco, then arrives, she quips, '[i]f I could bid the fifth welcome with so good heart as I can bid the other four farewell, I should be glad of his approach' (1.2.122–4). And yet, before the current group of strangers departs, Nerissa quizzes Portia on how she feels about them:

> Nerissa   But what warmth is there in your affection towards any of these princely suitors that are already come?
>
> Portia   I pray thee over-name them and, as thou namest them, I will describe them, and according to my description level at my affection.
> (1.2.31–36)

What follows is described by B. J. Sokol as 'a string of comically weak but possibly ethically acceptable "nationality" jokes' about the Neapolitan prince, the County Palatine, the French lord, Monsieur le Bon, Falconbridge, the English baron, the Scottish lord and the young German, the Duke of Saxony's nephew.[40] For Edward Berry, the play offers a good example of 'the exclusionary impulse behind Hobbesian laughter'.[41] Certainly for modern audiences, Portia's critique of the foreigners housed under her roof makes for uncomfortable listening. Everything racist and offensive which she says about the strangers would, under normal circumstances, be kept quiet: either left unsaid, or unheard by anyone other than an intimate confidant. However, by allowing us to eavesdrop on these rude, confidential insights into how Portia really feels towards her house guests, Shakespeare takes the time to provide us with a backstage glimpse into what goes on behind the scenes in the Belmont household. Here, as elsewhere in *The Merchant of Venice*, it is revealed that, beneath the polite ceremonies of hospitality and the outer façade of liberal cosmopolitanism and diversity, things can get quite ugly, so echoing the inscription on the gold casket: 'All that glisters is not gold' (2.7.65).

Portia's crude national stereotyping of her overseas visitors serves another purpose. Not only does it render audible things normally left unheard by guests and hosts, but her comments convey the arbitrary nature of hospitality's selection methods. In other words, her vetting of the suitors reveals the unfairness of clutching at straws in order to rationalise our often deeply subjective motives for welcoming certain outsiders even while we exclude others. The capriciousness of our personal tastes and whims is a theme which resonates across the text as a whole, for *The Merchant of Venice* makes a sustained connection between our idiosyncratic musical preferences and why we respond well to some people but not to everyone. Responding to Antonio's complaint at the beginning of the play that he does not understand why he feels so sad, Salanio says:

> Nature hath framed strange fellows in her time:
> Some that will evermore peep through their eyes
> And laugh like parrots at a bagpiper;
> And other of such vinegar aspect
> That they'll not show their teeth in way of smile
> Though Nestor swear the jest be laughable.
> (1.1.51–6)

Salanio's comforting reassurances to his friend are grounded on the commonplace notion that our emotions and impulses are unknowable to us and can sometimes cause us to behave irrationally. In Act 4, when Shylock is asked by the courtroom why he prefers to collect a pound of Antonio's flesh than receive the monetary value of the bond paid in full, he returns to Salanio's image of the bagpipes:

> I'll not answer that!
> But say it is my humour. Is it answered?
> What if my house be troubled with a rat,
> And I be pleased to give ten thousand ducats

> To have it baned? What, are you answered yet?
> Some men there are love not a gaping pig;
> Some that are mad if they behold a cat;
> And others when the bagpipe sings i'th' nose
> Cannot contain their urine: for affection
> Masters oft passion, sways it to the mood
> Of what it likes or loathes.
> (4.1.41–51)

During the course of this speech, which ranges widely over the dislike of some animals, gastronomic disgust, and different responses to hearing musical instruments, Shylock poses the Christians some interesting questions: where do our tastes come from? Why do we behave as we do?

Thus, when Shylock tells the listening court that his animosity towards Antonio is no more explicable than another man's dislike of the bagpipe music, he voices a connection upheld by the text between sounds we welcome inside our ears and those people we usher inside our homes. The unknowability of our emotions is mirrored, in each case, by the unjustifiability of our choices. Shakespeare's play invites us to reflect on the myriad of ways in which we go about selecting individuals whom we consider to be worthy or unworthy of our attention and hospitality. Derrida reminds us that hospitality is always reliant on a basic principle of exclusion:

> No hospitality, in the classic sense, without sovereignty of oneself over one's home, but since there is also no hospitality without finitude, sovereignty can only be exercised by filtering, choosing, and thus by excluding and doing violence. Injustice, a certain injustice, and even a certain perjury, begins right away, from the very threshold of the right to hospitality.[42]

We need to keep in mind that, when it comes to making a guest list, even the most generous of hosts is simultaneously making decisions about who is *not* welcome. For Derrida, we can never rationalise or explain this mysterious process by which we arrive at beneficiaries deemed to be deserving of our generosity: 'I can never justify this sacrifice, I must always hold my peace about it'.⁴³

Offering key choices between a gold, silver and lead casket, and between a legal bond or a pound of flesh, *The Merchant of Venice* is interested in decision-making in all its forms. The play interrogates on what grounds we make moral judgements about who or what we are prepared to welcome. One of Shakespeare's sources was a collection of fourteenth-century Italian short stories called *Il Pecorone* where, in one of the tales, a lady from Belmont plays a sly trick upon her wooers. It might initially seem as if the casket test in *The Merchant of Venice* is no more than another archaic trope drawn from the world of medieval Italian romance, but I suggest rather that Shakespeare is, in fact, encouraging a radical reassessment of whether the Belmont lottery is actually any different from the many other unfathomable ways in which we go about deciding which strangers to invite into our homes, cities or lives.

Jewish Soundscapes: Public and Private

Sensory historians have shed light on the myriad of sensations which accompanied cosmopolitan life across early modern Europe. In *Jewish Life in Renaissance Italy*, Robert Bonfil argues that, just as 'Jewish otherness conditioned the spatial and temporal universe, it also conditioned the universe of sound', not least because living regulations meant that Jews were subject to 'the overwhelming din of the stifling overpopulated ghettos'.⁴⁴ Accompanying the commotion that went with overcrowded living conditions, minorities were at risk of verbal abuse and violence. 'Flung out loosely and often indiscriminately,' Alexandra Walsham notes, 'nicknames index the irritation and hostility that could mark everyday interaction with those who espoused different faiths.'⁴⁵ In the dedication to his *Epistle*, Eustachi gives his patron, Francesco Alciati, a comparable justification as to why he presents this work on the ears. Addressing the defamation which he has been exposed to through the actions of 'certain malevolent men', Eustachi writes to Alciati that *'it was through your ears that you heard the evils and calumnies of individious men attempting to persecute me, but protected by your patronage I remained unharmed'* (my emphasis).⁴⁶ Jewish and Christian interactions in premodern Europe took place against a background which was, at times, loud and hostile. Cultural historian Daniel Jütte has found that Jewish homes routinely had their windows smashed.⁴⁷ Another aspect of the soundscape accompanying multi-ethnic life in densely populated urban areas, then, was the noise of breaking glass, an ominous precursor of Kristallnacht and the anti-Semitic demonstrations which took place across Germany in 1938.

Within the cosmopolitan and polyphonic setting of *The Merchant of Venice*, the selectivity of listening becomes paramount. Urban space can be interpreted as an ethical soundscape composed of micro inclusions and exclusions which in turn police the kinetics of daily life. Indeed, for the Jewish outsider, the Rialto is noisy, with clashes which sometimes erupt into violence. From the start of the play, the audience is made aware that Shylock has been publicly mistreated in the past by his Christian neighbours, including Antonio:

> You call me misbeliever, cut-throat dog,
> And spit upon my Jewish gabardine,
> And all for use of that which is mine own.
>   (1.3.107–9)

Open hostility towards Jews and their moneylending practices means that the soundscape of urban life in *The Merchant of*

Venice comprises racially motivated verbal abuse, name-calling and even spitting. Specifically, Shylock draws attention to how Antonio has humiliated him in the crowded districts of the city, including the place 'where merchants most do congregate' (1.3.45). The polyphonous din of the cosmopolitan soundscape is characterised by its varied acoustics and diverse ways of listening, speaking or being silent. This section considers Jewish aural experience in *The Merchant of Venice*. Comparing public and private soundscapes enables us to understand how Shylock's relationship with noise reflects his precarious citizenship and, in particular, his 'guest' status within the Republic.

I want to start, though, with the listening habits of the other members of Shylock's household. We first meet Lancelot the Clown when he is wondering aloud whether he should change employer:

> Certainly, my conscience will serve me to run from this Jew my master. The fiend is at mine elbow and tempts me, saying to me 'Gobbo, Lancelot Gobbo, good Lancelot', or 'Good Gobbo', or 'Good Lancelot Gobbo, use your legs, take the start, run away.' My conscience says 'No: take heed, honest Lancelot, take heed, honest Gobbo' – or (as aforesaid) – 'honest Lancelot Gobbo; do not run, scorn running with thy heels.'
> (2.2.1–8)

From these lines it is clear that Lancelot envisages himself as a type of Everyman in a medieval morality play, overhearing a dispute between the Devil and his conscience. The soliloquy is thick with reported speech, suggesting that he is hearing two separate voices. But whereas Everyman eventually comes to abandon worldly pleasure and think only of salvation, Lancelot's concerns never move beyond the material, and he is especially keen on his food. In a slapstick episode, Lancelot places his visually impaired father's hands on his own splayed fingers, pretending they are his bony ribs because he is so underfed in Shylock's home. Shylock also remarks on his employee's enormous appetite:

> The patch is kind enough, but a huge feeder,
> Snail-slow in profit, and he sleeps by day
> More than the wildcat.
>   (2.5.44–6)

Morality plays including *Everyman* and *Mankind* are dialogic and tend to feature the central character caught between good and evil figures who attempt either to intervene in his salvation or lead him to damnation. Lancelot's rhetorical self-fashioning is influenced by an unfashionable mode of drama, which brings with it an older style of listening behaviour. 'What the first Christians listen to', Roland Barthes argues, 'are still exterior voices, those of demons or angels; it is only gradually that the object of listening is internalised to the point of becoming pure conscience.'[48] Early on, Shylock's household becomes connected with the medieval iconography of the afterlife, as well as to older listening traditions.

In *Locating Privacy in Tudor London*, Lena Cowen Orlin discusses some of the challenges of private life in the early modern household. Building designs during the Tudor period reflected a growing trend for solitude in separate rooms, yet homes remained subject to overcrowding. Neighbourly snooping was, moreover, a time-honoured means of regulating local conduct. For the early moderns, then, the pursuit of privacy at home was difficult. Specifically on the 'eavesdropping household', Orlin writes that it was 'generally accepted that the domestic interior could not be trusted for what was called "private conference"'.[49] In *The Merchant of Venice*, it is just as hard to conduct a personal conversation in Shylock's home, since eavesdropping appears to be a routine occurrence, creating a claustrophobic atmosphere indoors. Secretly preparing to elope with the Christian gentleman Lorenzo, Jessica warns Lancelot, 'I would not have my father / See me in talk with thee' (2.3.8–9). Soon afterwards, we sure enough find Shylock attempting to eavesdrop on their conversation:

Lancelot	[*aside to Jessica*] Mistress, look out at window for all this: There will come a Christian by Will be worth a Jewess' eye.
Jew	What says that fool of Hagar's offspring, ha?
Jessica	His words were 'Farewell, mistress', nothing else.

(2.5.39–43)

But is there is a sympathetic reading of Shylock's failure to respect his daughter's privacy? Barthes makes an interesting point about sensory vigilance:

> For the mammal, its territory is marked out by odours and sounds; for the human being – and this is a phenomenon often underestimated – the appropriation of space is also a matter of sound: domestic space, that of the house, the apartment – the approximate equivalent of animal territory – is a space of familiar, *recognised* noises whose ensemble forms a kind of household symphony: differentiated slamming of doors, raised voices, kitchen noises, gurgle of pipes, murmurs from outdoors.[50]

As long as the house's soundscape stays reassuringly familiar, then it gives the occupant a powerful impression of safety. On the other hand, to detect strange noises is to awaken an older instinct for suspicious snooping. In *The Merchant of Venice*, Shylock's state of constant acoustic vigilance in a domestic setting is indicative of a broader disquiet within Venetian society. We might think of his eavesdropping as a form of defensive listening, a reaction to the verbal and physical abuse he has suffered at the hands of his Christian neighbours.

Considering the anti-Semitic abuse he has received in public, it is unsurprising that Shylock, like the Porter of the inner ear in Crooke's text, polices the acoustic boundaries of his own home. 'Immersing yourself in silence is a form of healing,' as French philosopher Michel Serres understands it.[51] Shylock is, in fact, acutely sensitive to the noise levels indoors. He reprimands Lancelot for shouting to Jessica without asking permission first – 'Who bids thee call? I do not bid thee call' (2.5.7) – and can be heard reminding those around him of the importance of fastening doors and windows. A welcoming home is one whose apertures are thrown invitingly open to the outside world. But Shylock is compulsive about ensuring his are kept firmly locked. Partly this is about religious practice, for his determination to keep his house quiet on the Sabbath means shutting out external noise. Shylock's instructions to his household emphasise the importance of insulating the interior against sounds drifting in from the street below:

> Well, Jessica, go in;
> Perhaps I will return immediately.
> Do as I bid you; shut doors after you.
> 'Fast bind, fast find.'
> A proverb never stale in thrifty mind.
>   (2.5.49–53)

An enduring attraction of the house has long been our capacity to control its soundscape. 'Beyond the reach of water,' Serres notes, 'beyond wind, cold, fog, light and dark – even beyond noise, in the past – the house protects us just as the belly of a vessel separates us from the cold of the sea.'[52] Our homes shelter us from the oceanic roar of noise which normally engulfs us in daily life. 'Sounds reach the monad softly, through doors and windows', and noise from the world outside can be shut out further still through the tactical use of 'shutters, windows, double-glazing, stained glass, net curtains, drapes, decorative pelmets, and until not so long ago, doorways and windows with deep alcoves'.[53] Commonplace characteristics of residential building design, such as the ones listed here, mean that, similar to a snail retreating further inside the recesses of its shell, the house seems capable of contracting into a deeper silence.

For the nervous homeowner, all apertures are the site of potential intrusions. Dismayed to hear from Lancelot that masques are planned for the same evening he plans to dine at Bassanio's place, Shylock instructs Jessica to soundproof his house. While this might appear a straightforward response to noisy neighbours, there are hints that Shylock is concerned about Jessica's chastity as well:

> What, are there masques? Hear you me, Jessica,
> Lock up my doors, and when you hear the drum
> And the vile squealing of the wry-necked fife,
> Clamber not you up to the casements then
> Nor thrust your head into the public street
> To gaze on Christian fools with varnished faces;
> But stop my house's ears – I mean my casements –
> Let not the sound of shallow foppery enter
> My sober house.
> (2.5.27–35)

Throughout this speech, Shylock's anthropomorphisation of the house overtly aligns it with his daughter's body. He says, 'stop my house's ears – I mean my casements'. Although he corrects himself immediately, the muddled directive reveals that Shylock is confusing Jessica's fleshy earlobes with the window casements. 'Early modern writers', Gina Bloom argues, 'figure closed ears as especially important for the maintenance of female chastity.'[54] Desdemona's 'greedy ear', for instance, through which she has devoured Othello's exotic travel narratives, is destabilising to an entire culture which venerates the patriarchal control of women's minds and bodies.⁵⁵ Shakespeare's overbearing fathers value selectively deaf ears alongside locked doors and windows.

In Act 3, Shylock's parental suspicions are justified when he learns from his friend Tubal that Jessica has eloped and taken with her his money and jewels:

> Why there, there, there, there! A diamond gone cost me two thousand ducats in Frankfurt! The curse never fell upon our nation till now, I never felt it till now. Two thousand ducats in that, and other precious, precious jewels! I would my daughter were dead at my foot, and the jewels in her ear: would she were hearsed at my foot, and the ducats in her coffin.
> (3.1.76–82)

Evocative of Catholic holy relics, which were sometimes decorated with ornate gemstones before interment, Shylock's lines extend his earlier conflation of house and body, as he envisages his daughter's corpse transformed into a storehouse for his gold and jewels. With her ear cavities stuffed full of jewels, and her coffin filled with ducats, Jessica becomes a perfectly sealed vessel, without even breath entering or leaving the body. Discussing Shakespeare's theatre, Valerie Traub suggests that 'the metaphoric displacement of sexually threatening women into jewels, statues and corpses attests that these plays contain rather than affirm female erotic power'.⁵⁶ Yet in *The Merchant of Venice*, Shylock's morbid fantasies remain ultimately unrealised, because Jessica and the jewels are, according to Tubal, nowhere to be found.

In his writings on hospitality, Derrida recognises the obvious truism that 'there is no home, no cultural home, no family home without some door, some opening and some ways of welcoming guests'.⁵⁷ However safe and cosy we may feel indoors, though, the house can never become an impermeable container, for there must always be some aperture which connects the quiet interior to the hum and whirr of the world outside. If there is no opening whatsoever – and this is where Jessica's betrayal leads Shylock – then what we have is a casket. But even the sole occupant of a coffin is not spared from the noisy intrusions of life, nor the appearance of unwanted guests, as reflected in the rich Renaissance tradition of presenting corpses as hospitable to worms and maggots. Hamlet puns on this concept of a banquet after death when he reveals the murder of Polonius:

> King Now, Hamlet, where's Polonius?
> Hamlet At supper.
> King At supper! Where?
> Hamlet Not where he eats but where 'a is eaten. A certain convocation of politic worms are e'en at him. Your worm is your only emperor for diet. We fat all creatures else to fat us, and we fat ourselves for maggots. Your fat king and your lean beggar is but variable service, two dishes but to one table.
> (4.3.16–24)

Karen Raber notes that *Hamlet* is a text about 'the experience of shared corporeality' and the question of 'what the body houses'.[58] I agree and would add that the representation of Jessica as a corpse makes a philosophical statement about the nature of hospitality in Shakespeare's *The Merchant of Venice*. Shylock's illusive fantasy of confinement fails because the coffin is no more a hermetically sealed vessel than the house. In reality, we are porous beings, continually acted upon or aggressed by our environments. Posthumously, what is left of our corporeal remains will then undergo a process of ecological transformation. If we were to listen very closely, we would hear not silence, but the infinitesimal sounds of worms and maggots burrowing, chewing, digesting, feasting.

Legal Hearings

This section changes location in order to explore the acoustics of the courtroom scene in *The Merchant of Venice*. I read the law court as a counter-space indicative of how relations between guest and host have become not only strained but stretched to breaking point. In this context, I define 'guest' as a foreigner or guest resident brought before an alien government. It is my intention, therefore, to expand our understanding of how hospitality works in practice in Shakespeare's play, moving from the private household to look at how governments, including the Venetian Republic, treat those whose citizenship status is seen as provisional or less secure.[59] My goals in this chapter section are twofold. First, I seek to demonstrate that violence against the stranger begins with the problem of translation, since non-native language users will inevitably be at a disadvantage when it comes to confronting the legal system of another country. Second, I argue that, *especially* when situated within a legal framework, hospitality is only ever conditional, remaining contingent on the guest's good behaviour.

Within the philosophical tradition, the law has long been a problem for hospitality and cosmopolitanism, and is where Derrida's definition of hospitality diverges from the one put forward earlier by Kant. The latter's *Toward Perpetual Peace* contends that we should think of hospitality in the following way:

> It is not the *right of a guest* that the stranger has a claim to (which would require a special, charitable contract stipulating that he be made a member of the household for a certain period of time), but rather a right to visit, to which all human beings have a claim, to present oneself to society by virtue of the right of common possession of the surface of the earth.[60]

Appropriately enough given the title of Kant's essay, a perceived benefit of this approach is that 'remote parts of the world can establish relations peacefully with one another, relations which ultimately become regulated by public laws and can thus finally bring the human species ever closer to a cosmopolitan constitution'.[61] By contrast, Derrida finds this legal underpinning to hospitality controversial to say the least. Engaging closely with *Perpetual Peace*, he argues that, 'in defining hospitality in all its rigour as a law (which counts in this respect as progress), Kant assigns to it conditions which make it dependent on state sovereignty, especially when it is a question of the *right of residence*'.[62] Within the Kantian framework of hospitality, the guest is required to abide by certain codes of conduct so as to ensure the continued goodwill of the hosting authority. In other words, 'as long as the stranger behaves peacefully where he happens to be, his host may not treat him with hostility'.[63] As Derrida rightly argues, though, one of the major limitations with this premise is the way in which:

> From the point of view of the law, the guest, even when he is well received, is first of all a foreigner, he must remain a foreigner. Hospitality is due to the foreigner, certainly, but remains, like the law, conditional, and thus conditioned in its dependence on the unconditionality that is the basis of the law.[64]

Should a guest fail to adhere to the terms and conditions of the host power, then their welcome on foreign soil is liable to be withdrawn at any time. In practice, this leaves the treatment of strangers open to exploitation by those in charge of the rulebook.

Seyla Benhabib gets to the heart of the matter, raising an intriguing question that is pertinent to my reading of the courtroom scene in *The Merchant of Venice*:

> Are the rights of asylum and refuge 'rights' in the sense of being *reciprocal moral obligations* which, in some sense or another, are grounded upon our mutual humanity? Or are these rights claims in the legal sense of being *enforceable norms* of behaviour which individuals and groups can hold each other to and, in particular, force sovereign nation-states to comply with?[65]

Benhabib makes a crucial differentiation between our *reciprocal moral obligations* towards other people and legally actionable *enforceable norms* of conduct. By Act 4 of *The Merchant of Venice*, this ethical distinction comes under intense pressure. We are led to understand that Antonio's ships, with their expensive merchandise, have all been lost at sea, meaning that, because he has defaulted on the clause named in the bond, Shylock is authorised by law to claim his pound of flesh. In the courtroom, when it still appears likely that the play is heading towards a violent climax, Portia (disguised as a legal clerk) tests Shylock on the nature of moral responsibility:

Portia	Have by some surgeon, Shylock, on your charge, To stop his wounds, lest he do bleed to death.
Shylock	Is it so nominated in the bond?
Portia	It is not so expressed, but what of that? 'Twere good you do so much for charity.
Shylock	I cannot find it, 'tis not in the bond.

(4.1.253–8)

During the exchange, Shylock refuses to look outside of the legal paperwork. When Portia counsels him that he should have a doctor present to save Antonio from bleeding to death, Shylock answers that – although this may be the ethical thing to do – since it is not a named condition of the bond, it is not legally enforceable. Through Shylock's rigid adherence to the letter of the law, *The Merchant of Venice* interrogates the sometimes wide gulf between what is officially permissible for people to do to one another and what is morally endurable.

But while Shylock uses the law to silence moral objections to his bond, he himself falls victim to what the law leaves unsaid. Legal language is open to evasion and equivocation, and it demands a special kind of listening in order to combat the silences, omissions and elisions encoded within it and which always risk creating an injustice within its own framework. In court, to be a foreign speaker is disadvantageous because, Derrida notes, the stranger 'risks being without defence before the law of the country that welcomes or expels him; the foreigner is first of all foreign to the legal language in which the duty of hospitality is formulated, the right to asylum, its limits, norms, policing, etc.'[66] Newcomers are less well versed in the legal rhetoric of the courtroom than a local resident would be and so are less able to listen out carefully for snares and loopholes. Shylock's unfamiliarity with the Republic's decrees is emphasised in Act 4 of *The Merchant of Venice*. When Portia gets the better of him, Shylock initially does not understand what is happening:

> *Portia* Tarry a little, there is something else.
> This bond doth give thee here no jot of blood:
> The words expressly are 'a pound of flesh'.
> Take then thy bond: take thou thy pound of flesh.
> But in the cutting it, if thou dost shed
> One drop of Christian blood, thy lands and goods
> Are by the laws of Venice confiscate
> Unto the state of Venice.
> *Gratiano*   O upright judge!
> Mark, Jew – O learned judge!
> *Jew*   Is that the law?
>   (4.1.301–10)

Shylock, struck by this unforeseen interpretation of his bond, wonders aloud about whether the law is what it says it is.

Portia's reply, that he 'shall see the act' (4.1.310), implies a sinister, overdue education in the minutiae of decrees permitting the persecution of aliens. Despite his own zeal for the letter of the law, Shylock does not read for gaps, and he consequently fails to notice the significance of the fact that the wording of the bond makes no provision for a 'jot of blood', awarding him *only* 'a pound of flesh'. *The Merchant of Venice* exposes how the difficulty of listening to the laws of a foreign country can be manipulated by representatives of the juridical system who, like Portia, are unsympathetic to outsiders.

Hospitality comes with its own unspoken rules and tacit acknowledgements that bind host and guest together in ways we do not always appreciate. Reading between the lines of an invitation, Derrida teases out the subtext: '"Please, come in, you're invited" – but of course as invited guest you won't disturb too seriously the order of the house, you're going to speak our language, eat the way we eat . . .'[67] The newcomer is expected to adapt to the status quo. This is the same universe which Derrida describes in the *Of Hospitality* seminars as one where 'the foreigner doesn't only have a right, he or she also has, reciprocally, obligations'.[68] So, if hospitality remains only conditional (and when doesn't it?), then the guest's invitation will have terms and clauses attached. What we might think of as the *fine print* of hospitality is likely to be inaudible to the naive or trusting foreigner. However, if the stranger fails to adhere to the unsaid rules, they may quickly discover that they have overstayed their welcome. For this reason, Étienne Balibar argues that nationalism 'allows the permanent stigmatization of any foreigner who does not consider his presence on national soil to be simply a revocable concession'.[69]

Following Portia's revelation of the legal loophole which prevents Shylock from cutting off his pound of flesh, Shakespeare's audience now learns that there is another subclause hidden away within the Republic's laws:

> Tarry, Jew,
> The law hath yet another hold on you.
> It is enacted in the laws of Venice,
> If it be proved against an alien
> That by direct, or indirect, attempts
> He seek the life of any citizen,
> The party 'gainst the which he doth contrive
> Shall seize the one-half his goods. The other half
> Comes to the privy coffer of the state,
> And the offender's life lies in the mercy
> Of the Duke only, 'gainst all other voice.
> (4.1.342–52)

Despite repeated assurances of the city's cosmopolitanism, referred to as 'the commodity that strangers have/ With us in Venice' (3.3.27–8), we find out about a nasty piece of legislation sanctioning the persecution of any aliens who overstep the mark. As it turns out, the hospitality that Shylock has been receiving from the state of Venice was only ever an interim arrangement reliant on his continued compliance and good behaviour, otherwise liable to be suspended at a moment's notice.

The Merchant of Venice requires its audience to listen carefully to what is going on beneath the polite façade of cosmopolitan integration. Shylock's presence in the city is tolerated until he seeks Antonio's life. Then, the hospitality of the Republic is revoked to be replaced instead with economic sanctions and a forced conversion to Christianity. By revealing how, this entire time, Shylock's life in Venice has been less free than he supposed, the play questions the extent to which outsiders can ever truly be at home.

Discordant Belmont

The Merchant of Venice concludes with music and hospitality in Portia's Belmont, producing an impression that harmony has been restored to Venetian society.[70] As the final act gets underway, the newlyweds Jessica and Lorenzo are sharing a quiet moment in the moonlit garden. Lorenzo says:

> The moon shines bright. In such a night as this,
> When the sweet wind did gently kiss the trees,
> And they did make no noise, in such a night
> Troilus methinks mounted the Troyan walls
> And sighed his soul toward the Grecian tents,
> Where Cressid lay that night.
> (5.1.1–6)

In contrast to the noisy clamour of the courtroom, Lorenzo's speech emphasises soothing sounds like the breeze, kissing and sighing. Despite the romantic setting, however, Shakespeare includes enough jarring notes as to problematise our initial sense of harmony and hospitality. Lorenzo's allusion to Cressida implies not only sexual infidelity, but the fall of Troy through the Greeks' treacherous gift of the wooden horse. His mention of the wind gently rustling the trees also recalls Shylock, who is repeatedly accused of hardheartedness and an inability to listen or be moved by the entreaties of others. Resigned to his fate earlier on, Antonio told the court:

> I pray you think you question with the Jew.
> You may as well go stand upon the beach
> And bid the main flood bate its usual height;
> You may as well use question with the wolf
> Why he hath made the ewe bleat for the lamb;
> You may as well forbid the mountain pines
> To wag their high tops and to make no noise
> When they are fretten with the gusts of heaven;
> You may as well do anything most hard
> As seek to soften that – than which what's harder? –
> His Jewish heart.
> (4.1.70–80)

Evoking the early modern association of emotion with motion, Antonio lists a series of examples all of which stress the movement of the landscape, from the ocean tides to the bleating of lambs to the pine trees rustling noisily in the wind. The vivacity and liveliness of the natural environment is intended to accentuate Shylock's fixed obduracy over the bond and make a wider point about the unnaturalness of his refusal to be swayed. *The Merchant of Venice* infers that the ability to be moved is not only a prerequisite of hospitality, but evidence of being part of our environment.

The ending of *The Merchant of Venice* articulates a compelling fantasy that the Christians are astute listeners. As they listen to the musicians together, Jessica confesses to her husband she is 'never merry' when she hears 'sweet music' (5.1.69). In response, Lorenzo praises her acoustic sensitivity, telling her that '[t]he reason is, your spirits are attentive' (5.1.170). Ignoring his wife's low mood, Lorenzo is eager to present the newly converted Jessica as an idealized Christian listener, an attribute which, as Folkerth has shown, was connected to contemporary ideas of femininity:

> The Protestant discourse pertaining to sound and hearing associates this entire perceptual domain with obedience, duty, receptivity and penetrability – all concepts which were gendered feminine in the period, and were officially codified as such with the state's sanction in the *Book of Common Prayer*.[71]

For women characters including Jessica and Desdemona, the sense of hearing is caught up in larger cultural discourses surrounding religion and sexuality.

Our impression of good listening habits is seemingly confirmed through Portia's speech about birdsong. Hearing the music playing on her approach to Belmont, she remarks to her travelling companion, Nerissa, how:

> The crow doth sing as sweetly as the lark
> When neither is attended; and I think
> The nightingale, if she should sing by day
> When every goose is cackling, would be thought
> No better a musician than the wren.
> How many things by season seasoned are
> To their right praise and true perfection.
> (5.1.102–8)

Comparing the melodies of different birds, Portia appears to be another sensitive listener who, like Antonio, is attuned to the rhythms of the natural environment. And yet, we have only to remember the immediately preceding courtroom drama to know that *The Merchant of Venice* is satirising these perceptive Christian hearers. For all the talk of auditory discretion, Bassanio did not recognise his wife's voice in court when she was dressed as the legal clerk Balthazar. Moreover, even when the Venetian characters *are* listening carefully in this play, the effect is often to cause harm. When it becomes clear that Shylock has lost the support of the law, Gratiano applauds Balthazar with the words, 'an upright judge, a learned judge!' (4.1.321). He deliberately echoes Shylock's earlier praise of Balthazar as a 'wise and upright judge' (4.1.247). Gratiano then goes on to compare Balthazar to '[a] Daniel, still say I; a second Daniel / I thank thee, Jew, for teaching me that word' (4.1.348–9). It is plain from these lines that Gratiano has been listening extremely closely to Shylock in the courtroom. And yet, these habits of attentive hearing – as with the cultural appropriation of Jewish biblical names – are not used to support social integration or cosmopolitanism, instead becoming a way to taunt the Jewish outsider. Shakespeare gives us every reason to suspect that such unkind mimicry of the foreigner will be intergenerational. Following Jessica's elopement, Solanio and Salarino have this conversation about Shylock's emotional distress:

> *Solanio* I never heard a passion so confused.
> So strange, outrageous, and so variable,
> As the dog Jew did utter in the streets
> [. . .]
> *Salarino* Why, all the boys in Venice follow him,
> Crying his stones, his daughter, and his ducats.
> (2.8.12–24)

Even though the Christian characters pride themselves on their aural discernment, the play depicts their listening behaviour in an unpleasant light, as when these children parrot after Shylock his words of incoherent pain. Like Gratiano, they cruelly impersonate the outsider's words, rather than emphasising with his predicament.

As I have shown, listening is an ethical act in *The Merchant of Venice*. Supposedly this play strives for harmony and cosmopolitanism between the city and its stranger communities. At the same time, symphonious social relations are too often premised on the unjust silencing of those who are distrusted. Thus, we can extend the private and bodily dimensions of ethics as a sensory activity into interrogations of the juridical systems through which communities constitute themselves and regulate otherness. Shakespeare's work loudly draws attention to the unvoiced injustices contained within how we, as individuals and societies, respond to strangers.

Silence

'Every society lives with silence', Amy Jo Murray and Kevin Durrheim argue, 'and the tensions created by absence. We choose to notice some aspects of our world, allowing others to fade into the background.'[72] *The Merchant of Venice* features many different kinds of silence. For instance, there is Bassanio's amazement after he wins the casket test. He tells Portia, 'you have bereft me of all words / Only my blood speaks to you in my veins' (3.2.175–7). Serres notes the microscopic biological processes, 'whose subliminal murmur our proprioceptive ear sometimes strains to hear: billions of cells dedicated to biochemical reactions, the likes of which should have us all fainting from the pressure of their collective hum'.[73] In these romantic few lines, Shakespeare draws our attention to the microscopic sounds not ordinarily perceptible. But the play is filled with other, negative depictions of silence and being silenced. As we have seen so far, there are gaps and exclusions, inattentiveness, selective deafness and refusals to listen or be swayed. In this context, silence might indicate complicity with injustice, or it can mean ignorance. In *The Inarticulate Renaissance: Language Trouble in an Age of Eloquence*, Carla Mazzio shows how silence can 'encode conceptions of inarticulate speech', as well as offering 'a convenient hiding place for the otherwise dumbfounded, or inarticulate, speaker'.[74] Gratiano's opinion is that 'silence is only commendable / In a neat's tongue dried and a maid not vendible' (1.1.111–12). In other words, silence only suits a bit of cured ox tongue, or an ugly spinster. The explicit sexism of these lines invites our reconsideration of who is entitled to speak and whose voices we, as a society, are prepared to tolerate. In *The Merchant of Venice*, there are some voices whom we never hear from, including the social demographics mentioned by Shylock when he confronts those present in the Venetian courtroom on their own inhospitable ethics:

> You have among you many a purchased slave,
> Which, like your asses, and your dogs and mules,
> You use in abject and in slavish parts,
> Because you bought them.
>   (4.1.89–92)

Further troubling our idea of Venice as a hospitable city, the play does not let us listen to its enslaved population, nor the voices of such marginal figures as the 'negro' woman who is pregnant with Lancelot's baby (3.5.35).

In conclusion, *The Merchant of Venice* also contains the unjust silence which accompanies the forceful suppression of any dissident voices. Shylock's defeat in court – the withdrawal of hospitality and imposition of retaliatory new rules and regulations – is a form of silencing. Before he leaves the courtroom, he says:

> I pray you, give me leave to go from hence.
> I am not well. Send the deed after me
> And I will sign it.
> (4.1.391–3)

Alongside Shylock's (momentary?) incapacitation in the law court, we should consider, too, the longer-term implications of what his silencing means in practice. The greatest impact will surely be on his capacity to participate in civic life. Deprived of half of his economic assets, and with a reduced amount of capital, Shylock's business transactions will be constrained. In effect, he is to be excluded from the soundscape of merchants trading on the Rialto. His enforced conversion to the Christian religion is, moreover, a segregation from the unique sounds and timbres of Jewish worship. In early modern Italy, Bonfil reminds us, 'the liturgical activity of the Jews was characterized by its loudness':

> Prayers were recited out loud, the more important sections were recited in unison, the poetical compositions of the liturgy (piyyutim) had refrains that the entire congregation recited along with the officiant. For a visitor entering the synagogue, nothing was more typical than this noise that defined beyond the shadow of a doubt the group's identity.[75]

Obligated to become a Christian, Shylock will no longer be able to join in with these noisy celebrations of Judaism.

While silence can be eloquent and signal openness and receptivity to strangers, it can communicate a lack of hospitality as well. 'Silences', as Murray and Durrheim conclude, 'come to define the society that keeps them, and its future depends on how these silences are identified, broken, or maintained.'[76]

Notes

1. Mikhail Bakhtin, *Rabelais and His World*, trans. Hélène Iswolsky (Bloomington: Indiana University Press, 1984), p. 281.
2. See, for instance: David Goldstein, *Eating and Ethics in Shakespeare's England* (Cambridge: Cambridge University Press, 2013); Kim F. Hall, 'Guess Who's Coming to Dinner? Colonisation and Miscegenation in *The Merchant of Venice*', *Renaissance Drama*, 23 (1992), 87–111; Julia Reinhard Lupton, *Citizen-Saints: Shakespeare and Political Theology* (Chicago: University of Chicago Press, 2005).
3. William Shakespeare, *The Merchant of Venice*, ed. John Drakakis (London: Bloomsbury, 2010), 1.3.30–4. All further references are to this edition and are given parenthetically in the text.
4. Ben Jonson, *Volpone, or The Fox*, in *Ben Jonson, Vol. 5: Volpone; Epicoene; The Alchemist; Catiline*, ed. C. H. Herford and Percy Simpson (Oxford: Oxford University Press, 2012), 1.2.83–4.
5. 'Gait, n.', *OED Online*.
6. William Shakespeare, *The Tempest*, ed. Stephen Orgel (Oxford: Oxford University Press, 2008), 4.1.102; William Shakespeare, *Othello*, ed. E. A. J. Honigmann (London: Bloomsbury, 1997), 5.1.23; William Shakespeare, *Julius Caesar*, ed. David Daniell (London: Thomson Learning, 2006), 1.3.132.
7. Patrick Bours and Adrian Evensen, 'The Shakespeare Experiment: Preliminary Results for the Recognition of a Person Based on the Sound of Walking', *2017 International Carnahan Conference on Security Technology* (2017), pp. 1–6, p. 1.

8. Jacques Derrida, *Adieu to Emmanuel Levinas*, trans. Pascale-Anne Brault and Michael Naas (Stanford: Stanford University Press, 1999), p. 100.
9. Bruce R. Smith, *The Acoustic World of Early Modern England: Attending to the O-Factor* (Chicago: University of Chicago Press, 1999), p. 6.
10. Jacques Derrida, 'Ulysses Gramophone: Hear Say Yes in Joyce', in *A Derrida Reader: Between the Blinds*, ed. Peggy Kamuf (New York: Columbia University Press, 1991), pp. 569–601, p. 572.
11. Derrida, *Adieu to Emmanuel Levinas*, p. 22.
12. Jennifer Linhart Wood, *Sounding Otherness in Early Modern Drama and Travel: Uncanny Vibrations in the English Archive* (London: Palgrave, 2019). p. 8.
13. Lisbeth Lipari, 'Rhetoric's Other: Levinas, Listening, and the Ethical Response', *Philosophy & Rhetoric*, 45:3 (2012), 227–45, pp. 229–40.
14. Lisbeth Lipari, 'Listening Otherwise: The Voice of Ethics', *International Journal of Listening*, 23:1 (2009), 44–59, pp. 45–56.
15. Krista E. Hughes, 'Cultivating Listening as a Civic Discipline', in *Ecological Solidarities: Mobilizing Faith and Justice for an Entangled World*, ed. Krista E. Hughes, Dhawn B. Martin and Elaine Padilla (Philadelphia: Pennsylvania State University Press, 2019), pp. 201–7, p. 206.
16. Jean-Luc Nancy, *Corpus*, trans. Richard A. Rand (New York: Fordham University Press, 2008), p. 161.
17. Judith Still, *Derrida and Hospitality: Theory and Practice* (Edinburgh: Edinburgh University Press, 2010), p. 13.
18. Bartolomeo Eustachi, *An Epistle on the Organs of Hearing: An Annotated Translation*, trans. C. D. O'Malley, *Clio Medica*, 6 (1971), 49–62, pp. 58–9.
19. Eustachi, *An Epistle on the Organs of Hearing*, p. 57.
20. Eustachi, *An Epistle on the Organs of Hearing*, p. 60.
21. Helkiah Crooke, *Microcosmographia* (London, 1616), p. 696.
22. Crooke, *Microcosmographia*, p. 697.
23. 'Window, n.', *OED Online*.
24. Crooke, *Microcosmographia*, p. 592.

25. Crooke, *Microcosmographia*, pp. 585–92.
26. Gina Bloom, *Voice in Motion: Staging Gender, Shaping Sound in Early Modern England* (Philadelphia: University of Pennsylvania Press, 2007), p. 2.
27. Eustachi, *An Epistle on the Organs of Hearing*, p. 57.
28. Eustachi, *An Epistle on the Organs of Hearing*, p. 59.
29. Crooke, *Microcosmographia*, p. 586.
30. The authoritative work on this topic is Arnold Hunt, *The Art of Hearing: English Preachers and Their Audiences, 1590–1640* (Cambridge: Cambridge University Press, 2010). See, too, Daniel Jütte, 'Sleeping in Church: Preaching, Boredom, and the Struggle for Attention in Medieval and Early Modern Europe', *American Historical Review*, 125:4 (2020), 1146–74, and Ceri Sullivan, 'The Art of Listening in the Seventeenth Century', *Modern Philology*, 104:1 (2006), 34–71.
31. Jennifer Rae McDermott, '"The Melodie of Heaven": Sermonizing the Open Ear in Early Modern England', in *Religion and the Senses in Early Modern Europe*, ed. Wietse de Boer and Christine Göttler (Leiden: Brill, 2012), pp. 177–97, pp. 183–7.
32. Rae McDermott, 'Sermonizing the Open Ear', p. 187.
33. Robert Wilkinson, *Sermon of hearing, or, A jewell for the eare* (London, 1643), p. 7.
34. William Shakespeare, *Coriolanus*, ed. Peter Holland (London: Bloomsbury, 2013), 4.5.11–36.
35. Tanya Pollard, *Drugs and Theatre in Early Modern England* (Oxford: Oxford University Press, 2005).
36. Wes Folkerth, *The Sound of Shakespeare* (London: Routledge, 2002), p. 73.
37. William Shakespeare, *Hamlet*, ed. Ann Thomson and Neil Taylor (London: Thomson Learning, 2006), 1.5.63–7.
38. Geraldo de Sousa, '"My hopes abroad": The Global/Local Nexus in *The Merchant of Venice*', in *Shakespeare and Immigration*, ed. Ruben Espinosa and David Ruiter (Farnham: Ashgate, 2014), pp. 37–59, p. 46.
39. Critics have done much to debunk the supposed impartiality of the casket test. See Geraldo de Sousa, *Shakespeare's Cross-Cultural Encounters* (Basingstoke: Macmillan, 1999).

Cosmopolitan Soundscapes in the *Merchant of Venice* [101

De Sousa shows how the lottery disadvantages Morocco and the other foreign suitors because they are less well acquainted with deciphering European texts and artefacts.

40. B. J. Sokol, *Shakespeare and Tolerance* (Cambridge: Cambridge University Press, 2009), p. 16.
41. Edward Berry, 'Laughing at "Others"', in *The Cambridge Companion to Shakespearean Comedy*, ed. Alexander Leggatt (Cambridge: Cambridge University Press, 2002), pp. 123–38, p. 125.
42. Jacques Derrida, *Of Hospitality: Anne Dufourmantelle Invites Jacques Derrida to Respond*, trans. Rachel Bowlby (Stanford: Stanford University Press, 2000), p. 55.
43. Jacques Derrida, *The Gift of Death*, trans. David Wills (Chicago: University of Chicago Press, 1995), p. 70.
44. Robert Bonfil, *Jewish Life in Renaissance Italy*, trans. Anthony Oldcorn (Berkeley: University of California Press, 1994), pp. 233–6. Many critics have noticed that Shakespeare either ignores or was unaware that in 1516 a Jewish ghetto was established in Venice, choosing to situate Shylock's household in the middle of the Christian district.
45. Alexandra Walsham, *Charitable Hatred: Tolerance and Intolerance in England, 1500–1700* (Manchester: Manchester University Press, 2006), p. 127.
46. Eustachi, *An Epistle on the Organs of Hearing*, p. 52.
47. Daniel Jütte, 'They Shall Not Keep Their Doors and Windows Open: Urban Space and the Dynamics of Conflict and Contact in Premodern Jewish-Christian Relations', *European History Quarterly*, 46:2 (2016), 209–37.
48. Roland Barthes, *The Responsibility of Forms: Critical Essays on Music, Art and Representation*, trans. Richard Howard (Berkeley: University of California Press, 1991), pp. 250–2.
49. Lena Cowen Orlin, *Locating Privacy in Tudor London* (Oxford: Oxford University Press, 2007), pp. 231–7.
50. Barthes, *Responsibility of Forms*, p. 246.
51. Michel Serres, *The Five Senses: A Philosophy of Mingled Bodies*, trans. Margaret Sankey and Peter Cowley (London: Continuum, 2008), p. 88.

52. Serres, *Five Senses*, p. 147.
53. Serres, *Five Senses*, p. 107, p. 146.
54. Bloom, *Voice in Motion*, p. 133.
55. Shakespeare, *Othello*, 1.3.150.
56. Valerie Traub, 'Jewels, Statues, and Corpses: Containment of Female Erotic Power in Shakespeare's Plays', in *Shakespeare and Gender: A History*, ed. Deborah E. Barker and Ivo Kamps (London and New York: Verso, 1995), pp. 120–42, p. 137.
57. Jacques Derrida, *Deconstruction Engaged: The Sydney Seminars*, ed. Paul Patton and Terry Smith (Sydney: Power, 2001), p. 97.
58. Karen Raber, *Animal Bodies, Renaissance Culture* (Philadelphia: University of Pennsylvania Press, 2014), p. 111.
59. Kevin Curran argues that this play is 'using hospitality to think beyond the horizons of the individual'; *Shakespeare's Legal Ecologies: Law and Distributed Selfhood* (Evanston: Northwestern University Press, 2017), p. 77.
60. Immanuel Kant, 'Toward Perpetual Peace: A Philosophical Sketch', in *Toward Perpetual Peace and Other Writings on Politics, Peace, and History*, ed. Pauline Kleingeld, trans. David L. Colclasure (New Haven and London: Yale University Press, 2006), pp. 67–109, p. 82.
61. Kant, 'Toward Perpetual Peace', p. 82.
62. Jacques Derrida, *On Cosmopolitanism and Forgiveness*, trans. Mark Dooley and Michael Hughes (London: Routledge, 2001), p. 22.
63. Kant, 'Toward Perpetual Peace', p. 82.
64. Derrida, *Of Hospitality*, pp. 71–3.
65. Seyla Benhabib, *The Rights of Others: Aliens, Residents, and Citizens* (Cambridge: Cambridge University Press, 2012), p. 29.
66. Derrida, *Of Hospitality*, p. 15.
67. Derrida, *Deconstruction Engaged*, p. 98.
68. Derrida, *Of Hospitality*, p. 23.
69. Étienne Balibar, *We, the People of Europe? Reflections on Transnational Citizenship*, trans. James Swenson (Princeton and London: Princeton University Press, 2004), p. 37.

70. Stephen Greenblatt says of Portia that 'her special values in the play are bound up with her house at Belmont and all it represents: its starlit garden, enchanting music, hospitality, social prestige', *Learning to Curse: Essays in Early Modern Culture* (New York and London: Routledge, 1990) (p. 43).
71. Folkerth, *The Sound of Shakespeare*, p. 51.
72. Amy Jo Murray and Kevin Durrheim, 'Introduction: A Turn to Silence', in *Qualitative Studies of Silence: The Unsaid as Social Action*, ed. Amy Jo Murray and Kevin Durrheim (Cambridge: Cambridge University Press, 2019), pp. 1–20, p. 1.
73. Serres, *The Five Senses*, p. 106.
74. Carla Mazzio, *The Inarticulate Renaissance: Language Trouble in an Age of Eloquence* (Philadelphia: University of Pennsylvania Press, 2009), pp. 3–5.
75. Bonfil, *Jewish Life in Renaissance Italy*, p. 239.
76. Murray and Durrheim, 'Introduction', p. 1.

CHAPTER 3

TROILUS AND CRESSIDA: MILITARISED ENCOUNTERS

Stoking concerns about unchecked immigration along the United States border during the 2016 presidential election campaign, the Republican nominee Donald Trump compared the situation to the Trojan Horse. Speaking at a rally in Portland, he told attendees that even legal immigrants pose a threat to homeland security:

> They're the ones we know about. There are so many that we don't know about. You're going to have problems like you've never seen [. . .] We don't know where these people are. You know when the government puts them around [. . .] for the most part, very few people know where they even are. We don't even know where they are located. I'm telling you, I've said it before: This could be the great Trojan horse of all time. They're coming in. They're coming in.[1]

The *Oxford English Dictionary* retains the classical context of political sabotage by providing this definition of the Trojan Horse: 'according to epic tradition, the hollow wooden horse in which Greeks were concealed to enter Troy; *figurative* a person, device, etc., insinuated to bring about an enemy's downfall; a person or thing that undermines from within'.[2]

Throughout western culture, the emblem of the wooden horse of Troy embodies underlying fears about being the victim of unsuspected violence at the hands of outsiders.

In Elizabethan England, retellings of the siege and eventual destruction of Troy were immensely popular.[3] One of the major sources was Virgil's *Aeneid*, where the Trojan warrior Aeneas narrates what happened:

> Broken by war and rebuffed by the Fates
> For so many years, the Greek warlords
> Built a horse, aided by the divine art
> Of Pallas, a horse the size of a mountain,
> Weaving its ribs out of beams of fir.
> They pretended it was a votive offering
> For their safe return home. So the story went.
> But deep within the horse's cavernous dark
> They concealed an elite band, all their best,
> Stuffing its huge womb with men at arms.[4]

Despite never appearing onstage in *Troilus and Cressida*, the wooden horse casts a shadow over the performance. In Act 1, the old Greek warrior Nestor says:

> But let the ruffian Boreas once enrage
> The gentle Thetis, and anon behold
> The strong-ribbed bark through liquid mountains cut,
> Bounding between the two moist elements
> Like Perseus' horse. Where's then the saucy boat
> Whose weak untimbered sides but even now
> Co-rivalled greatness?[5]

In combination with the ship's 'strong-ribbed' wooden frame, Nestor's allusion to 'Perseus' horse' establishes a prophetic mood, foreshadowing the eventual fall of Troy.

Myths surrounding the Trojan War foreground the body as the site of treachery. At least since the *Aeneid*, where its hollow innards are likened to a 'huge womb', pregnancy has been the metaphor most commonly used to describe the Greeks' military stratagem. As many critics have noted, *Troilus and Cressida* seems fascinated by the body and what it conceals on the inside. David Hillman argues that Shakespeare breaks with literary tradition when he 'makes the belly the origin rather than the culmination of the tale'.[6] Patricia Parker suggests that 'the play itself is all distended middle, figuring the grotesque possibility of a bloated simulacrum of pregnancy'.[7] Expanding on his concept of 'intestine hospitality', Jacques Derrida blends imagery of pregnancy together with the Trojan Horse:

> Hospitality, what belabours and concerns hospitality at its core [*ce qui travaille l'hospitalité en son sein*], what works at it like a labour, like a pregnancy, like a promise as much as like a threat, what settles in it, within it [*en son dedans*], like a Trojan horse, the enemy (*hostis*) as much as the *avenir*, intestine hospitality, is indeed a contradictory conception.[8]

The Trojans brought the wooden horse, presented to them as a gift, inside their city walls. As soon as darkness fell, however, elite warriors poured out of its hollow belly and devoured the host city from within. The Greeks' counterfeit gift, which ended the lengthy siege of Troy, is one of the earliest cautionary tales of hospitality in the western literary tradition.[9] In the extract above, the legendary wooden horse becomes, for Derrida, an evocative way of articulating the fact that we can never know for certain the inward intentions of hosts or guests to one another. While obviously intensified during wartime, there is always a latent possibility that hospitality might end in violence, for what the Trojan Horse so memorably demonstrates is our innate capacity to harbour violent designs beneath a welcoming exterior.

This chapter focuses on Shakespeare's representation of inwardness and interiority, arguing that it informs the play's ethics of hospitality. I begin inside the garrisoned city of Troy, where a romantic relationship is developing between Cressida and Troilus. My analysis considers ideas of disarmament, unveiling and the revelation of the secret, to show how, at the moment of greeting, Shakespeare redirects our attention onto the body and its internal processes. The play's uncomfortable or inept salutations reveal how a sense of shame or bodily embarrassment can dominate in situations where we are faced with the stranger. The second section returns to the counterfeit gift to examine how easily hospitality can be feigned or impersonated for personal gain. Situating my reading within economic criticism of the play's proto-capitalist marketplace, I ask what it means to think of hospitality as a currency that can be counterfeited. As I understand it, hospitality in *Troilus and Cressida* is entrenched in the spirit of the marketplace; furthermore, the wartime setting lends an urgency to interpersonal relations, with time emerging as a valuable commodity in its own right. In the third section, I analyse the battlefield encounters between Greek and Trojan combatants. The absurdity of wartime adversaries who not only respect one another, but greet each other warmly, is an important, if critically neglected, component of Shakespeare's pacifism. Time is again relevant to my argument. Social encounters between those caught on opposing sides of the conflict are always 'time-locked' and can exist only in a perpetual present, under temporary ceasefire conditions. The fourth and final section revisits the concept of disarmament in relation to hospitality. One of the foundational questions of hospitality is what happens when we take down our defences. Being truly welcoming requires exposing oneself to a degree of risk, and this vulnerability cannot be eradicated without sacrificing the conditions necessary for hospitality. The classical heroes in this play speak about feeling vulnerable when confronted with the other. I thus concentrate my reading on the bowels and entrails because, for the early moderns, the bowels were the seat of compassion. The manner in which the compassionate Trojan prince Hector is surprised on the battlefield reminds us that leaving oneself open and defenceless before strangers can be a shocking experience.

It is a critical commonplace that *Troilus and Cressida* is bleak in tone. Nonetheless, I find in the play's representation of hospitality glimmers of hope. The Trojan warriors agree that the civilian and military sacrifices implied in keeping Helen as their guest any longer, and therefore prolonging the Trojan War, are too great, but they continue to do so anyway. Hector is warned by everyone around him of the danger of displaying sympathy towards the Greeks and trusting that they will do the same, yet he still decides to put his faith in strangers and let his guard down. Each of these decisions has destructive consequences, yet there is something inspiring to be found in the way that hospitality in *Troilus and Cressida* moves beyond thought or calculation. To watch this play performed is to become spectators to an overwhelming impulse to be welcoming in spite of the incalculable costs involved.

Blush

Entering the stage in armour, the Prologue explains that the action begins in the middle of the Trojan War and that Troy is strongly garrisoned against the invading Greek army:

> Priam's six-gated city –
> Dardan and Timbria, Helias, Chetas, Troien
> And Antenorides – with massy staples
> And corresponsive and fulfilling bolts,
> Spar up the sons of Troy.
> (1.0.15–19)

By taking the time to itemise the city's six gates, the Prologue to *Troilus and Cressida* emphasises how Troy has blockaded itself against outsiders. As soon as the play begins, however, our initial impression of homeland security and tight border control is undermined. First to speak is the Trojan prince, Troilus, who is complaining about his (seemingly) unrequited adoration of Cressida:

> Call here my varlet; I'll unarm again.
> Why should I war without the walls of Troy,
> That find such cruel battle here within?
>   (1.1.1–3)

From the outset, Shakespeare deflates our expectation that we are about to see a chivalric contest, since Troilus decides to remove his armour and stay home from the battlefield. After carefully enumerating some of the measures we take to protect ourselves against strangers – such as securely defended cities and armoured bodies – the play then immediately undermines these fortifications. Comparing himself unfavourably with the Greek soldiers a few lines later, Troilus' effeminised self-portrayal reinforces the sense of bodily exposure to harm:

> But I am weaker than a woman's tear,
> Tamer than sleep, fonder than ignorance,
> Less valiant than the virgin in the night
>   (1.1.9–11)

For readers and audience members accustomed to the heroic male bodies of classical literature, Shakespeare's characterisation of Troilus as 'womanish' (1.1.103) may be unexpected.

Remaining with the Trojan characters, Cressida's entrance in the next scene establishes the same narrative trajectory from armament to a rapid dismantling of those defences.

While in conversation with her uncle, Pandarus, Cressida playfully says that she lies:

> Upon my back to defend my belly, upon my wit to defend my wiles, upon my secrecy to defend mine honesty, my mask to defend my beauty, and you to defend all these; and at all these wards I lie, at a thousand watches.
> (1.2.251–5)

In this short speech, Cressida portrays herself as the epitome of circumspect femininity. Consistent with gendered norms of conduct across early modern Europe, she speaks about safeguarding her virginity, her chaste reputation, and the whiteness of her facial skin, which was highly esteemed in contemporary conceptions of female beauty. In addition, Cressida's state of watchfulness associates her with the besieged city of Troy and its sentries. 'Because the city is walled for most of its history,' Gail Kern Paster notes, 'it is early associated with the female principle.'[10] Similar to Trojan military tactics, Cressida appears determined to keep her suitors at bay. Irrespective of such intentions, though, her wariness comes under pressure when she meets Troilus alone for the first time.

The encounter between the lovers, presided over by the sleazy Pandarus offering encouragement and instructions, is extremely embarrassing for both of them, yet is far from being the only uncomfortable meeting in *Troilus and Cressida*. Shakespeare presents us with so many fumbling and shamefaced salutations that it seems at times as if nobody in this play knows how to welcome one another properly. In Act 3, for instance, Pandarus waylays Paris' servant:

> *Pandarus* I come to speak with Paris from the Prince Troilus. I will make a complimental assault upon him, for my business seethes.

Servant	Sodden business! There's a stewed phrase indeed.
	(3.1.37–41)

With an amusing pun on Pandarus' comment that his message 'seethes', or demands urgent attention, the servant calls his words 'stewed' in the culinary sense of being overcooked. Pandarus' salutation to Paris and Helen shortly afterwards is no less overdone:

Pandarus	Fair be to you, my lord, and to all this fair company! Fair desires, in all fair measure, fairly guide them! – especially to you, fair queen. Fair thoughts be your fair pillow!
Helen	Dear lord, you are full of fair words.
	(3.1.42–6)

As Helen's witty response makes clear, Pandarus' exaggerated repetition of the word 'fair' lends his polite greeting an absurd quality. Inept salutations like these occur all the way through the play. When being introduced to the Greek warrior Menelaus, Hector manages to put his foot in it as well:

Hector	O, you, my lord? By Mars his gauntlet, thanks! Mock not that I affect th'untraded oath; Your quondam wife swears still by Venus' glove. She's well, but bade me not commend her to you.
Menelaus	Name her not now, sir; she's a deadly theme.
Hector	O, pardon! I offend.
	(4.5.178–83)

Considering Venus betrayed her husband, Vulcan, Hector's oath is comically inappropriate. It is a reminder that – just as Venus had an affair with her lover Mars – so Menelaus has been cuckolded, for Helen's elopement with Paris instigated the conflict. The Trojan War was rooted in inhospitality, as

Paris was a guest in Sparta when he abducted Helen. *Troilus and Cressida* offers an absurd take on this cultural history, presenting us with salutations which are clumsy, tactless or uncomfortable.

The meeting between the lovers in Act 3 comprises a series of embarrassing confessions and other denudings. Cressida comes on stage veiled and remains covered until Pandarus chides her, 'draw this curtain, and let's see your picture' (3.2.45). Cressida's removal of her veil not only anticipates the sensual undressing to follow when she and Troilus will spend the night together, but leads on to other secret revelations. Confessing to Troilus that she has actually been in love with him for many months, Cressida concedes that she was:

> Hard to seem won; but I was won, my lord,
> With the first glance that ever – pardon me;
> If I confess much, you will play the tyrant.
> I love you now, but till now not so much
> But I might master it. In faith, I lie;
> My thoughts were like unbridled children, grown
> Too headstrong for their mother. See, we fools!
> Why have I blabbed? Who shall be true to us
> When we are so unsecret to ourselves?
> (3.2.113–21)

Developing the theme of unveiling, Cressida's discovery of her secret fondness for Troilus is another form of nakedness. According to the *Oxford English Dictionary*, the linguistic associations of 'naked' can also denote 'free from concealment or reserve; plain, straightforward; outspoken'.[11] Here, having 'blabbed' her inward thoughts aloud to Troilus, and seemingly unable to 'lie' to him, Cressida characterises herself as truthful and lacking in artifice. Her reference to tyranny and forced confession in the third line evokes the partitioning of bodies on the Renaissance scaffold where, through means of torture, the condemned individual was made to divulge their innermost secrets. 'The traitor', Katharine Eisaman Maus writes, 'comes to the scaffold quite literally to spill his guts, to have the heart plucked out of his mystery.'[12] Cressida's allusion to the apparatus of state power is not as incongruous as it could appear in this romantic setting because she, too, makes a number of 'unsecret' confessions which leave her exposed, further complicating the Prologue's intimation that we are ever capable of securely guarding ourselves against outsiders.

In another sleazy attempt to magnify the sexual tension between the couple, Pandarus guides Troilus' attention to the fact that his niece is blushing and short of breath or, in other words, that she is sexually aroused by the latter's presence: 'She does so blush, and fetches her wind so short, as if she were frayed with a sprite. I'll fetch her. It is the prettiest villain! She fetches her breath as short as a new-ta'en sparrow' (3.2.29–32). Escorting Cressida on stage a few lines later, Pandarus tells her, 'what need you blush? Shame's a baby' (3.2.38–9). Blushing causes capillaries to dilate and the complexion to appear red and inflamed, making the inner workings of the body momentarily visible beneath the surface of the skin. Complaining about the futility of war near the start of the play, Troilus says:

> Peace, you ungracious clamours! Peace, rude sounds!
> Fools on both sides! Helen must needs be fair,
> When with your blood you daily paint her thus.
> (1.1.85–7)

Troilus pictures Helen using the blood of wounded soldiers as a rouge cosmetic to add colour to her complexion and so beautify it. The gory conceit encapsulates Jonathan Sawday's argument that some hidden parts of the human anatomy, including the blood and other bodily fluids, are revealed to the naked eye only during 'moments of trauma or potential danger'.[13]

Blushing has another confession for the world, which is to say that it exhibits a self-conscious awareness of our environmental surroundings. It is the body's most visible response to the sensation of shame, and its colour provides a pseudo-covering for the embarrassed subject. In *Blush: Faces of Shame*, Elspeth Probyn notes that shame is 'the only feeling that physically covers the face. In French, one blushes to the whites of the eyes, to the ears, and to the roots of one's hair. The tentacles of the blush, of blood rushing to the face, attest to the inner cringe.'[14] Scholars working on shame are unanimous in their agreement that it is an *interpersonal* emotion dependent on coming into close contact with other people and of being uncomfortably conscious of that immediacy. In *The Expression of the Emotions in Man and Animals* (1872), Charles Darwin claimed that the mental states which cause blushing 'consist of shyness, shame, and modesty; the essential element in all being self-attention', for it is 'not the simple act of reflecting on our own appearance, but the thinking what others think of us, which excites a blush. In absolute solitude the most sensitive person would be quite indifferent about his appearance.'[15] For Probyn, 'shame teaches us about our relations to others. Shame makes us feel proximity differently, understood as the body's relationship to its self.'[16] 'Shakespearean shame', Ewan Fernie suggests, 'turns out to be the way to relationship with the world outside the self.'[17] Chaperoned by sordid Pandarus, the encounter between the lovers in *Troilus and Cressida* is cringingly embarrassing, with pink faces galore. The red blood perceptible within the blush links the play's love and war plots, reminding us that, like hospitality, shame is a relational construct, defined through its soft and fragile exposure to other bodies.

'A gilt counterfeit'

Economic criticism of *Troilus and Cressida* is largely in agreement that Shakespeare's play represents an emergent capitalist society, albeit one that is contaminated or diseased.[18] Douglas Bruster finds that '*Troilus and Cressida* echoes traditional reservations over mercantile exchange and merchant adventurism, locating the source of the city's ills in the uncontrolled dynamism of the market.'[19] The centrality of the wooden horse to the Troy myth lends the play a suspicion about counterfeit gifts, deepened through Shakespeare's proto-capitalist economy. Throughout, there are image clusters of counterfeiting: fakes, forgeries, pirate copies and other spurious reproductions. Writing about early modern imprinting techniques, Margreta de Grazia notes that 'with all stamping techniques – whether of wax, coins or paper – there is always the possibility of forgery'.[20] In *Troilus and Cressida*, the danger of fraud reinforces the recurring theme of illegitimacy and doubtful parentage. The rascally Greek warrior Thersites brings this up when he has a skirmish in the combat zone with another self-proclaimed bastard:

Thersites	What art thou?
Margareton	A bastard son of Priam's.
Thersites	I am a bastard too; I love bastards. I am bastard begot, bastard instructed, bastard in mind, bastard in valour, in everything illegitimate.

(5.8.6–10)

To Nestor, meanwhile, Thersites is:

A slave whose gall coins slanders like a mint –
To match us in comparisons with dirt,
To weaken and discredit our exposure
(1.3.193–5)

In the same way that forged coins can disrupt the financial market by complicating the correct valuation of goods, Nestor worries that Thersites' satire will cheapen or 'discredit' the reputation of the Greek army. Counterfeit money, Derrida notes, is 'a sign without value'.[21] In *Troilus and Cressida*, the counterfeit achieves a comparable effect, implying that there is something empty or worthless underneath the outer exterior. Thersites calls Patroclus, Achilles' lover in the Greek camp, 'a gilt counterfeit' (2.3.23), later saying of the pair that 'Hector shall have a great catch an 'a knock out either of your brains. 'A were as good crack a fusty nut with no kernel' (2.1.97–9). In this section, I consider the economic logic suffusing welcoming scenes in *Troilus and Cressida*, asking what it means to think of Shakespearean hospitality as a currency that can be forged.

In any commercial society grounded on the principles of free trade and economic exchange, the question of how to distinguish fraudulent copies from legal tender is imperative and can have expensive repercussions if misjudged. As we saw in the previous chapter on *The Merchant of Venice*, a sense of discernment is equally important for two or more subjects in a hospitality relationship. Indeed, Shakespeare's tragedies are filled with cautionary stories of failing to recognise in time the ill-intentioned host or guest. Yet in *Troilus and Cressida*, the ability to assess the true aims and motivations of the stranger stumbles at the first hurdle owing to the peculiarly widespread difficulty of recognising other people. Not only do the characters seem unable to greet one another politely, but they struggle even to *identify* each other.[22] As they stand watching the Trojan warriors returning home from the day's fighting, Pandarus promises Cressida that he will point Troilus out to her. After a few men have passed over the stage, Cressida asks her uncle, '[w]hat sneaking fellow comes yonder?' (1.2.218). Pandarus replies: 'Where? Yonder? That's Deiphobus. – 'Tis Troilus! There's a man, niece! Hem! Brave Troilus, the prince of chivalry!' (1.2.219–21). We might be able to put Pandarus' embarrassing mistake down to the fact that Deiphobus and Troilus are probably dressed in similar armour if the lack of differentiation did not extend to the play's civilian encounters as well. Consider, for instance, this conversation between Paris' servant and Pandarus:

Servant	Marry, sir, at the request of Paris my lord, who is there in person; with him, the mortal Venus, the heart-blood of beauty, love's visible soul –
Pandarus	Who, my cousin Cressida?
Servant	No, sir, Helen. Could you not find that out by her attributes?

(3.1.29–35)

While the exchange is intended to make a satirical statement about Helen's unparalleled beauty, it is still indicative of a prevalent issue in the play, regarding the inability to differentiate.

Troilus and Cressida's paranoia over the counterfeit and confusion about identity has implications for hospitality as well, making it more difficult to separate genuine from false displays of welcome. Hospitality is, after all, disturbingly easy to impersonate. Moving to the Greek camp, in Act 3, Ulysses has this to say on the subject:

> For Time is like a fashionable host
> That slightly shakes his parting guest by th' hand,
> And, with his arms outstretched as he would fly,
> Grasps in the comer. Welcome ever smiles,
> And Farewell goes out sighing.
>   (3.3.166–70)

Hospitality lends itself to instantly recognisable gestures, which is why it is so easy to pretend to be welcoming even if one is not. In *Macbeth*, for instance, Lady Macbeth counsels her husband to be conscious of his body language so as to dispel suspicion that they wish their royal guest Duncan any harm:

> Your face, my Thane, is as a book, where men
> May read strange matters. To beguile the time,
> Look like the time; bear welcome in your eye,

> Your hand, your tongue: look like th'innocent flower,
> But be the serpent under't.[23]

Pleasure at receiving visitors is a universal body language, whose gestures and expressions can be counterfeited by the unscrupulous individual.

Before giving an example, it is worth noting the connection between time and economics, since this will be relevant to my argument later. In a text filled with prostitution and infectious diseases like syphilis, welcoming with open arms is regarded as cheap and somehow suspect. Consequently, Shakespeare's characters delay extending their hospitality in order to inflate their personal worth, ensuring their salutations remain coveted and sought after. Economists term this the 'scarcity principle', meaning that a shortfall in the chain of supply and demand (often overstated by retailers or artificially engineered) allows rare commodities to achieve greater desirability among consumers. If we compare the encounter between the lovers with their farewell the morning afterwards, we witness the scarcity principle in action. The pair spend ages shyly hesitating before going to bed together. In fact, a great deal of the humour of this scene comes from Pandarus' efforts to hurry things along. He says to them: 'What, blushing still? Have you not done talking yet?' (3.2.96–7). Troilus' departure from Pandarus' house the next morning could not be more different, for it looks to Cressida as if he cannot get away fast enough:

> Prithee, tarry. You men will never tarry.
> O foolish Cressid, I might have still held off,
> And then you would have tarried!
> (4.2.17–19)

Yet Troilus' hurried departure slows when he learns from a messenger that Cressida is to be sent to the Greek camp as part of a prisoner exchange:

> We two, that with so many thousand sighs
> Did buy each other, must poorly sell ourselves
> With the rude brevity and discharge of one.
> Injurious Time now with a robber's haste
> Crams his rich thiev'ry up, he knows not how.
> As many farewells as be stars in heaven,
> With distinct breath and consigned kisses to them,
> He fumbles up into a loose adieu
> And scants us with a single famished kiss,
> Distasted with the salt of broken tears.
>   (4.4.38–47)

Couching their goodbye in economic image clusters, Troilus implies that the rushed nature of his separation from Cressida is impoverishing to them both. The lines demonstrate the extent to which hospitality in *Troilus and Cressida* is shaped by the values of a proto-capitalist society, and how many of the characters have internalised a connection between leisurely salutations and increased personal capital.

Even if the figures on stage are only *pretending* to be welcoming or not, the play confirms an association between hospitality and economics. In Act 2, Agamemnon, commander of the Greek army, decides to pay a visit to his star warrior, Achilles, who has recently been absent from the battlefield. But Achilles refuses to greet the visitor, instead staying inside his tent, while sending Patroclus to make a feeble excuse:

> Achilles bids me say he is much sorry
> If anything more than your sport and pleasure
> Did move your greatness, and this noble state,
> To call upon him; he hopes it is no other
> But for your health and your digestion sake,
> An after-dinner's breath.
>   (2.3.105–10)

In response, an irritated Agamemnon warns that if Achilles 'overhold his price so much / We'll none of him,' (2.3.131–2). Agamemnon thinks that Achilles is being purposely unwelcoming, with the intention of increasing his market value within the Greek camp. Continuing to speak in coded economic terms, Agamemnon now tells Patroclus that Achilles' good qualities

> Do in our eyes begin to lose their gloss,
> Yea, like fair fruit in an unwholesome dish,
> Are like to rot untasted.
> (2.3.117–19)

Through this reference to rottenness and nutritional waste, Agamemnon threatens to take his leading warrior off the market altogether. Because Achilles begins the play already rich in international reputation, suspending his hospitality in this manner is interpreted as triggering a dangerous move towards economic inflation.

As discussed earlier, the Trojan War had its origins in inhospitality and bad guest behaviour which, in Shakespeare's retelling of events, gives rise to its own economic logic. James A. W. Heffernan notes that 'whenever hosts or guests mistreat or offend one another, the system of benign reciprocity that governs hospitality as an exchange of benefits can all too readily turn into its dark double, retaliation'.[24] In *Troilus and Cressida*, retaliatory guest and host conduct is theorised in economic terms. While debating whether they should return Helen to Sparta, for example, Troilus says that the 'theft' (2.2.92) was originally conceived as 'vengeance' (2.2.73) for the Greeks' prior abduction of Priam's sister, Hesione: 'Why keep we her? The Grecians keep our aunt' (2.2.80). He also reasons that:

> We turn not back the silks upon the merchant
> When we have soiled them; nor the remainder viands

> We do not throw in unrespective sieve
> Because we now are full.
> (2.2.69–72)

The imagery is hardly flattering of Helen, now seen as soiled or leftover food. Perverting the customary ethics of generosity, hospitality in *Troilus and Cressida* is an exchange economy of stolen goods.

'This blended knight, half Trojan and half Greek'

That the play seems scathing in its treatment of the Trojan War has long been noted by critics. Steven Marx argues that the text 'marks a turning point' in Shakespeare's career, because he 'mounts an attack on classical war heroes and on the very arguments for going to war he had supported earlier, and he undermines the whole set of values and symbols that constitute Renaissance military culture'.[25] In this section, I suggest that the strange combination of hospitality and hostility which we find throughout *Troilus and Cressida* (what Derrida would call 'hostipitality'), can be understood as an important aspect of Shakespeare's pacificism, if one that has yet to receive scholarly attention.

A striking example of Shakespeare's dramatization of 'hostipitality' in the play takes place in Troy, where Aeneas is welcoming as his guest the Greek warrior Diomedes:

> *Aeneas* Welcome to Troy! Now by Anchises' life,
> Welcome indeed! By Venus' hand I swear,
> No man alive can love in such a sort
> The thing he means to kill more excellently.
> *Diomedes* We sympathise. Jove, let Aeneas live,
> If to my sword his fate be not the glory,
> A thousand complete courses of the sun!
> But in mine emulous honour let him die,
> With every joint a wound, and that tomorrow!

Aeneas	We know each other well.
Diomedes	We do, and long to know each other worse.
Paris	This is the most despiteful'st gentle greeting, The noblest hateful love, that e'er I heard of.

(4.1.23–35)

Wishing someone good health and a long life is a standard salutation in many world cultures. Diomedes' desire that Aeneas might go on to live a 'thousand complete courses of the sun' is, however, ironic considering that he could easily be killed 'tomorrow' by the Greeks. The gap between twenty-four hours and a thousand years highlights the absurd and jarring nature of the soldierly greeting, which, in turn, supports the play's pacifist sentiment.

Throughout *Troilus and Cressida*, Shakespeare uses metaphors of impurity, contamination and dirtied liquids to express the utter impossibility of separating hospitality from a wider culture of violence. After being rudely snubbed by some Greek visitors who walk past his tent, Achilles reflects that his mind is 'troubled, like a fountain stirred / And I myself see not the bottom of it' (3.3.309–10). During their private meeting, Troilus inquires of Cressida why she is still unsure:

Troilus	What too-curious dreg espies my sweet lady in the fountain of our love?
Cressida	More dregs than water, if my fears have eyes.

(3.2.63–5)

Preparing to leave the city as part of the prisoner swap, Cressida returns again to the metaphor of muddied waters to emphasise to her uncle how her sorrow is undiluted in its essence:

Why tell you me of moderation?
The grief is fine, full, perfect that I taste,
And violenteth in a sense as strong
As that which causeth it. How can I moderate it?

> If I could temporize with my affection,
> Or brew it to a weak and colder palate,
> The like allayment could I give my grief.
> My love admits no qualifying dross;
> No more in grief, in such a precious loss.
>   (4.4.2–10)

The irony is that we will soon be made voyeurs to Cressida's sexual infidelity in the Greek encampment. Yet her insistence on uncomplicated grief captures the play's concern with pollution.

During the encounters between enemy soldiers, the imagery of adulterated liquids conveys an extraordinary blend of emotion. Before their chivalric combat, we find out from Aeneas that the Trojan prince Hector and the Greek warrior Ajax are, in fact, blood relations:

> This Ajax is half made of Hector's blood,
> In love whereof half Hector stays at home;
> Half heart, half hand, half Hector comes to seek
> This blended knight, half Trojan and half Greek.
>   (4.5.84–7)

After the contest has been going on for a while, Hector abruptly calls for an end to the hostilities on account of his conflicted feelings towards Ajax:

> Why, then will I no more.
> Thou art, great lord, my father's sister's son,
> A cousin-german to great Priam's seed.
> The obligation of our blood forbids
> A gory emulation 'twixt us twain.
> Were thy commixtion Greek and Trojan so
> That thou couldst say, 'This hand is Grecian all,
> And this is Trojan; the sinews of this leg
> All Greek, and this all Troy; my mother's blood
> Runs on the dexter cheek, and this sinister

> Bounds in my father's', by Jove multipotent,
> Thou shouldst not bear from me a Greekish member
> Wherein my sword had not impressure made
> Of our rank feud. But the just gods gainsay
> That any drop thou borrowed'st from thy mother,
> My sacred aunt, should by my mortal sword
> Be drained.
> (4.5.120–36)

'In Hector's fantasy', Matthew A. Greenfield notes, 'Ajax's mixed bloods are separated and his dual nationalities untangled.'[26] But since this is an impossibility, Hector interrupts the combat. In spite of the characters' persistent talk of purification, within the polluted atmosphere of *Troilus and Cressida*, decontamination is ultimately shown to be unattainable. This is, after all, a drama which concludes with Pandarus describing the hot sweats induced by the traditional tub bath treatments for venereal disease. In the end, any attempted extraction of pure hospitality from contaminated elements remains only an unrealised ideal.

John Bayley, in an influential essay on 'Time and the Trojans', makes a compelling case for the significance of the present to *Troilus and Cressida*. Due to the fact that the Troy legend is so deeply ingrained in our cultural imaginary, he argues that '[t]he only surprise here must be a perpetual present'.[27] From here, we might add that, in wartime, the present is also the time of the temporary ceasefire. After the contest ends, Hector is welcomed to the Greek camp by Agamemnon:

> Worthy of arms! As worthy as to one
> That would be rid of such an enemy –
> But that's no welcome. Understand more clear:
> What's past and what's to come is strewed with husks
> And formless ruin of oblivion;
> But in this extant moment, faith and troth,
> Strained purely from all hollow bias-drawing,

Bids thee, with most divine integrity,
From heart of very heart, great Hector, welcome.
   (4.5.164–72)

This poetic speech symbolises another effort to separate hospitality from the surrounding military conflict. Agamemnon returns us to the idea of distillation when he reassures Hector his welcome has been '[s]trained purely from all hollow bias-drawing'. Agamemnon stresses the importance of the present, consciously differentiating a heartfelt greeting in 'this extant moment' from the violent past and an uncertain future.

Troilus and Cressida stages hospitality under extraordinary circumstances, finding moments of pause amid the ongoing horror and death. In the end, though, and irrespective of polite intentions on both sides, the text proves how unfeasible it is to eradicate all traces of hostility from hospitality. While the play navigates this dilemma, it says something philosophical about the composite nature of the hospitality relationship. Set against the backdrop of the Trojan War, encounters are never far from violence. But, as we have seen throughout this book, the same could be said of many of Shakespeare's peacetime plays. Notwithstanding the failure to extract pure or uncomplicated acts of hospitality from the surrounding military aggression, the implications are not as bleak as we may presume. Even though hospitality keeps collapsing into wartime hostilities, the figures on stage still long to forge meaningful connections with one another in spite of the devastating risks involved. Indeed, what we ultimately find in *Troilus and Cressida* is a reckless striving to be hospitable regardless of the consequences.

Disarming Hector

I want to end by revisiting the theme of vulnerability and disarmament looked at earlier in relation to the love plot, only here I focus on Hector, who is associated throughout with imagery of unarming. Near the middle of the play, for example, Paris asks Helen to help unbuckle Hector's armour:

> Sweet Helen, I must woo you
> To help unarm our Hector. His stubborn buckles,
> With these your white enchanting fingers touched,
> Shall more obey than to the edge of steel
> Or force of Greekish sinews. You shall do more
> Than all the island kings: disarm great Hector.
> (3.1.143–8)

Paris' eroticised portrayal of his brother undressed by Helen's 'white enchanting fingers' assumes sinister connotations in Act 5, when the other members of Hector's family plead with him to stay home from the battlefield because they have had dreams and premonitions of violent death. Andromache entreats her husband to '[u]narm, unarm, and do not fight today' (5.3.3), and his sister Cassandra echoes these words when she urges him to '[u]narm, sweet Hector' (5.3.25). However, Hector unwisely ignores their prophecies, and it will not be long before he disarms on the battleground within full sight of the enemy Greeks.

Even before he removes his armour, Hector's legendary compassion renders him vulnerable around members of the enemy camp. Troilus admonishes Hector that his misplaced sympathy for the weaker fighters in the Greek army is inappropriate in wartime: 'Brother, you have a vice of mercy in you / Which better fits a lion than a man' (5.3.37–8). Hector's empathy does not go unnoticed among the Greek warriors either. Ulysses remarks on how 'Hector in his blaze of wrath subscribes / To tender objects' (4.5.106–7). Nestor gives the following account of witnessing Hector's pity in action:

> When thou hast hung thy advanced sword i'th'air,
> Not letting it decline on the declined,

That I have said to some my standers-by:
'Lo, Jupiter is yonder, dealing life!'
   (4.5.189–92)

In the early modern period, the bowels were thought to be the body's main site of compassion. As Bruce R. Smith puts it, 'compassion begins in the guts'.[28] It is perhaps unsurprising, then, that in *Troilus and Cressida*, Hector is connected to the innards or entrails. He alludes to his own softheartedness when he tells his father:

There is no lady of more softer bowels,
More spongy to suck in the sense of fear,
More ready to cry out 'Who knows what follows?'
Than Hector is.
   (2.2.11–14)

Near the end of the play, while she is trying to persuade her brother to break his promise to meet the Greeks and keep away from the fighting on that particular day, the prophetess Cassandra assures him that:

The gods are deaf to hot and peevish vows.
They are polluted off'rings, more abhorred
Than spotted livers in the sacrifice.
   (5.3.16–18)

Shakespeare's descriptions of the liver and the soft and spongy bowels in conjunction with the characterisation of Hector reproduces the early modern understanding of compassionate conduct. Kristine Steenbergh has shown how 'the capacity to share in another person's suffering was determined by the softness and openness of one's bowels'.[29] She notes that, whereas 'closed and dry bowels were inimical to the experience of compassion',

> The early modern compassionate body is not self-contained. After the initial movement within, there follows a movement outward. The bowels of the person who experiences compassion are described in early modern texts as expanding, dilating, opening and pouring out towards the person they feel compassion with. The compassionate self is porous, extending beyond the boundaries of the physical body, stretching towards the other.[30]

For people in the sixteenth and seventeenth centuries, open bowels were a useful metaphor for expressing the ethics of emotional receptiveness or fellow feeling with others.

French philosophy has reinvigorated the early modern motif of the compassionate bowels as a way of theorising sympathy and neighbourliness. 'Every love or every hatred of a neighbour', Emmanuel Levinas argues, 'presupposes this prior vulnerability, this mercy, this "groaning of the entrails"'.[31] Following Levinas, Derrida writes that 'the tender' implies 'a movement toward appeasement, a moment of peace, and a disarming, which insistently reaches into the violence of a violation'.[32] This idea relates to Derrida's thinking on pure or unconditional hospitality, which would require condoning the dangers involved in welcoming the stranger without first seeking to impose limitations on them: 'you have to accept the risk of the other coming and destroying the place, initiating a revolution, stealing everything, or killing everyone. That is the risk of pure hospitality and pure gift, because a pure gift might be terrible too.'[33] Of course, the shock waves arising from a condition of passivity may be disturbing:

> To be hospitable is to let oneself be overtaken [*surprendre*], *to be ready to not be ready*, if such is possible, to let oneself be overtaken, to not even *let* oneself be overtaken, to be surprised, in a fashion almost violent, violated and raped [*violée*], stolen [*volée*] (the whole question of violence and violation/ rape and of expropriation and de-propriation is

waiting for us), precisely where one is not ready to receive – and not only *not yet ready* but *not ready, unprepared* in a mode that is not even that of the 'not yet'.³⁴

It is crucial to recognise that Derrida is *not* suggesting rape or any other intimate violence is a hospitable act. Judith Still clarifies how 'Derrida uses the term *violé* (raped) for the general effect of the surprise visitor whose arrival may be experienced as a violent intrusion by the unprepared host'.³⁵ Conditional hospitality means that the individual or the authority who issues the invitation remains in control of the hosting situation at all times and the guest is required to abide by certain rules and norms of social conduct. Unconditional hospitality, on the other hand, is given without reservations or limits, creating an environment where the host is left completely exposed.

Hector's murder at the hands of Achilles and his Myrmidons, which takes place at the end of the play, is graphic in its staging of mass violence:

> Hector   Now is my day's work done. I'll take good breath.
> Rest, sword; thou hast thy fill of blood and death.
> [*He starts to disarm.*]
>   *Enter Achilles and his Myrmidons.*
> Achilles   Look, Hector, how the sun begins to set,
> How ugly night comes breathing at his heels.
> Even with the vail and dark'ning of the sun
> To close the day up, Hector's life is done.
> Hector   I am unarmed. Forgo this vantage, Greek.
> Achilles   Strike, fellows, strike! This is the man I seek.
> (5.9.3–10)

Hector's trust in the ethics of 'fair play' (5.3.43) gives him a misplaced sense of confidence that the Greek soldiers will not attack him as long as he is unarmed. In reality, they do not hesitate to surround Hector and bayonet him with their weapons. 'Seen in the terms that Achilles himself provides,' Smith notes, 'the slaughter of Hector becomes an act of sexual consumation, a homosexual gang rape that Achilles and his Myrmidons carry out on their unarmed victim.'[36] While Smith is surely correct in his reading of homosexual assault in this scene, I want to end with a different suggestion. As the compassionate Hector pauses for breath and removes his armour in the middle of the combat zone, Shakespeare's text questions what it means to take down our defences. Foreshadowing the breaching of Troy's city walls, the bayonetting of Hector shows how placing our trust in strangers can be a terrible thing.

Notes

1. https://www.washingtonpost.com/news/post-politics/wp/2016/08/05/donald-trump-now-says-even-legal-immigrants-are-a-security-threat/ [accessed September 2021].
2. 'Trojan, adj. and n.', *OED Online*.
3. For more on the Troy legend in the early modern period, see: John Tatlock, 'The Siege of Troy in Elizabethan Literature, Especially in Shakespeare and Heywood', *PMLA*, 30:4 (1915), 673–770; Heather James, *Shakespeare's Troy: Drama, Politics, and the Translation of Empire* (Cambridge: Cambridge University Press, 1997).
4. Virgil, *Aeneid*, trans. Stanley Lombardo (Indianapolis: Hackett Publishing Company, Inc., 2005), Book 2, ll. 17–26.
5. William Shakespeare, *Troilus and Cressida*, ed. David Bevington (London: Cengage Learning, 1998), 1.3.38–44. All further references are to this edition and are given parenthetically in the text.
6. David Hillman, *Shakespeare's Entrails: Belief, Scepticism and the Interior of the Body* (Basingstoke and New York: Palgrave Macmillan, 2007), p. 67.
7. Patricia Parker, *Shakespeare from the Margins: Language, Culture, Context* (Chicago: University of Chicago Press, 1996), p. 226.

8. Jacques Derrida, 'Hostipitality', in *Acts of Religion*, ed. Gil Anidjar (London and New York: Routledge, 2002), pp. 356–421, p. 359.
9. James A. W. Heffernan, *Hospitality and Treachery in Western Literature* (New Haven and London: Yale University Press, 2014).
10. Gail Kern Paster, *The City in the Age of Shakespeare* (Athens, GA: University of Georgia Press, 1985), p. 4.
11. 'Naked, adj. and n.', *OED Online.*
12. Katharine Eisaman Maus, *Inwardness and Theatre in the English Renaissance* (Chicago: University of Chicago Press, 1995), p. 195.
13. Jonathan Sawday, *The Body Emblazoned: Dissection and the Human Body in Renaissance Culture* (London and New York: Routledge, 1995), p. 8.
14. Elspeth Probyn, *Blush: Faces of Shame* (Minneapolis and London: University of Minnesota Press, 2005), p. 2.
15. Charles Darwin, *The Expression of the Emotions in Man and Animals*, ed. Francis Darwin (Cambridge: Cambridge University Press, 2010), Chapter 13, p. 345.
16. Probyn, *Blush*, p. 35.
17. Ewan Fernie, *Shame in Shakespeare* (London and New York: Routledge, 2002), p. 1.
18. For economic criticism on the play, see: Hugh Grady, *Shakespeare's Universal Wolf: Studies in Early Modern Reification* (Oxford: Oxford University Press, 1996); Lars Engle, *Shakespearean Pragmatism: Market of his Time* (Chicago: Chicago University Press, 1993); Jonathan Gil Harris, *Sick Economies: Drama, Mercantilism, and Disease in Shakespeare's England* (Philadelphia: University of Pennsylvania Press, 2004).
19. Douglas Bruster, *Drama and the Market in the Age of Shakespeare* (Cambridge: Cambridge University Press, 1992), p. 99.
20. Margreta de Grazia, 'Imprints: Shakespeare, Gutenburg and Descartes', in *Alternative Shakespeares*, vol. 2, ed. Terence Hawkes (London: Routledge, 1996), pp. 63–95, p. 75.

21. Jacques Derrida, *Given Time: I. Counterfeit Money*, trans. Peggy Kamuf (Chicago: University of Chicago Press, 1992), p. 85.
22. 'The *Hamlet* question, "Who's there?" is asked over and over' in this play, Alexander Leggatt notes in *Shakespeare's Tragedies: Violation and Identity* (Cambridge and New York: Cambridge University Press, 2005), adding that '[e]ven familiar identities need to be constantly checked' (p. 86).
23. William Shakespeare, *Macbeth*, ed. Kenneth Muir (London: Methuen & Co. Ltd., 2006), 1.5.62–6.
24. James A. W. Heffernan, *Hospitality and Treachery in Western Literature* (New Haven and London: Yale University Press, 2014), p. 14. In an historicist account, Felicity Heal demonstrates 'the nexus of obligation and reciprocity that was an inevitable part of private hospitality'; *Hospitality in Early Modern England* (Oxford: Oxford University Press, 1990), p. 218.
25. Steven Marx, 'Shakespeare's Pacifism', *Renaissance Quarterly*, 45:1 (1992), 49–95, p. 59.
26. Matthew A. Greenfield, 'Fragments of Nationalism in *Troilus and Cressida*', *Shakespeare Quarterly*, 51:2 (2000), 181–200, p. 195.
27. John Bayley, 'Time and the Trojans', *Essays in Criticism*, 25:1 (1975), 55–73, p. 58.
28. Bruce R. Smith, 'The Ethics of Compassion in Early Modern England', in *Compassion in Early Modern Literature and Culture: Feeling and Practice*, ed. Kristine Steenbergh and Katherine Ibbett (Cambridge: Cambridge University Press, 2021), pp. 25–43, p. 30.
29. Kristine Steenbergh, 'Mollified Hearts and Enlarged Bowels: Practising Compassion in Reformation England', in *Compassion in Early Modern Literature and Culture*, ed. Steenbergh and Ibbett, pp. 121–38, p. 130. Also relevant is Jennifer Clement, 'Bowels, Emotion, and Metaphor in Early Modern English Sermons', *The Seventeenth Century*, 35:4 (2020), 435–51.
30. Steenbergh, 'Mollified Hearts', pp. 128–9.
31. Emmanuel Levinas, 'No Identity', in *Collected Philosophical Papers*, trans. Alphonso Lingus (Dordrecht and London: Kluwer Academic, 1993), pp. 141–53, pp. 146–7.

32. Jacques Derrida, *On Touching – Jean-Luc Nancy*, trans. Christine Irizarry (Stanford: Stanford University Press, 2005), p. 93.
33. Jacques Derrida, 'Hospitality, Justice and Responsibility: A Dialogue with Jacques Derrida', in *Questioning Ethics: Contemporary Debates in Philosophy*, ed. Richard Kearney and Mark Dooley (London: Routledge, 1999), pp. 65–83, p. 71.
34. Derrida, 'Hostipitality', in *Acts of Religion*, p. 361.
35. Judith Still, *Derrida and Hospitality: Theory and Practice* (Edinburgh: Edinburgh University Press, 2010), p. 123.
36. Bruce R. Smith, *Homosexual Desire in Shakespeare's England: A Cultural Poetics* (Chicago: University of Chicago Press, 1991), p. 61.

CHAPTER 4

TIMON OF ATHENS AND PARASITOLOGY

As William Shakespeare and Thomas Middleton's *Timon of Athens* opens, Timon is intent on being the most generous of hosts, lavishly entertaining friends and neighbours at his home in Athens with an extravagant banquet and bankrolling them through a series of gifts and financial loans. Even when his own financial situation deteriorates, and his debts accumulate to the extent that he runs into problems with his creditors, Timon still holds on to the idea of the communal meal, using it as an imaginative means to get revenge on his former acquaintances. This second 'mock banquet' marks a turning point in the play for, shortly afterwards, Timon goes into solitary exile in the woods outside of Athens, claiming that he is a misanthrope who hates mankind. His unexplained death and burial in an isolated locale at the end of the drama only confirms his estrangement from human society. It should be clear from this brief synopsis that *Timon of Athens* shows a sustained interest in the ethics of hospitality, generosity and neighbourliness. Throughout, the theme of indebtedness is a means to interrogate the question of what really binds us to other people, whether they are our neighbours, our creditors or our mourners. As I seek to show, it is nevertheless vital to expand the traditional boundaries of the economic in order to appreciate more fully both the nature of Timon's debts as well as his supposed acts of generosity.

I begin this chapter by examining Timon's wasteful expenditure in the early part of the play, arguing that his outpouring of generosity is expressed through a fluid symbolism of wine, other libations and emotional tears. Feasts may be good to hold, but they can be risky social events. Boring conversation, choking hazards or exposing oneself to harm are just a few examples of what can go wrong when a group of strangers gather around a table together. I consider the dangers of dining out in *Timon of Athens*, focusing on Shakespeare and Middleton's imagery of cannibalism and ritual sacrifice. Turning my attention in the second section to the 'mock banquet', I show how hospitality is complicated by debt. Through an underlying dynamic of coercion, and as a result of Timon's insistence on remembering the gift, the recipients of his earlier generosity end up becoming bound to him. This section concludes by engaging with the work of anthropologist Claude Lévi-Strauss, who has studied the cultural symbolism of the boiled and the roast in native culinary myths. In the third section, I draw on writings by Michel Serres and Jacques Derrida with the aim of defining the relationship between hospitality and parasitism. Timon accuses his dinner guests of being parasites because they have taken advantage of his generosity. His zoological imagery illuminates the ways in which an ethically inflected vocabulary of hospitality has historically been grafted onto the science of parasitology. In the second part of this section, I move from Athens to the isolated woods. Timon, who was earlier so disapproving of his sponging guests, now lives parasitically off of the natural environment. Developing Coppélia Kahn's feminist psychoanalytic theory, I suggest that Timon's anger in the latter half of the text is directed at the natural fecundity and hospitality of Mother Nature. I end by picking up Lévi-Strauss's category of rotted foodstuffs, arguing that, in

Shakespeare and Middleton, this is an important misogynist trope. Section four revisits the play's emblem of emotional tears to put forward a reading of hospitality that encompasses Timon's strange death and the experience of bereavement on the part of those left behind. Weeping can be read in terms of an economic symbolism that links together acts of hospitality and mourning. Due to their mysterious opacity, tears draw out questions concerning the insincerity of ritual and encourage a reconsideration of hospitality's limitations as well as raising doubts about the nature of generosity. I compare the play to Sophocles' *Oedipus at Colonus*, another text which ends in the hostile landscape outside of Athens and one that is similarly intrigued by the correlation between cultures of hospitality and rituals of mourning and bereavement. Just as Oedipus' death becomes a gift to his host city, Timon's burial can be understood as one last attempt at generosity. In the end, though, there are no easy solutions to the problem of giving. Hospitality and mourning each disclose a spirit of calculation that is disquieting.

'This great flood of visitors'

In Act 1, a large crowd of guests is gathering outside Timon's house, leading the Poet to remark on 'this confluence, this great flood of visitors'.[1] In their Arden edition, Anthony Dawson and Gretchen Minton note how this language 'expresses the fluidity, even the liquidity, of exchange, both monetary and social, that characterises the interaction in the early parts of the play'.[2] Early on, then, Shakespeare and Middleton introduce the watery imagery which will accompany Timon's generosity for the remainder of the action, even foreshadowing his final resting place by the sea. Greeting one another outside Timon's residence, a lord of Athens now asks another, 'shall we in and taste lord Timon's bounty?' (1.1.281), to which the second replies:

> He pours it out; Plutus, the god of gold,
> Is but his steward: no meed but he repays
> Sevenfold above itself, no gift to him
> But breeds the giver a return exceeding
> All use of quittance.
>   (1.1.283–6)

The lord's classical allusion to 'the god of gold' as a 'steward', pouring from his cornucopia, is one of many mentions in the play of their host's desire to give without recompense.

Timon's sumptuous banquet in the second scene is a chance for the audience to witness his hospitality in action. Once his guests are seated at the banquet table, the copious helpings of wine are compared to the ocean surges as Timon passes the cup around his friends:

> *Timon*   My lord, in heart, and let the health go round.
> *2 Lord*   Let it flow this way, my good lord.
> *Apemantus*   Flow this way? A brave fellow! He keeps his tides well; those healths will make thee and thy state look ill, Timon.
>   (1.2.53–7)

Here, as elsewhere, it is the sceptical Apemantus who sounds a note of concern at Timon's excessive generosity, drawing our attention to the fact that 'tides' can suddenly become dangerous. In his anthropological study of the gift, Marcel Mauss points out that, for the ancient Germans and Scandinavians, the archetypal gift was pourable. According to Mauss, 'one can see that the uncertainty about the good or bad nature of the presents could have been nowhere greater than in the case of the customs of the kind where the gifts consisted essentially of drinks taken in common, in libations offered or to be rendered'.[3] The drink's inscrutable quality encapsulates its potential to be poisonous. Even at this early stage in the proceedings, Apemantus is modelling a far more cautious response to commensality.

Partway through the banquet, Timon proposes an emotional toast to his guests. He says to the banquet table:

> O, what a precious comfort 'tis to have so many like brothers commanding one another's fortunes. O, joy's e'en made away ere't can be born – mine eyes cannot hold out water, methinks. To forget their faults, I drink to you.
> (1.2.101–6)

Timon's sentimental crying as he drinks in honour of his friends gives his toast an exceptionally wet quality. In 1658, Thomas Hobbes would note that '[t]hose that weep the greatest amount and more frequently are those, such as women and children, who have the least hope in themselves and the most in friends.'[4] Timon's weepiness is thus effeminising and indicative of his trusting nature at this point in the play. Emotional tears can, moreover, be interpreted as a visible expression of his uneconomical behaviour. Deborah Lupton writes that, in spite of being perceived as 'the most symbolically "clean" of the bodily fluids', tears still 'bespeak a loss of control'.[5] Bridget Escolme has shown how the early moderns valued moderate displays of grief, linking self-control with economics: 'For Thomas Playfere in his sermon on *The Mean in Mourning* (1595), crying is compared to the weather: too much weeping is like an economically unproductive, physically destructive storm.'[6] Timon has no control over his spending or his tearful excretions. A fitting emblem for the early part of the play, the imagery of water reflects the protagonist's cash flow problems.

Because Timon wants to give unreservedly to those around him, he maintains an open-house policy in Athens. Everyone is welcome indoors for there is '[n]o porter at his gate / But rather one that smiles and still invites / All that pass by' (2.1.10–12).

In this respect, Timon is said to be like 'tapsters that bade welcome / To knaves and all approachers' (4.3.214–15). Flavius, the loyal steward, touches on some of the problems this causes when he reprimands his master's generosity:

> So the gods bless me,
> When all our offices have been oppressed
> With riotous feeders, when our vaults have wept
> With drunken spilth of wine, when every room
> Hath blazed with lights and brayed with minstrelsy,
> I have retired me to a wasteful cock
> And set mine eyes at flow.
> (2.2.157–63)[7]

Flavius relates the spilt wine of the rowdy visitors to his own empathetic weeping in an image that again captures the liquid quality of Timon's spending. His unflattering description of the dinner guests emphasises their poor social etiquette. And yet, for pure or absolute hospitality to occur, Derrida suggests that we must be prepared to relinquish control of the threshold:

> Even if the other deprives you of your mastery or your home, you have to accept this. It is terrible to accept this, but that is the condition of unconditional hospitality: that you give up the mastery of your space, your home, your nation. It is unbearable. If, however, there is pure hospitality it should be pushed to this extreme.[8]

At the start of the play, Timon would appear to be pursuing an agenda of unconditional hospitality in the sense that he lets his guests take over the house, in the process leaving his property and person susceptible to damage. However, Timon is *not* as altruistic as he would like to imagine. Rather, he knowingly manipulates hospitality's tendency to accrue debts and commitments in a way that undermines his generosity from the beginning. Such numerical calculations dilute the gift. Before long, Timon's guests will discover that their host's bounty comes with a number of stipulations attached.

As well as the reported damage to Timon's household furnishings, at the first banquet, it starts to look as if the host himself is in danger of suffering violence at the hands of his guests. Again, it is Apemantus who provides a cynical commentary in the middle of the celebrations. Seated apart from the main banquet table, he has these words to say on the dangers of eating in company:

> I scorn thy meat, 'twould choke me 'fore I should e'er flatter thee. O you gods, what a number of men eats Timon and he sees 'em not! It grieves me to see so many men dip their meat in one man's blood, and all the madness is, he cheers them up too.
> I wonder men dare trust themselves with men,
> Methinks they should invite them without knives –
> Good for their meat and safer for their lives.
> There's much example for't: the fellow that sits next him, now parts bread with him, pledges the breath of him in a divided draft, is the readiest man to kill him – 't has been proved. If I were a huge man I should fear to drink at meals,
> Lest they should spy my windpipe's dangerous notes;
> Great men should drink with harness on their throats.
> (1.2.38–52)

Maggie Kilgour writes that 'feasts are dangerous places', and Judith Still notes, 'hospitality obviously carries the risk of creating the conditions of possibility for theft, assault or murder'.[9] Apemantus has plainly internalised this viewpoint since his speech is filled with references to violent death, whether through choking or on account of the dangerous number of knives at the table.

Evoking religious iconography, Apemantus envisages his host's blood as the communal dipping bowl and his flesh as meat for the table when he says: 'O you gods, what a number of men eats Timon and he sees 'em not! It grieves me to see so many men dip their meat in one man's blood' (1.2.38–40). Dawson and Minton suggest that the line alludes to Judas' betrayal of Christ: 'He that dippeth his hand with me in the dish, he shall betray me.'[10] Reminiscent of the symbolism of the Eucharist, Apemantus' words convert Timon into a Christlike figure, offering up his body and blood for the guests to sate their hunger on. The votive connotations recall Sigmund Freud's argument in *Totem and Taboo* that 'a sacrifice involves a feast and a feast cannot be celebrated without a sacrifice'.[11] J. Hillis Miller notes the etymology of 'host' and its inherent sacrificial logic:

> the host is himself the food, his substance consumed without recompense, as when one says, 'He is eating me out of house and home.' The host may then become the host in another sense, not etymologically connected. The word 'Host' is of course the name for the consecrated bread or wafer of the Eucharist, from Middle English *oste*, from Old French *oiste*, from Latin *hostia*, sacrifice, victim.[12]

Timon of Athens preserves these religious and sacrificial associations, as Timon allows himself to be consumed by his guests' greed.

The masque of the five senses at the end of the meal reiterates some of the risks of commensality. On behalf of the masquers, Cupid says:

> Hail to thee, worthy Timon, and to all that of his bounties taste! The five best senses acknowledge thee their patron and come freely to gratulate thy plenteous bosom.
> There taste, touch, all, pleased from thy table rise,
> They only now come but to feast thine eyes.
>   (1.2.121–6)

Cupid personifies the five senses as guests all rising satisfied from Timon's banquet table. The senses perform in miniature our vulnerability in the act of reception. As Kilgour puts it, '[t]he body must incorporate elements from outside itself in order to survive. The need for food exposes the vulnerability of individual identity, enacted at a wider social level in the need for exchanges, communion, and commerce with others.'[13] The danger is that sensory perception, as with social interactions, entails a hazardous mingling of the foreign with the native. Derrida describes the olfactory and gustatory senses, those most associated with eating, as 'more subjective than objective. The sense of taste is activated when the organ of the tongue, the gullet, and the palate come into touch with an external object. The sense of smell is activated by drawing in air which is mixed with alien vapours.'[14] In the same way that our nourishment must be absorbed *within* the body, we do not keep a safe distance from visitors, nor do we wear defensive armour when we eat out as Apemantus recommends. If we truly want to be hospitable, as Timon does, then we hold our arms open to dinner guests, even knowing that they may be carrying knives.

Remembering the Gift

Needing his generosity to be unreciprocated, at the start of the play, Timon refuses to accept repayment on any money he has loaned to friends. Julia Lupton notes that 'Timon aspires to a kind of economic martyrdom'.[15] Thus, when his friend Ventidius offers to reimburse the bail money which he had previously borrowed while he was in prison, Timon interrupts him with the words:

> O, by no means,
> Honest Ventidius, you mistake my love:
> I gave it freely ever, and there's none
> Can truly say he gives if he receives.
>   (1.2.8–11)

Yet, by Act 2, Timon's own financial situation has become desperate. Creditors are gathering outside his house and *now* he wants his money back. He sends one of his servants to Ventidius' home with instructions to remind his friend:

> When he was poor,
> Imprisoned and in scarcity of friends,
> I cleared him with five talents. Greet him from me,
> Bid him suppose some good necessity
> Touches his friend which craves to be remembered
> With those five talents
> (2.2.224–9)

Interwoven with the salutation is a demand for economic repayment. Of course, by requesting that Ventidius give back his gift, Timon annuls his earlier promise that it was freely given without hope of future reimbursement. In fact, it soon becomes apparent that Timon regards his friends as an alternate bank account for a rainy day. With his own capital depleted, he is reliant on having made sound financial investments (or so he thinks) among his Athenian friends and neighbours.

Given Time: I. Counterfeit Money is Derrida's most extensive investigation into the gift's relationship to economy and, above all, how any calculations of return on investment prevent the gift from ever being given freely. 'Now the gift, if there is any', Derrida argues, 'would no doubt be related to economy. One cannot treat the gift, this goes without saying, without treating this relation to economy, even to the money economy. But is not the gift, if there is any, also that which interrupts economy? That which, in suspending economic calculation, no longer gives rise to exchange?'[16] Derrida notes that remembering is a problem for the gift:

> The gift is not a gift, the gift only gives to the extent it *gives time*. The difference between a gift and every other operation of pure and simple exchange is that the gift gives

time. *There where there is gift, there is time*. What it gives, the gift, is time, but this gift of time is also a demand of time. The thing must not be restituted *immediately and right away*. There must be time, it must last, there must be waiting – without forgetting [*l'attente – sans oubli*].[17]

Timon's waiting without forgetting for an opportune moment when he will ask for the gift to be returned to him undermines his generosity from the beginning. In the above example, he tells his servant that the money he lent to Ventidius now 'craves to be remembered'. Timon purposely keeps the notion of repayment alive. This does not make him bountiful, though; instead, the insistence on remembering his former gifts demonstrates how attempts at generosity in this play are curtailed by an economic cycle of exchange. It does not matter whether he refers to an account book or relies on his memory, by calling in his loan, *Timon of Athens* dramatizes the darker side of giving, showing how the money which Timon advanced to Ventidius was only ever borrowed time and not the pure gift that he had imagined.

We might think of Timon's display of emotion as subject to the same economic logic as the gift. Consider, for instance, Timon's weepy toast at the banquet table which at first resembles a spontaneous outpouring of joy as he contemplates being surrounded by so many loyal friends. On closer inspection, however, the guests feel compelled to emulate their host's outburst. Sure enough, Timon's tears immediately elicit a flood of weeping from the rest of the table:

2 Lord	Joy had the like conception in our eyes
	And at that instant like a babe sprung up.
Apemantus	Ho ho, I laugh to think that babe a bastard.
3 Lord	I promise you, my lord, you moved me much.
	(1.2.108–11)

Punning on the second lord's imagery of conception, Apemantus satirises the watery scene, implying that the guests are shedding only crocodile tears. The host, too, comes in for his share of criticism when Apemantus says, '[t]hou weep'st to make them drink, Timon' (1.2.107). The insinuation being that Timon's own tears are pregnant with ulterior motives. Derrida reminds us that, if guest and host are bound to one another in some way, 'this hospitality of paying up is no longer an absolute hospitality, it is no longer graciously offered beyond debt and economy'.[18] The mass emotional weeping in *Timon of Athens* evidences an equivalent dynamic of coercion. In other words, Timon makes demands on his guests in ways that are not solely financial.

'In their essence', Marjory Lange writes, 'tears, like all expressions of feeling, are ultimately mysterious.'[19] Their opacity comes from never knowing for sure whether they are false or genuine. Evolutionary theories have sought to uncover why weeping is predisposed to self-interest. While Charles Darwin thought tears were a meaningless biological side effect, recent studies have refuted this point. In *Why Only Humans Weep: Unravelling the Mysteries of Tears*, Ad Vingerhoets suggests that emotional weeping may have served a vital evolutionary purpose by making us look defenceless and so deterring predators.[20] Human tears, then, likely evolved out of the need to coerce other people, and even different species, into behaving in a certain way. At least, this is what happens in *Timon of Athens*, where the dinner guests feel obliged to reciprocate their host's display of sentiment, whether they want to or not. The scene proves that it is not just the monetary economy of Athens which is heavily indebted. Timon's weepy toast can perhaps best be compared to a form of emotional blackmail, offering a corrective to the idea that hospitality accumulates only economic debts and arrears.

In any case, when Timon *does* ask for his money back, he is left frustrated. Flaminius is one of several servants

Timon sends out begging for money in order to appease his creditors. After being turned away by his master's old friend, Lucullus, he says angrily:

> Has friendship such a faint and milky heart
> It turns in less than two nights? O you gods,
> I feel my master's passion. This slave
> Unto this hour has my lord's meat in him:
> Why should it thrive and turn to nutriment,
> When he is turned to poison?
> (3.1.52–7)

Flaminius uses cookery imagery appropriate to Timon's hospitality to liken their friendship to curdled milk that has gone sour. What makes Lucullus' ingratitude worse is that his body is still digesting and so being nourished by the rich food he was served at Timon's house. Having had a bellyful of his friends' ungratefulness and angered at their collective refusal to give him his money back, Timon's thoughts again turn to entertaining. In Act 3, he instructs Flavius to 'invite them all, let in the tide / Of knaves once more: my cook and I'll provide' (3.5.11–12). Mirroring the watery allusions from the first banquet, the text invites us to compare the two feasts. Chris Meads suggests that they 'are structurally a pair; the first being a statement of the accepted Athenian hierarchy and the second depicting the breaking down of that order'.[21] Understood in Bakhtinian terms, the second banquet is a carnivalesque inversion of the earlier one.

A good deal of the cunning which goes into preparations for the 'mock banquet' comes from the way Timon deliberately whets his guests' appetites. The stage directions specify that a banquet is brought in, while the visitors speculate on what sort of delicious meal they are about to enjoy:

2 Lord	All covered dishes!	
1 Lord	Royal cheer, I warrant you.	
3 Lord	Doubt not that, if money and the season can yield it.	

(3.7.48–50)

Covered dishes arouse the senses by creating an illusion that the edibles underneath are extravagant and therefore need to be kept warm. Keeping up the pretence that a hot, delectable meal is about to be dished up, Timon urges the visitors not to worry about the social hierarchy when it comes to the seating arrangements but to sit themselves anywhere: 'your diet shall be in all places alike. Make not a city feast of it to let the meat cool ere we can agree upon the first place. Sit, sit' (3.7.66–7). Continuing to adhere to the polite ceremonies of hospitality, Timon then says grace:

> The gods require our thanks:
> You great benefactors, sprinkle our society with thankfulness
> [. . .] For these my present friends, as they are to me nothing,
> so in nothing bless them and to nothing are they welcome.
> Uncover, dogs, and lap! [*The dishes are uncovered and prove to be full of lukewarm water.*]
> (3.7.68–84)

Submerged in the lukewarm water are some stones which Timon, in a parody of the generous host, throws at his hastily departing guests.

The substitution of stones in the place of culinary delicacies evokes the logic of transferral which René Girard has identified as the basis for all sacrificial proceedings. In *Violence and the Sacred*, Girard shows how a scapegoat figure can protect the rest of the community from harm:

> Society is seeking to deflect upon a relatively indifferent victim, a 'sacrificeable' victim, the violence that would

otherwise be vented on its own members [. . .] with these qualities goes the strange propensity to seize upon surrogate victims, to actually conspire with the enemy and at the right moment toss him a morsel that will serve to satisfy his raging hunger.[22]

Appropriately for *Timon of Athens*, Girard cites stone as the classic example of a surrogate morsel, noting that '[t]he fairy tales of childhood in which the wolf, ogre, or dragon gobble up a large stone in place of a small child could well be said to have a sacrificial cast'.[23] Although the scapegoat depends on misdirection, it 'must never lose sight entirely, however, of the original object, or cease to be aware of the act of transference from that object to the surrogate victim; without that awareness no substitution can take place'.[24] Equally, when Timon presents the dinner guests with stones, his revenge is effective because we never lose sight of the fact that tasty nibbles should be underneath the covered dishes. Anthropologist Claude Lévi-Strauss has taken the ogre and stone analogy one step further. In *The Raw and the Cooked: Introduction to a Science of Mythology*, he suggests that 'the episode of the ogre shows how the hero tricked his abductor by leaving him a stone to eat instead of a body. Stone, or rock, appears, then, as the symmetrical opposite of human flesh.'[25] According to Lévi-Strauss's structuralist approach to native culinary myths, stone epitomises the inedible and is the symbolic reverse of cannibalism. In *Timon of Athens*, the mode of Timon's revenge on his friends and neighbours also relies on a structuralist method, which sees meat replaced with stone, a transferral which neutralises the cannibalistic overtones of the earlier feast.

Deepening the religious allegory of the 'mock banquet', Timon sprinkles the tepid water in his guests' faces, telling them, '[s]moke and lukewarm water / Is your perfection' (3.7.88–9). Water was commonly associated with duplicity in the early modern period, which is why Desdemona in *Othello* is said to be 'false as water'.[26] In *Timon of Athens*, the tepid temperature is emblematic of the Athenians' lukewarm gestures of politeness. Earlier, Flavius spoke scathingly about their 'half-caps and cold-moving nods' (2.2.212), with the implication being that they only go through the motions of civility, therefore making an incomplete show of good manners. Dawson and Minton argue that the lukewarm water is a reference to the Book of Revelation 3:15–16: 'because thou art lukewarm, and neither cold nor hot, it will come to pass, that I shall spew thee out of my mouth'.[27] In a reversal of his former hospitality, Timon's revenge is grounded on an ethic of anti-ingestion, which includes references to spitting out of the mouth and the provision of indigestible stones in place of delicious food. The dialogue at the 'mock banquet' also alludes several times to '[s]moke' (3.7.88) and 'reeking' (3.7.92) 'vapours' (3.7.96), implying that the covered bowls are emitting clouds of hot steam. As well as stimulating his guests' appetites, these vaporous mists create a convincing impression of boiled food.

In *The Origin of Table Manners*, Lévi-Strauss makes an interesting distinction between the boiled and the roast in world mythology. The third volume in the *Mythologiques* series, *The Origin of Table Manners* develops Lévi-Strauss's investigations into raw, cooked and rotten foodstuffs. Here, though, the basic categories are expanded to include the boiled and the roast, which, in many native cultures, signify the main difference in cooking method:

> What, then, constitutes the opposition between the roast and the boiled? Roasted food, being directly exposed to fire is in a relationship of *non-mediatized conjunction*, whereas boiled food is the product of a two-fold process of mediation: it is immersed in water and both food and water are contained within a receptacle.

> So, on two counts, the roast can be placed on the side of nature, and the boiled on the side of culture. Literally, since boiled food necessitates the use of a receptacle, which is a cultural object; and symbolically, in the sense that culture mediates between man and the world, and boiling is also a mediation, by means of water, between the food which man ingests and that other element of the physical world: fire.[28]

On boiling, Lévi-Strauss goes on to say:

> Boiling takes place inside (a receptacle), whereas roasting is cooking from the outside: one suggests the concave, the other the convex. Thus, the boiled often belongs to what might be called 'endo-cooking', intended for private use and for a small closed group. This is most forcefully expressed in the Hidatsa language, where the same word *mi dá ksi* is used for the fence surrounding the village, the cooking pot and the pan, since all three delimit an enclosed space.[29]

Whereas the roast 'belongs to "exo-cooking", the kind that is offered to strangers', across numerous world cultures boiling signifies a much more intimate method of food preparation.[30] Analysing the rich vocabulary of gastronomic symbolism ingrained in these various cooking techniques, Lévi-Strauss concludes that '[b]oiled meat could thus connote a strengthening of family and social ties, and roast meat a weakening of these ties'.[31] In *Timon of Athens*, Timon's culinary-themed revenge corresponds to the cultural anthropology of boiled food as put forward by Lévi-Strauss. That is to say, the warm vapours drifting upwards from the bowls of steaming water seemingly promise the guests that an intimate and special meal is about to be served.

Lévi-Strauss makes a final point about the mythology of boiled food that is relevant to my reading of hospitality in *Timon of Athens*. Comparing the boiled and the roast, he notes, 'boiling provides a method of preserving all the meat and its juices, whereas roasting involves destruction or loss. One suggests economy, the other waste.'[32] As the first banquet is laid out on stage, it is sure to consist of a rich variety of roast meat. Near the beginning of Jonathan Miller's production, for instance, Timon's guests tuck into chicken and roast pork.[33] Roasting is an uneconomical cooking method because it produces a lot of waste. Roasting techniques tend to scorch the meat, leaving it blackened and charred on the outside, while the fatty juices drain out, sometimes running untasted into the fire. The roast is characteristic of Timon's uneconomical attitude towards food and drink in the early part of the play. For the 'mock banquet', though, he favours the boiled, a far more frugal gastronomic technique, which conserves all of the cooking liquid (as well as any juices) inside the boiling pot. Not only that, but this time he does not even add food to the container. Timon's change in cooking methods, from the roast to the boiled, accompanies the transformation in his economic situation, which moves from waste to punishing austerity.

'Smiling, smooth, detested parasites'

In his book on *The Parasite*, Michel Serres draws on beast fables and cultural customs to better understand the science of parasitology. 'The basic vocabulary of this science', he writes, 'comes from such ancient and common customs and habits that the earliest monuments of our culture tell of them, and we still see them, at least in part: hospitality, table manners, hostelry, general relations with strangers.'[34] Hospitality and other social exchanges lent themselves to discourses of parasitology because man was, in fact, the original parasite, long before the classification was ever applied to the natural world and plant, animal or insect life. Anders M. Gullestad notes that 'until the mid-seventeenth century (when it also came to designate plants living on other plants), the term "parasite" was used solely for people, and it was only after the natural sciences of the early nineteenth century adopted the term that it became applied to sponging animals and insects'.[35] Shakespeare typically uses the word 'parasite' as an insult to mean a sycophant at the court. Thus, Bolingbroke in *Richard II* is described as 'a flatterer / A parasite'.[36] In *Coriolanus*, Martius distinguishes between soldierly and civilian life when he says:

> When drums and trumpets shall
> I'th' field prove flatterers, let courts and cities be
> Made of false-faced soothing. When steel grows soft
> As the parasite's silk, let him be made
> An ovator for th' wars.[37]

Parasitology in these examples is a *social* concept, albeit with negative associations of self-serving behaviour and sponging. One result of the grafting of human behaviour onto the natural sciences was, Gullestad points out, to create an unforeseen moral slant by causing scientists to 'understand the relationship between parasite and host in ethical terms foreign to nature'.[38]

Cursing his former friends for taking advantage of his generosity, Timon labels them parasites:

> Live loathed and long,
> Most smiling, smooth, detested parasites,
> Courteous destroyers, affable wolves, meek bears –
> You fools of fortune, trencher-friends, time's flies,
> Cap-and-knee slaves, vapours and minute-jacks!
> (3.7.92–6)

Timon blends together social and zoological examples of the parasite in order to foreground our attention onto the precise nature of the bonds between him and the recipients of his generosity. Critiquing their hypocrisy and the lack of sincerity behind everyday social pleasantries, Timon accuses his Athenian neighbours of being 'trencher-friends', implying that they are only after a free meal.

Through its emphasis on the parasite, the text reiterates Timon's one-directional view of the hospitality relationship. Whereas earlier he imagined his generosity towards his guests as a flood, now he complains that the same people have sucked him dry. And yet, the bond between parasite and host organism was not always seen as unequal. In an influential essay, 'The Critic as Host', J. Hillis Miller reminds us of the implications behind the etymology:

> 'Parasite' comes from the Greek, *parasitos*, etymologically: 'beside the grain,' *para*, beside (in this case) plus *sitos*, grain, food. 'Sitology' is the science of foods, nutrition, and diet. 'Parasite' was originally something positive, a fellow guest, someone sharing the food with you, there with you beside the grain. Later on, 'parasite' came to mean a professional dinner guest, someone expert at cadging invitations without ever giving dinners in return.[39]

For Serres, too, companionship is a significant factor in the cultural history of parasitology. 'The parasite', he argues, 'is invited to the *table d'hôte*; in return, he must regale the other diners with his stories and his mirth. To be exact, he exchanges good talk for good food; he buys his dinner, paying for it in words. It is the oldest profession in the world.'[40] These mutually beneficial advantages are firmly ingrained within the history of social parasitism. Because the earliest parasite was an expert dinner guest, and because the stories he narrated to the rest of the table enhanced the communal enjoyment of the meal, the parasite would effectively pay his way. The same is true of nature. Organic life forms prosper from the presence of parasites, which perform an important evolutionary function for the plant, insect and animal kingdoms. 'Evolution', Serres explains, 'has a parasitic structure. It would not favour parasites as much as it does if it were not more or less favoured by them.'[41] When a parasite invades a new host, it accelerates the biological mechanisms responsible for natural selection and adaptation, enhancing the evolutionary capabilities of the larger organism which is forced to evolve at a quicker rate than is usual. Parasites also coerce their hosts into improving their immunity against other predators. Contrary to the negative perception of parasites, then, they are extremely valuable to the organisms they frequent.

This is surely the case with Timon, who feeds off the sycophantic adoration of everybody around him. Despite his repeated efforts to give without return, he is, in fact, the recipient of flattery, good company, gifts, accolades and entertainments, including Cupid's masque of the senses. While it might seem as if Timon's guests are the ones with insatiable appetites – intent on eating him out of house and home – this is not quite the whole story, for the host, as well, satisfies his own desires on the newcomers. Ben Jelloun touches on this idea in *French Hospitality: Racism and North African Immigrants*:

> Moroccan expressions of welcome are very instructive. For example, to convey the pleasure and satisfaction you feel when you receive another person into your home you say, 'You have filled up my house' or 'You have filled up our house with us (or for us).' If you want to say something nice to someone you say: 'May your house always be full (of people, friends, love, blessings)'. When guests finally leave you call them back and tell them: 'After you've gone (or without you) the house will be empty.' [. . .] The act of entertaining a guest is something that both honours and humanises the host. But as well as filling his heart it does something more. It makes the guest recognise me, the host, as someone capable of sharing. It improves my status, as someone capable of existing in relation to others.[42]

Jelloun evocatively captures the many benefits that the guest brings to the host's household, demonstrating how these sentiments have entered the very language of Morocco. As Jelloun continues, '[w]hen another person comes to my house, he teaches me things about myself. His mere presence makes me confront myself. He upsets my space and my habits and teaches me what I am.'[43] Indeed, the pleasurable, instructional and world-building rewards that the visitor contributes are so abundant that it is difficult to say who is the principal beneficiary of hospitality. In negative discourses on the parasite, these gains are sometimes lost. While acknowledging that some parasites are destructive, Gullestad warns against striving for a world in which they do not exist, concluding that 'a lack of parasites should therefore not be understood as a sign of health, but rather the opposite, pointing to a world out of balance'.[44]

Before turning to environmental perspectives on the parasite in *Timon of Athens*, it is worth noting that the science of parasitology is haunted by a classificatory indeterminacy. It is surprisingly hard for experts to agree on what constitutes a parasite.[45] When it comes to hospitality and other social interactions, we are faced with the same problem. 'How can we distinguish between a guest and a parasite?', Derrida wonders, before going on to say that:

> Not all new arrivals are received as guests if they don't have the benefit of the right to hospitality or the right of asylum, etc. Without this right, a new arrival can only be introduced 'in my home', in the host's 'at home' as a parasite, a guest who is wrong, illegitimate, clandestine, liable to expulsion or arrest.[46]

Whether the newcomer is a guest or a parasite depends on the spirit in which they are received by the host. As we have seen in this book, there is only ever a fine line separating welcomed guest from illegal alien. During the 'mock banquet' scene, Timon theatrically revokes his hospitality, pelting the strangers with stones and lukewarm water as they rush to depart. His change of heart shows how even the most treasured of guests is only ever one misstep away from becoming an unwanted parasite.

In Act 4, newly homeless and poor, Timon leaves Athens and heads for the deserted woods. Once outside the city walls, he muses on his change in circumstance:

> But myself –
> Who had the world as my confectionary,
> The mouths, the tongues, the eyes and hearts of men
> At duty more than I could frame employment,
> That numberless upon me stuck as leaves
> Do on the oak, have with one winter's brush
> Fell from their boughs and left me open, bare
> For every storm that blows
>   (4.3.258–65)

Like a child in a sweet shop, Timon had his pick of willing admirers in Athens, the mention of 'confectionary' redolent of the lavish sugary desserts served at the end of early modern banquets.[47] Friendless, though, he is now a leafless tree, uncovered to the winter weather. Seasonal imagery recalls Sonnet 73, where the older speaker says to the young man:

> That time of year thou mayst in me behold,
> When yellow leaves, or none, or few do hang
> Upon those boughs which shake against the cold.[48]

Autumnal branches denote hair loss and indicate exposure to the elements. When he meets the prostitutes in the woods, Timon similarly advises them to make wigs to keep their heads warm:

> And thatch your poor thin roofs
> With burdens of the dead – some that were hanged –
> No matter, wear them, betray with them.
> (4.3.144–6)

Laurie Shannon coins the term 'pelt envy' to convey our species jealousy at the mammal who 'comes armed with a good coat already on its back'.[49] Not only must we rely on fur, wool, feathers, leather or silks to keep ourselves warm and dry, but humankind is the only animal to spend time mediating in his gastronomic environment by means of food preparation and cookery, instead of consuming nutrition raw. But when Timon leaves Athens behind him, he is removed from the fledgling sanitation of the early modern kitchen.

Timon's woodland diet of raw roots is a recipe for humankind's unaccommodated state and our inability to survive easily in the wilderness. Comparable to other desert regions, food is (seemingly) hard to come by in the forest, and when we first encounter Timon he is digging hungrily in the soil looking for something to eat, while still cursing Athenian society:

> Therefore be abhorred
> All feasts, societies and throngs of men!
> His semblance, yea himself, Timon disdains.
> Destruction fang mankind! Earth, yield me roots.
> [*Digs in the earth.*]
> (4.3.20–3)

As Timon consumes the roots which he has dug out of the soil, the text collapses any distinction between humankind and wild animals who get their nourishment raw and sometimes freshly bloodied. Joan Fitzpatrick notes: 'Timon's foraging for roots as much as his desire for solitude would have struck an early modern audience as distinctly bestial, indeed pig-like.'[50] Vegetarianism was seen by many people in the seventeenth century as a peculiar lifestyle choice. Timon's vegan diet designates him a foreigner and heightens his estrangement from civilization. Yet there are hints that he is holding on to his old eating habits. While he eats the root, he says: 'That the whole life of Athens were in this / Thus would I eat it' (4.3.281–2). The line resonates with Girard's argument in *Violence and the Sacred* that, '[w]hen unappeased, violence seeks and always finds a surrogate victim. The creature that excited its fury is abruptly replaced by another, chosen only because it is vulnerable and close at hand.'[51] Timon may have gone vegan out of necessity, but he retains the sacrificial logic of the carnivorous feast.

Timon of Athens blurs the categories of guest, host and parasite. In the woods, Timon – vocal critic of his guests' freeloading behaviour – now lives parasitically off his new woodland home. French philosophy has encouraged us to rethink humankind's parasitic relationship with nature. 'The earth', Derrida argues, 'gives hospitality before all else'.[52] For Serres:

> But let us descend to the level of a tree. It gives shelter, decoration, flowers, fruits, and shade. And in return for its wages or more accurately for its rent – for it shelters and produces a territory – it is felled. The tree judges man to be an ingrate [. . .] history hides the fact that man is the universal parasite, that everything and everyone around him is a hospitable space. Plants and animals are always his hosts; man is always necessarily their guest. Always taking, never giving.[53]

Timon of Athens stages its own example of sylvan inhospitality when Timon sarcastically tells the Athenian senators that he will help them to escape Alcibiades and his army:

> I have a tree which grows here in my close
> That mine own use invites me to cut down,
> And shortly must I fell it. Tell my friends,
> Tell Athens, in the sequence of degree

> From high to low throughout, that whoso please
> To stop affliction, let him take his haste,
> Come hither ere my tree hath felt the axe
> And hang himself.
> (5.2.90–7)

Timon's repeated use of possessive pronouns, and metaphors of urban architecture, implies a sense of proprietorship towards his woodland surroundings.

In hypocritical fashion, Timon in the woods becomes the definitive parasite. Apemantus teases him on this very subject:

> What, think'st
> That the bleak air, thy boisterous chamberlain,
> Will put thy shirt on warm? Will these mossed trees
> That have outlived the eagle page thy heels
> And skip when thou point'st out? Will the cold brook,
> Candied with ice, caudle thy morning taste
> To cure thy o'ernight's surfeit?
> (4.3.220–6)

Apemantus teases Timon that the ancient woods are indifferent to his needs and the comforts he enjoyed in Athens. And yet, the guest *does* receive hospitality from his surroundings.

In a feminist psychoanalytic reading of *Timon of Athens*, Kahn argues that the text is organised around a core 'fantasy of maternal bounty and maternal betrayal'.[54] Whereas Kahn focuses on Lady Fortune, I am interested in Timon's relationship with Mother Nature. I suggest that Timon's envy is triggered by a correlation between hospitality and maternity. Anne Dufourmantelle writes that motherhood is the original hospitality we receive:

> Our birth in fact constitutes the first act of hospitality – offered to, not by, us – and not a psychological, but an

ontological, existential problem: We come from a mother's womb, we begin our beings as cells splitting and growing, until we finally part, indeed 'disassemble' ourselves from another human being who has nourished and (preferably) loved us, but at least carried us long enough to be born.[55]

We begin life as parasites, housed in the womb for nine months and nurtured by the hospitable maternal body. *Timon of Athens* presents a male protagonist who is envious of the lush green hospitality of the natural world. In contrast, Timon's money problems are framed in a language of infertility and abnormally generative breeding. As an Athenian senator puts it:

> If I want gold, steal but a beggar's dog
> And give it to Timon, why, the dog coins gold.
> If I would sell my horse and buy twenty more
> Better than he, why, give my horse to Timon –
> Ask nothing, give it him – it foals me straight
> And able horses.
>   (2.1.5–10)

Timon blames his insolvency on an inability to renew organically like the cosmos. Embittered by his losses, he degrades the gravitational pull of the stars and the ocean tides through a comparison to theft:

> The sun's a thief and with his great attraction
> Robs the vast sea; the moon's an arrant thief
> And her pale fire she snatches form the sun;
> The sea's a thief whose liquid surge resolves
> The moon into salt tears; the earth's a thief
> That feeds and breeds by a composture stol'n
> From general excrement.
>   (4.3.431–7)

Timon's comment about how the soil 'feeds and breeds' is telling of a more general obsession with women's reproductive parts.

If we return to the agricultural episode where Timon is digging in the soil for roots to eat, he addresses nature directly when he says:

> Common mother – thou
> Whose womb unmeasurable and infinite breast
> Teems and feeds all, whose selfsame mettle
> Whereof thy proud child, arrogant man, is puffed,
> Engenders the black toad and adder blue,
> The gilded newt and eyeless venomed worm,
> With all th'abhorred births below crisp heaven
> Whereon Hyperion's quickening fire doth shine –
> Yield him who all the human sons do hate
> From forth thy plenteous bosom one poor root.
> Ensear thy fertile and conceptious womb,
> Let it no more bring out ungrateful man. [. . .]
> Dry up thy marrows, vines and plough-torn leas,
> Whereof ungrateful man with liquorish draughts
> And morsels unctuous greases his pure mind,
> That from it all consideration slips –
> (4.3.176–95)

In this long soliloquy, Timon personifies 'mother' nature, lingering over her sexually reproductive organs: her 'womb unmeasurable and infinite breast', her 'plenteous bosom' and 'fertile and conceptious womb'. Clearly it is the fecundity of nature which Timon finds repellent. Conflating botanical and corporeal imagery, Timon curses the soil: 'Dry up thy marrows, vines and plough-torn leas'. The line recalls Lear's violent wish for his daughter: 'Dry up in her the organs of increase'.[56] Lear is angered by Goneril's refusal to accommodate him. On the other hand, Timon would appear to have the reverse problem because he claims to be appalled at the indiscriminate hospitality of this maternal source. He complains that nature's 'proud child, arrogant man' receives no special care and attention, for the ground gives identical nourishment to the most poisonous, creeping animals, such as the toad, adder, newt and worm. In his diseased imagination, Timon pictures nature as a sluttish hostess who serves up 'liquorish draughts' and 'morsels unctuous' to every hungry guest. Soon afterwards, Timon returns to this theme when he comments on the woods' rich storehouse of culinary provisions:

> Behold, the earth hath roots,
> Within this mile break forth a hundred springs,
> The oaks bear mast, the briars scarlet hips,
> The bounteous housewife Nature on each bush
> Lays her full mess before you.
> (4.3.412–16)

In Athens, hospitality is male, dependent on the culinary mediation of the kitchen, and vulnerable to depletion. Conversely, sylvan hospitality is feminine, vegetarian and immeasurable.

As evidence of his growing bitterness at the verdant hospitality of his alfresco home, Timon starts becoming fixated on malodorous smells. Cursing again, he says:

> O blessed breeding sun, draw from the earth
> Rotten humidity, below thy sister's orb
> Infect the air!
> (4.3.1–3)

Timon sees the planet festering under an adverse microclimate which is rotten and humid. The line looks ahead to his hope that the invading Alcibiades will destroy Athens:

> Be as a planetary plague when Jove
> Will o'er some high-viced city hang his poison
> In the sick air.
> (4.3.108–10)

As part of his ethnography of native culinary myths, Lévi-Strauss notices a misogynist triangulation between nature, stench and femininity. 'We are dealing with stench and decay,' he writes, 'which, as has already been established, signify nature, as opposed to culture, but this time they are expressed in terms of anatomical coding. And woman is, everywhere synonymous with nature.'[57] Referring back to the ethnographic source material, he explains how:

> In their sexual life the Brazilian Indians are particularly susceptible to the smells of the female body [. . .] Seeing a rotten fruit full of worms, Mair, the Urubu demiurge, exclaimed: 'That would make a nice woman!' And straightaway the fruit turned into a woman. In a Tacana myth the jaguar decides not to rape an Indian woman after he has caught the smell of her vulva, which seems to him to reek of worm-ridden meat. A Mundurucu myth, which has already been quoted, relates that after the animals had made vaginas for the first women, the armadillo rubbed each of the organs with a piece of rotten nut, which gave them their characteristic smell.[58]

Within the European tradition, the misogynist parallel between women and rottenness, especially decayed or smelly food, is every bit as well established. In *Much Ado About Nothing*, Claudio cautions Leonato regarding his daughter Hero: 'Give not this rotten orange to your friend / She's but the sign and semblance of her honour.'[59] Lucio implies a sexual slur when he says of the Duke of Vienna in *Measure for Measure* he 'would eat mutton on Fridays [. . .] he would mouth with a beggar though she smelt brown bread and garlic'.[60] For the early moderns, gone-off fresh produce, such as mouldy fruit and vegetables, or meat that was long past its best, was culinary slang for lapsed female chastity. In *Timon of Athens*, Timon associates femininity and rotten food when he refuses to kiss the prostitutes: 'I will not kiss thee, then the rot returns / To thine own lips again' (4.3.65–6). Apemantus then offers Timon some fruit to eat, which he also declines:

> *Apemantus*   There's a medlar for thee – eat it.
> *Timon*   On what I hate I feed not.
> *Apemantus*   Dost hate a medlar?
> *Timon*   Ay, though it look like thee.
>   (4.3.304–7)

The medlar is a small fruit, eaten when soft, pulpy and partially rotten, and it was slang for the female genitalia and prostitution. Lucio in *Measure for Measure* calls a prostitute a 'rotten medlar'.[61]

Kahn's psychoanalytic approach to *Timon of Athens* feels convincing and I hope to have extended her analysis into a discussion of hospitality in the woods. Following Kahn, we could perhaps best understand Timon's unwillingness to eat the medlar, and his refusal to kiss the prostitutes, as a phobic intolerance of the female part. Confronted by female hostesses real and metaphorical, all proffering up food, Timon's dietary policy in the woods increasingly becomes nil by mouth.

Balance Sheet

This chapter ends by returning to the symbolism of tears in *Timon of Athens* to put forward a reading of hospitality which encompasses Timon's mysterious death and burial in the final part of the play. Welcoming guests and burying the dead are at once the mundane and extraordinary limits of experience and share a concern with ideas of ritual, commemoration, the relationship to place, and nationality. Marjorie Garber suggests that:

> Rites of incorporation for the dead are often thought of as congruent with hospitality rites among the living: the new

arrival is supposedly offered food or other gifts by those who have gone before him, or by the divine inhabitants of the other world. Such rites are by their nature taboo for the living if they wish to return to earth after their sojourn among the dead. Thus, Proserpina, eating the seeds of a pomegranate, unwittingly accepted Pluto's hospitality and was incorporated for six months a year into his kingdom.[62]

In *Timon of Athens*, the accrual of debts and obligations connects cultures of hospitality to mourning rites. Throughout, the text explores what binds people to one another or sets them at odds. Social exchanges between guest and host, debtor and creditor, are replaced, in the closing scenes, with the relationship between the mourner and the deceased. 'What grief displays', according to Judith Butler,

> is the thrall in which our relations with others hold us, in ways that we cannot always recount or explain, in ways that often interrupt the self-conscious account of ourselves that we might try to provide, in ways that challenge the very notion of ourselves as autonomous and in control [. . .] Let's face it. We're undone by each other. And if we're not, we're missing something.[63]

Shakespeare and Middleton, I contend, do not offer us a way out of this thraldom in *Timon of Athens*. If anything, as the play concludes it implies that being held to account by one another is still everything. Nevertheless, the final scenes give us a deeper sense of the debts and accountabilities that grief and hospitality accumulate and which are important if we are to appreciate more fully the nature of generosity.

Compared to Shakespeare's other tragic protagonists, Timon's death is puzzling because he dies offstage and in unknown circumstances. His parting words to the senators are:

> Come not to me again, but say to Athens
> Timon hath made his everlasting mansion
> Upon the beached verge of the salt flood,
> Who once a day with his embossed froth
> The turbulent surge shall cover
> (5.2.99–103)

A soldier confirms the sea-soaked burial place when he brings news of Timon's death to Alcibiades, who reads out the epitaph: '*Here lie I, Timon, who alive all living men did hate / Pass by and curse thy fill, but pass and stay not here thy gait*' (5.5.70–1). Combined with the remote coastal location of his grave, Timon's rude epitaph seeks to dissuade mourners from lingering to pay their respects. His emotional weeping from earlier on now gives way to a desire for *no* sentimentality. And yet, while Timon's suspension of his own mourning rituals might strike us as inhospitable, Derrida can help us to understand this moment differently as the most generous of farewell gifts.

It is here that a comparison with Sophocles' *Oedipus at Colonus* is instructive. A. D. Nuttall suggests that '*Timon of Athens* has an oddly Greek feel to it', and there are other similarities between the two plays: both culminate in the lonely scenery outside of Athens and omit the normal burial customs.[64] Oedipus tells Theseus, the ruler of Athens, never to disclose the location of his last resting place to anyone, not even to his family. Derrida shows how this occasions mourning for the loss of mourning. 'She complains', he says of Antigone, 'that her father has died in a foreign land and moreover is buried in a place foreign to any possible localization. She complains of the mourning not allowed, at any rate of a mourning without tears, a mourning deprived of weeping.'[65] Oedipus' actions seem needlessly unkind:

> It is as if he wanted to depart without leaving so much as an address for the mourning of the women who love him. He acts as if he wanted to make their mourning infinitely worse, to weigh it down, even, with the mourning they can no longer do. He is going to deprive them of their mourning, thereby obliging them to go through their mourning of mourning. Do we know of a more generous and poisoned form of the gift?[66]

Derrida's question has implications for how we might interpret the strange ending of *Timon of Athens*. Timon, like Oedipus, forgoes all customary mourning rites, depriving his surviving loved ones of an opportunity to grieve over his death. Although this legacy appears cruel, it can also be seen as extraordinarily compassionate. By allowing no tears of remembrance or burial customs, Timon liberates the citizens of Athens from their work of mourning.

Outstanding debts still continue to complicate the gift economy of *Timon of Athens* even after the central character's death and burial. Timon's generous insistence that he does not want any sorrow or remembrance paradoxically ends up leaving his mourners bound to him through this last attempt at uncompensated giving. The visual iconography of balance sheets and account books surrounding representations of death has been well documented. Philippe Ariès notes that, in the medieval period, depictions of death became gradually more consistent with the idea that '[e]ach man is to be judged according to the balance sheet of his life. Good and bad deeds are scrupulously separated and placed on the appropriate side of the scales. Moreover, these deeds have been inscribed in a book.'[67] Throughout western culture, dying is the ultimate settling of spiritual accounts, often expressed in terms of a far more worldly settling up of the financial account books. Mourning, too, involves calculations, as the bereaved person is left behind to come to terms with dues that will forever be outstanding.

Bereavement can assume a materialistic quality as the person left behind struggles to account for unresolved debts and grievances. In his *Mourning Diary: October 26, 1977 – September 15, 1979*, begun on his mother's death, Roland Barthes confesses to an uncomfortable feeling 'of a *lack of generosity*'.[68] Derrida touches on the indebted economy of bereavement in one of the texts gathered in *The Work of Mourning*, suggesting that '[t]here come moments when, as *mourning* demands [*deuil oblige*], one feels obligated to declare one's debts. We feel it our duty to say what we owe to the friend.'[69] Bereavement compels us to behave in ways we cannot easily predict or reckon with. Another entry in Barthes' diary reflects how 'she wants everything, total mourning, its absolute (but then it's not her, it's I who is investing her with the demand for such a thing)'.[70] According to Derrida, the sensation of finality which comes from settling our accounts with the deceased can be unbearable:

> Inadmissible, not because one would have problems recognising one's debts or one's duty as indebted, but simply because in declaring these debts in such a manner, particularly when time is limited, one might seem to be putting an end to them, calculating what they amount to, pretending then to be able to recount them, to measure and thus limit them, or more seriously still, to be able to settle them in the very act of exposing them.[71]

We *long* to be held in arrears to one another, especially after death.

Having read aloud the epitaph, Alcibiades feels obliged to say a few words in remembrance of Timon:

> These well express in thee thy latter spirits.
> Though thou abhorred'st in us our human griefs,
> Scorned'st our brains' flow and those our droplets which

> From niggard nature fall, yet rich conceit
> Taught thee to make vast Neptune weep for aye
> On thy low grave, on faults forgiven.
> (5.5.72–7)

Michael Neill notes how 'Alcibiades is driven, even in the absence of a body, to improvise a funeral rite of sorts to revive the memory of a man he wants to think of as "noble Timon"'.[72] Alcibiades translates the unfriendly epitaph into an uplifting message. He reinterprets Timon's disgust at emotional weeping ('human griefs', 'brains' flow' and 'droplets') into a 'rich conceit', whereby the waves crashing over Timon's grave become a form of environmental grief, with teary-eyed Neptune as chief mourner. As part of this improvised eulogy, Alcibiades comforts the people of Athens, reassuring them that Timon leaves behind him all 'faults forgiven'. By restoring (against his wishes) the protagonist's suspended burial rites, the play attests to the spirit of obligation inscribed in works of mourning.

Timon of Athens, a play long recognised for its interest in money, raises a number of ethical calculations which philosophy can help us to better understand. The reminder of debts and obligations delimits the scope for generosity. And yet, though the gift of hospitality again turns out to be less free than we imagine, it might still help to blot out what wrongs have passed.

Notes

1. William Shakespeare and Thomas Middleton, *Timon of Athens*, ed. Anthony B. Dawson and Gretchen E. Minton (London: Bloomsbury, 2008), 1.1.43. Further references are all to this edition and given in the body of the text.
2. Dawson and Minton, 'Introduction', *Timon of Athens*, pp. 1–145, p. 94.

3. Marcel Mauss, 'Gift, Gift', in *The Logic of the Gift: Toward an Ethic of Generosity*, ed. Alan D. Schrift (London and New York: Routledge, 1997), pp. 28–33, p. 30.
4. Thomas Hobbes quoted by Marjory E. Lange in *Telling Tears in the English Renaissance* (Leiden: Brill, 1996), p. 30.
5. Deborah Lupton, *The Emotional Self: A Sociocultural Exploration* (London: SAGE, 1998), pp. 74–87.
6. Bridget Escolme, *Emotional Excess on the Shakespearean Stage: Passion's Slaves* (London and New York: Bloomsbury, 2014), p. xiv.
7. For continued discussion of Flavius' role in the play, see: Maurice Hunt, 'Qualifying the Good Steward of Shakespeare's *Timon of Athens*', *English Studies*, 82:6 (2001), 507–20; Ellorasrhee Maitra, 'Toward an Ethical Polity: Service and the Tragic Community in *Timon of Athens*', *Renaissance Drama*, 41 (2013), 173–98; Drew Daniel, 'Syllogisms and Tears in *Timon of Athens*', *English Studies*, 94:7 (2013), 799–820. In 'Thinking Hospitably with *Timon of Athens*: Toward an Ethics of Stewardship', in *Shakespeare and Hospitality: Ethics, Politics, and Exchange*, ed. David Goldstein and Julia Lupton (London and New York: Routledge, 2016), pp. 242–64, Michael Noschka offers a reading of the play that 'seeks to shift critical attention away from gift exchange, biblical or otherwise, in order to better attend to hospitality in its vocation as stewardship' (p. 244).
8. Jacques Derrida, 'Hospitality, Justice and Responsibility', in *Questioning Ethics: Contemporary Debates in Philosophy*, ed. Richard Kearney and Mark Dooley (London and New York: Routledge, 1999), pp. 65–83, p. 70.
9. Maggie Kilgour, *From Communion to Cannibalism: An Anatomy of Metaphors of Incorporation* (Princeton: Princeton University Press, 1990), p. 89, and Judith Still, *Derrida and Hospitality: Theory and Practice* (Edinburgh: Edinburgh University Press, 2010), pp. 13–14.
10. *Timon of Athens*, 1.2.39–41*n*.
11. Sigmund Freud, *The Origins of Religion: Totem and Taboo, Moses and Monotheism and Other Works*, trans. James Strachey (London: Penguin, 1990), p. 195.

12. J. Hillis Miller, 'The Critic as Host', *Critical Inquiry*, 3:3 (1977), 439–47, p. 442.
13. Kilgour, *Communion to Cannibalism*, p. 6. In a psychoanalytic reading of *Coriolanus*, '"Anger's My Meat": Feeding, Dependency, and Aggression in *Coriolanus*', Janet Adelman suggests that 'the taking in of food is the primary acknowledgement of one's dependence on the world, and as such, it is the primary token of one's vulnerability', *Shakespearean Tragedy*, ed. John Drakakis (London and New York: Longman, 1992), pp. 353–73 (p. 356).
14. Jacques Derrida, 'Economimesis', trans. Richard Klein, *Diacritics*, 11:2 (1981), 3–25, p. 23.
15. Julia Lupton, *Thinking with Shakespeare: Essays on Politics and Life* (Chicago: University of Chicago Press, 2011), p. 146.
16. Jacques Derrida, *Given Time: I. Counterfeit Money*, trans. Peggy Kamuf (Chicago: University of Chicago Press, 1992), p. 7.
17. Derrida, *Given Time*, p. 41.
18. Jacques Derrida, *Of Hospitality: Anne Dufourmantelle Invites Jacques Derrida to Respond*, trans. Rachel Bowlby (Stanford: Stanford University Press, 2000), p. 83.
19. Lange, *Telling Tears in the English Renaissance*, p. 2.
20. Ad Vingerhoets, *Why Only Humans Weep: Unravelling the Mysteries of Tears* (Oxford: Oxford University Press, 2013).
21. Chris Meads, *Banquets Set Forth: Banqueting in English Renaissance Drama* (Manchester: Manchester University Press, 2001), p. 147.
22. René Girard, *Violence and the Sacred*, trans. Patrick Gregory (London and Baltimore: Johns Hopkins University Press, 1977), p. 4.
23. Girard, *Violence and the Sacred*, p. 5.
24. Girard, *Violence and the Sacred*, p. 5.
25. Claude Lévi-Strauss, *The Raw and the Cooked: Introduction to a Science of Mythology*, trans. J. and D. Weightman (London: Pimlico, 1994), p. 153.
26. In his edition of *Timon of Athens* (Cambridge: Cambridge University Press, 2001), Karl Klein makes the same comparison at 3.4.76–7n.

27. *Timon of Athens*, 3.7.84n.
28. Claude Lévi-Strauss, *The Origin of Table Manners: Introduction to a Science of Mythology*, vol. 3, trans. J. and D. Weightman (London: Cape, 1978), pp. 479–80.
29. Lévi-Strauss, *The Origin of Table Manners*, pp. 482–3.
30. Lévi-Strauss, *The Origin of Table Manners*, p. 483.
31. Lévi-Strauss, *The Origin of Table Manners*, p. 483.
32. Lévi-Strauss, *The Origin of Table Manners*, p. 484.
33. Dawson and Minton note in their 'Introduction' how 'in the BBC version Jonathan Pryce's Timon did not participate in the indulgences of the feast; watching with anxious affection while the guests gnawed on chicken and roast pig, he ate nothing (the camera twice moving to his empty plate)' (p. 48).
34. Michel Serres, *The Parasite*, trans. Lawrence R. Schehr (Minneapolis: University of Minnesota Press, 2007), p. 6.
35. Anders M. Gullestad, 'Literature and the Parasite', *Deleuze Studies*, 5:3 (2011), 301–23, p. 305.
36. William Shakespeare, *Richard II*, ed. Charles R. Forker (London: Bloomsbury, 2002), 2.2.69–70.
37. William Shakespeare, *Coriolanus*, ed. Peter Holland (London: Bloomsbury, 2013), 1.9.42–6.
38. http://www.politicalconcepts.org/issue1/2012-parasite/ [accessed September 2021].
39. Hillis Miller, 'The Critic as Host', p. 442.
40. Serres, *The Parasite*, p. 34.
41. Serres, *The Parasite*, p. 186.
42. Ben Jelloun, *French Hospitality: Racism and North African Immigrants* (New York: Columbia University Press, 1999), p. 2.
43. Jelloun, *French Hospitality*, p. 3.
44. Gullestad, 'Literature and the Parasite', p. 309.
45. In 'Literature and the Parasite', Gullestad wryly points out that 'this is seldom a problem for those working in the field – they recognise a parasite perfectly well when they see one. It is only when they are forced to attempt a definition that they run into problems' (p. 308).
46. Derrida, *Of Hospitality*, pp. 59–61.

47. For more on early modern sugary desserts, see Julia Reinhard Lupton's chapter 'Room for Dessert in *The Winter's Tale*', in her *Shakespeare Dwelling: Designs for the Theater of Life* (Chicago: Chicago University Press, 2018), pp. 195–220.
48. William Shakespeare, *Shakespeare's Sonnets*, ed. Katherine Duncan-Jones (London: Methuen Drama, 2010), Sonnet 73, ll. 1–3.
49. Laurie Shannon, *The Accommodated Animal: Cosmopolity in Shakespearean Locales* (Chicago: University of Chicago Press, 2013), p. 142.
50. Joan Fitzpatrick, *Food in Shakespeare: Early Modern Dietaries and the Plays* (Aldershot: Ashgate, 2007), p. 118.
51. Girard, *Violence and the Sacred*, p. 2.
52. Jacques Derrida, *Adieu to Emmanuel Levinas*, trans. Pascale-Anne Brault and Michael Naas (Stanford: Stanford University Press, 1999), p. 93.
53. Serres, *The Parasite*, p. 24.
54. Coppélia Kahn, '"Magic of Bounty": *Timon of Athens*, Jacobean Patronage, and Maternal Power', *Shakespeare Quarterly*, 38 (1987), 34–57, p. 35.
55. Anne Dufourmantelle, 'Hospitality – Under Compassion and Violence', in *The Conditions of Hospitality: Ethics, Politics, and Aesthetics on the Threshold of the Possible*, ed. Thomas Claviez (New York: Fordham University Press, 2013), pp. 13–23, p. 17. For more on female hospitality, see Tracy McNulty, *The Hostess: Hospitality, Femininity, and the Expropriation of Identity* (Minneapolis: University of Minnesota Press, 2007).
56. William Shakespeare, *King Lear*, ed. R. A. Foakes (London: Thomson Learning, 1997), 1.4.271.
57. Lévi-Strauss, *The Raw and the Cooked*, pp. 269–70.
58. Lévi-Strauss, *The Raw and the Cooked*, p. 269.
59. William Shakespeare, *Much Ado About Nothing*, ed. Claire McEachern (London: Bloomsbury, 2006), 4.1.30–1.
60. William Shakespeare, *Measure for Measure*, ed. J. W. Lever (London: Thomson Learning, 2006), 3.2.175–8.
61. *Measure for Measure*, 4.3.171–2.

62. Marjorie Garber, *Coming of Age in Shakespeare* (London and New York: Routledge, 1981), p. 215.
63. Judith Butler, *Precarious Life: The Powers of Mourning and Violence* (London and New York: Verso, 2004), p. 23.
64. A. D. Nuttall, *Shakespeare the Thinker* (New Haven and London: Yale University Press, 2007), p. 320.
65. Derrida, *Of Hospitality*, p. 111. Compare *Specters of Marx: The State of Debt, the Work of Mourning and the New International*, trans. Peggy Kamuf (New York: Routledge, 1994), where Derrida suggests that '[n]othing could be worse, for the work of mourning, than confusion or doubt: one *has to know* who is buried where' (p. 9).
66. Derrida, *Of Hospitality*, p. 93.
67. Philippe Ariès, *Western Attitudes toward Death from the Middle Ages to the Present*, trans. Patricia M. Ranum (London: Marion Boyars, 1974), p. 32.
68. Roland Barthes, *Mourning Diary: October 26, 1977 – September 15, 1979*, trans. Richard Howard (New York: Hill & Wang, 2010), p. 92.
69. Jacques Derrida, *The Work of Mourning*, ed. and trans. Pascale-Anne Brault and Michael Naas (Chicago: University of Chicago Press, 2001), p. 223.
70. Barthes, *Mourning Diary*, p. 32.
71. Derrida, *The Work of Mourning*, pp. 223–4.
72. Michael Neill, *Issues of Death: Mortality and Identity in English Renaissance Tragedy* (Oxford: Oxford University Press, 1997), p. 296.

CHAPTER 5

SECRETIVE HOSTS IN *PERICLES*

If critics remain undecided on whether to call them romances, tragicomedies, the late plays or something else, they agree that what makes this group of texts distinctive is their mixed mode. Verna A. Foster, in *The Name and Nature of Tragicomedy*, argues that Shakespeare's tragicomedies 'integrate tragic and comic effects in such complex ways that the plays' meanings depend on an understanding of how their comic and tragic elements work with or against one another'.[1] Lawrence Danson suggests that they are 'infused throughout, and not only by turns, with the energies of compounded genres'.[2] *Pericles*, *The Winter's Tale*, *Cymbeline* and *The Tempest* combine the tragic experience with wonder and miraculous scenes of reunion and forgiveness.

Even a cursory glance at the plot of *Pericles*, an adaptation of the Apollonius of Tyre story, thought to have been written by Shakespeare and George Wilkins, makes clear that we are dealing with a composite genre. In this play of journeys and contrasts, fourteenth-century poet John Gower acts as Chorus, guiding the action through an incredible breath of geographical settings. The play is every bit as expansive in its representation of hospitality, presenting us with the extreme ends of what this relationship is capable of achieving. *Pericles* has incest, murderous hosts, wicked foster parents and failed ecosystems. Yet it encompasses extraordinary gestures of humanitarian aid, notably that of a guest who disembarks in a famine-stricken country with a boat full of wheat, not to mention several scenes of welcome which are miraculously healing to body and mind. Echoing the mixed genre of tragicomedy, the chapter begins by examining how hospitality in *Pericles* is part of the tragic universe, involving guests and hosts in nightmarish scenarios. Then, in the second section, I turn to some of the play's later recuperative scenarios. Across both halves of the argument, I contend that there is a philosophical connection between hospitality and environmental ethics. As I will show, *Pericles* equates conduct towards strangers with what Randall Martin refers to as 'an early modern ecological consciousness'.[3]

Antiochus' Riddle

When Pericles arrives in Antioch at the beginning of the play, he enters a world full of secrets. He has come to the city – 'fairest in all Syria' – to make a politically advantageous marriage with King Antiochus' beautiful daughter.[4] First, however, he has to pass the riddle put to all potential suitors and which reads as follows:

> *I am no viper, yet I feed*
> *On mother's flesh which did me breed.*
> *I sought a husband, in which labour*
> *I found that kindness in a father.*
> *He's father, son, and husband mild;*
> *I mother, wife, and yet his child.*
> *How they may be, and yet in two,*
> *As you will live resolve it you.*
> (1.1.65–72)

Riddles are cleverly encoded language games, but their mystery dissipates as soon as the player has guessed the right answer. 'After its solution', Katelijne Schiltz notes, 'the riddle is no longer a riddle, as the veils have been removed and the tension has dissolved. What remains is a text.'[5] In *Pericles*, on the other hand, solving the riddle only reveals another secret: the 'foul incest' (1.1.127) between father and daughter. The culture of secrecy which pervades Antiochus' court operates on the same principle as nested Chinese boxes, whereby the most disturbing secret – in this case, the social taboo of incest – is concealed within another, less difficult puzzle. Secrets in *Pericles* (and perhaps more generally) have a pervasive presence and resist being solved or dispelled. The solution itself becomes another problem.

In his influential study of *The Poetics of Space*, Gaston Bachelard touches on this phenomenon as part of a wider discussion of drawers, chests and wardrobes. 'An anthology devoted to small boxes, such as chests and caskets', Bachelard writes, 'would constitute an important chapter in psychology. These complex pieces that a craftsman creates are very evident witnesses of the *need for secrecy*, of an intuitive sense of hiding places.'[6] On the function of architectural space in our psychological imaginary of secrecy, Bachelard goes on to say that 'rather than challenge the trespasser, rather than frighten him by signs of power, it is preferable to mislead him. This is where boxes that fit into one another come in. The least important secrets are put in the first box, the idea being that they will suffice to satisfy his curiosity, which can also be fed on false secrets.'[7] At Antioch, secrets are hidden within other secrets, creating a nested effect similar to what Bachelard describes above. Consequently, this places the newcomer in an impossible position because he is unable to reveal the first secret (the answer to the riddle) without simultaneously broadcasting the incest between the king and his daughter.

Social relations in the early part of the play are primarily mediated through hospitality and interconnected ideas of eating and welcoming guests. Bachelard's notion of the trespasser being 'fed on false secrets' establishes a connection between appetite and secrecy. The riddle foregrounds unwholesome eating patterns: '*I am no viper, yet I feed / On mother's flesh which did me breed*' (1.1.65–6). 'Vipers', Suzanne Gossett glosses in her Arden edition, 'were traditionally believed to eat their way out of their mother's body.'[8] In Shakespeare, food is an index of hospitality and of the cultural expectation that we should nurture and shelter the stranger at the door. However, the Antioch scenes disrupt anticipation of a warm welcome. Newly arrived at Antiochus' court, Pericles is tasked with solving the riddle and we are quickly made aware that, if he fails, then he will be executed. Subverting the usual norms of hospitality, secrets contribute to the unwelcoming atmosphere of the Antioch court. Pericles' hostile reception is compounded by the wording of the riddle where, in place of any nourishing commensality between guest and host, the parasite cannibalistically destroys its host organism from within. Elizabeth Archibald, in her book *Incest and the Medieval Imagination*, notes the affinity between incest and abnormal consumption, arguing that the sexual taboo was 'seen as the most extreme manifestation of lust and bodily appetite'.[9] *Pericles* develops the association between desire and gastronomic appetite through its repetition of food imagery equating the daughter with 'the fruit of yon celestial tree' (1.1.22) and again with 'golden fruit, but dangerous to be touched' (1.1.29). Blending biblical and classical allusions to the forbidden knowledge of the tree in the Garden of Eden, and the golden apples guarded by a dragon which comprised one of the Labours of Hercules, such caveats about proscribed foodstuffs and the dangers of eating only confirm that bonds between guest and host have become poisoned.

As soon as he discovers the incest between his prospective wife and father-in-law, Pericles revisits the symbol of the venomous serpent to convey his horror:

And she an eater of her mother's flesh,
By the defiling of her parents' bed;
And both like serpents are who, though they feed
On sweetest flowers, yet they poison breed.
   (1.1.131–4)

The allusion to venom here is literalised in horrible fashion towards the end of this scene when Antiochus, realising that his guest has worked out the riddle, attempts to have him murdered. Entrusting his chamber attendant Thaliard with the commission, Antiochus provides him with 'poison' (1.1.155). Indicative of the extent to which social relations in Antioch are perverted, the norms of hospitality, including the duty to accommodate the stranger, are replaced with secretive behaviour, disordered eating habits, and actions intended to cause harm.

As Bachelard notes, our cultural imaginary of secrecy is architectural and spatial. Conceptualising the relational dynamics of secrecy in this way helps us understand how architecture can be used to create zones of exclusion. Discussing the controversial installation of anti-homeless spikes in central London within the last ten years, James Petty defines hostile architecture as a 'method of environmental coercion'.[10] As a forerunner to these spiky installations which are found everywhere in modern urban planning, early modern London had its own form of coercive or disciplinary architecture. For playgoers crossing London Bridge to reach the Southbank theatres, the heads of convicted traitors impaled on spikes and set on the gatehouse would, as Tiffany Stern notes, have served as a 'grim reminder' of the consequences of transgressive conduct.[11] From the condemned subject's forced confession to the torture and eventual display of their parboiled, perhaps tarred head, public visibility and revelation was incorporated into the spectacle of early modern punishment, symbolically counteracting the individual's earlier furtiveness and their secret crimes against the state. 'The traitor', Katharine Eisaman Maus argues, 'comes to the scaffold quite literally to spill his guts, to have the heart plucked out of his mystery.'[12] Through spectacular torture, the body of the condemned was made to disclose its innermost secrets.

In *Pericles*, the row of heads impaled on spikes at Antiochus' court similarly functions as a form of hostile architecture intended to keep the secret safe. Gower first draws our attention to the 'yon grim looks' (1.0.40) of the former contestants. Presumably, they have failed to solve the riddle or else been too afraid to confront the king with his incest, hence they have been butchered and their heads impaled on spikes as a warning to future contenders. As with modern-day hostile architecture, this gruesome installation is aimed at dissuading a single demographic: the princes who have travelled to Antioch to seek a wife. Antiochus gestures towards the court's disciplinary architecture when encouraging Pericles to turn back:

> Yon sometimes famous princes [*indicating the heads*], like thyself,
> Drawn by report, adventurous by desire,
> Tell thee with speechless tongues and semblance pale
> That without covering save yon field of stars
> Here they stand, martyrs slain in Cupid's wars,
> And with dead cheeks advise thee to desist
> From going on death's net, whom none resist.
> (1.1.35–41)

In a parody of the Petrarchan lover's blazon, Antiochus catalogues the 'speechless tongues', 'semblance pale' and 'dead cheeks' of the murdered guests. As yet unaware of the incest, Pericles is doubtless still trying to impress his future father-in-law. Responding politely to the gory sight, he assures Antiochus that the 'fearful objects' (1.1.44) are an instructive memento mori which 'hath taught / My frail mortality to know itself' (1.1.42–3). The opening scene of *Pericles* thus continues to disrupt any prospect of a warm welcome, replacing the conventional hospitable hearth with an installation meant to discourage strangers. Hospitality always involves some willingness on the part of the host to shelter their guest, and this remains the case even after death. But in another violation of his ethical responsibilities as host, Antiochus displays the dismembered body parts of the earlier visitors, now left unsheltered and exposed to the elements and to the night sky.

A great deal of excellent scholarship has been done on secrets and the clever uses of architectural design *within* the private household, but Shakespeare scholars have not sufficiently drawn on the rich body of work related to the role of visible and civic architectures in the maintenance of secrecy and the policing of social conduct.[13] In *Pericles*, the row of heads executed and mounted on spikes forms a symbolic (and perhaps literal) boundary to the court of Antiochus. More subtle is the way that the culture of secrecy erects its own invisible borders, walls and thresholds. Given their highly divisive nature, it is surely unsurprising that modern theorists of the secret frequently rely on an architectural vocabulary. In his persuasive analysis of secret societies, for instance, the German sociologist Georg Simmel uses architectural imagery to define the operation of the secret. For the privileged few in the know, he suggests, the secret 'encircles them like a boundary'.[14] Simmel goes on to point out that the secret 'sets barriers between men', because 'secrecy and pretense of secrecy (*Geheimnistnerei*) are means of building higher the wall of separation'.[15] French philosopher Anne Dufourmantelle makes a related comparison to defensive architecture in her 2021 book *In Defense of Secrets*, proposing that the secret 'structures society according to the principle of inclusion and exclusion, erecting barriers between those who have access to a certain knowledge and those who are not aware of what remains inaccessible'.[16] Secrets convey the architecture of political power, for they are divisive, can separate people into factions and conceal knowledge, while generating an atmosphere of suspicion and mistrust. Moreover, what each of these thinkers captures is the way in which secrets are themselves architectural.

Secrets and a lack of hospitality interconnect in Shakespeare and Wilkins's *Pericles* in ways that may be surprising. Comparable to how the reception of strangers involves displacement and temporary accommodation, secrets, too, complicate conventional notions of home and belonging. 'A secret', Jacques Derrida notes, 'doesn't belong, it can never be said to be at home or in its place [*chez soi*].'[17] One explanation for the secret's nomadism is that it is most noticeable in circulation, passed among members of a chosen clique, while excluding those not privy to its confidences. Seen in a constructive light, this means that possession of the secret can foster intimacy by encouraging a sense of community among the group invited to share in its mystery. In the case of occult societies, Simmel has shown how the initiated 'constitute a community for the purpose of mutual guarantee of secrecy'.[18] Dufourmantelle agrees that in the right circumstances the secret can be 'an assembling force'.[19] In *Pericles*, on the other hand, the secret has no benefit for the aristocratic community gathered at Antioch. Quite the reverse as, far from being a unifying agent, Pericles' newly acquired knowledge of Antiochus' sexual relationship with his daughter nearly gets him killed. We might conclude that being granted privileged access to the monarch's secrets is every visitor's nightmare. Although the guest and host relationship inevitably requires some degree of physical proximity, *Pericles* stages the acute discomfort produced by an unwanted emotional intimacy. Drawing on the metaphor of the codex, Pericles says: 'Who has a book of all that monarchs do / He's more secure to keep it shut than shown' (1.1.95–6). Thaliard, the reluctant assassin, reiterates this sentiment when he remarks, 'I perceive he was a wise fellow and had good discretion that, being bid to ask what he would of the king, desired he might know none of his secrets' (1.3.3–6).

The strange power imbued in the hospitality relationship, which Émile Benveniste traces back to its etymological associations with mastery and the desire for control, is amplified in *Pericles* through the secret's intensity. Secrecy can accumulate a dominating force, even an eroticism. It is surely no coincidence, then, that theorists writing about secrecy often use an overtly sexualised language in which the exposure of the secret is its own kind of ejaculation. 'Secrecy', Simmel suggests, 'involves a tension which, at the moment of revelation, finds its release.'[20] For Dufourmantelle, the secret 'often resides in the folds of the sexual, there where shame, jouissance, excitement, memory, and fantasy exist side by side', prompting the question: if '[e]very secret carries in itself the potential charge of violence. How to be delivered from it without exploding with it?'[21] Australian anthropologist Michael Taussig makes a related point when he concludes that there is 'something so absurdly pleasurable at breaking through the skin of the secret'.[22] Modern theorists of secrecy turn to bodily imagery of arousal, penetration and orgasm in their attempts to express something of the secret's irresistibly tempting hold over us. What Taussig terms 'the fetish power of the secret' structures social and familial relations in *Pericles*, both through the taboo erotic desire which circulates between the king and his daughter and via the unethical treatment of any strangers who come to Antioch to try their luck at the riddle contest.[23] Should a visitor to the court answer the riddle correctly, then not only is their life in danger but they are immediately inducted into the most intimate knowledge of their host's sex life. Ordinarily, to put trust in a stranger by taking them into one's confidence is an act which inspires warmth and trust. In *Pericles*, however, the secret has become degraded in the same manner that the normal family relationship is perverted into a sexual one.

Once Pericles gives a tactfully evasive response to the riddle, Antiochus promises to allow him to safely extend his stay in Antioch:

> Forty days longer we do respite you;
> If by which time our secret be undone
> This mercy shows we'll joy in such a son.
> And until then your entertain shall be
> As doth befit our honour and your worth.
> (1.1.117–21)

The Arden edition points out that, in a 'seagoing play' like *Pericles*, the reprieve of forty days likely implies biblical connotations and 'may recall the dangerous period when Noah's Ark sailed in the rain'.[24] With its scriptural subtext of refuge and shelter from the storm, the pledge of hospitality only serves to worsen Antiochus' treachery, for he now engages Thaliard to murder his guest, determining that, given Pericles knows about the incest, 'instantly this prince must die' (1.1.149), otherwise he will 'live to trumpet forth mine infamy' (1.1.146). Antiochus' efforts to wrest back control of the situation creates a treacherous *double timeframe* of hospitality: superficially, it seems that the host will grant his guest a generous reception for another forty days but, at the same time, Antiochus is planning for Pericles' immediate assassination.

This dual timeframe of hospitality echoes and reinforces the extensive temporal disruption caused by the other secrets. To begin with, the incest has put the time spectacularly out of joint. Addressing his bride, Pericles says:

> You are a fair viol, and your sense the strings,
> Who, fingered to make man his lawful music,

Would draw heaven down and all the gods to hearken;
But, being played upon before your time,
Hell only danceth at so harsh a chime.
   (1.1.82–6)

Combining an obscene metaphor of the 'fair viol' being 'fingered' to make music, with the contemporary association between celestial harmony and social order, he compares the unnamed daughter to an instrument 'played upon before your time'. Soon afterwards, Pericles reproaches his prospective father-in-law for simultaneously fulfilling the separate roles of 'a father and a son / By your untimely claspings with your child' (1.1.128–9). The incest is considered *untimely* because, by prematurely enjoying the marital 'pleasures' (1.1.130) which should be reserved for an unknown future son-in-law, Antiochus' wrongdoing has interrupted the normal passage of time and thrown into disarray his ancestral line.

Supplementing these disordered temporalities as they relate to and reflect the disruption caused to hospitality and genealogy, the secret possesses its own complex relationship with time. Corinne Squire has shown how secrets 'always exist after themselves, already betrayed, as what we could call postsecrets or partial secrets', which leads her to conclude that 'there is no simple present for secrets. The secret that is known, or known about now, belongs to the past.'[25] We notice this curious temporal paradox at work in *Pericles*. Required by the rules of the contest to give an answer to the riddle, Pericles speaks vaguely about wickedness and the womb, indirectly hinting that he knows about the incest. In an obscure excerpt, Pericles reassures Antiochus that his secret is safe:

For vice repeated is like the wandering wind
Blows dust in others' eyes to spread itself;
And yet the end of all is bought thus dear:

> The breath is gone and the sore eyes see clear.
> To stop the air would hurt them. The blind mole casts
> Copped hills towards heaven, to tell the earth is thronged
> By man's oppression, and the poor worm doth die for't.
> (1.1.98–103)

Pericles uses environmental imagery of the wind and creaturely life forms with the purpose of subtly conveying to his host the message that he is conscious of the enormous personal risks involved in being the bearer of bad news. The irony, as Steven Mullaney puts it, is that Pericles' 'offer to keep the king's secret safe only reveals, of course, that it is no longer either a secret or his own'.[26] Mullaney's interpretation is surely right, and these veiled reassurances have the unintentional effect of nullifying the secret by making it a thing of the past. In the end, the secret is that there is no secret.

Shakespeare and Wilkins's interlacing of secrecy and hospitality is brought to a satisfying resolution at the end of the play, when the hero is reunited with his daughter, Marina, who presents him with a second riddle. Under the erroneous impression that she was murdered by her foster parents, Pericles has become consumed by grief. While in a catatonic state, not speaking and hardly eating, the sea brings his ship to Mytilene, where Lysimachus the governor comes aboard curious to know why a vessel decorated with black mourning colours has anchored in the town during the festive period. Learning of the stranger's bereavement and ensuing catatonia, Lysimachus is eager to help and sends for Marina, hoping that her 'sacred physic' will revive their 'kingly patient' (5.1.64–7). Marina's riddle – given in response to Pericles' question of where she was born – provides a positive reclamation of the secret:

> *Pericles* Here of these shores?
> *Marina*   No, nor of any shores.

> Yet I was mortally brought forth and am
> no other than I appear.
>   (5.1.94–6)

The miraculously curative effect which Marina has on her father and, by extension, the happy ending of *Pericles* is bound up with the resolution of secrets. The instant Marina starts to disclose snippets of her remarkable personal history, she awakens in Pericles an overwhelming curiosity to know more about her life. Thus, while he was introduced to Lysimachus at the beginning of this scene as '[a] man who for this three months hath not spoken / To anyone' (5.1.20–1), Pericles' urgent questions to this stranger now come thick and fast:

> But are you flesh and blood?
> Have you a working pulse and are no fairy?
> Motion as well? Speak on. Where were you born?
> And wherefore called Marina?
>   (5.1.143–6)

Notwithstanding the risks and the disturbing revelations which can unfold, Dufourmantelle is undoubtedly right to argue that, in spite of everything, 'the secret is still the very thing we often wish to possess in another being'.[27] Indeed, this logic applies to *Pericles*, where the mystery surrounding Marina's oceanic birthplace and her unknown parentage arouse in Pericles an intense urge to know this stranger's secret and, in the end, it is this inquisitiveness which jolts him out of his catatonic state. The secret brings Pericles back to life.

Although the incest and riddle are specific to the Apollonius of Tyre narrative, the secret itself is at the heart of all human encounters. Charles Barbour argues that secrecy 'is a condition of our relations with others, or a condition of interaction, and we can only reveal ourselves to one another, and indeed to anything other (including all of those things we call both subjects and objects), in so far as, at the exact same moment, we conceal as well.'[28] Problematising Simmel's basic premise, which differentiates between secret and ordinary societies, Barbour suggests that 'all society is structured or formed by the secret, and thus by the possibility of concealment and mendacity, prevarication and deceit'.[29] At the same time, he continues, 'secrecy or concealment are not only things that distinguish or separate us from others; they are also an integral part of what relates us to others, or keeps us within one another's orbit'.[30] *Pericles* reaches the same conclusion, showing us that, even though some secrets are lethal or politically explosive, there are others which strengthen our connections with others, take us outside ourselves, remake our world and reveal something new. Hospitality or any other type of social exchange would be unthinkable without an opacity which permits us always to keep something back for ourselves. The secret thus exposes an underlying truth about society, that there is something veiled and unseen within all human relationships. American author Willa Cather compares the heart of another to a dark forest. What her sylvan analogy so eloquently communicates is the reality that even our most intimate interactions with other people are based on nothing more than trust in the good intentions of strangers and close acquaintances alike. Of course, this fact may be uncomfortable and ripe for exploitation by unscrupulous individuals but, as Shakespeare and Wilkins know, the secret can lead to encounters which are moving, surprising and life-affirming.

Refugee Bodies

To cite a well-known statistic, water covers 71 per cent of the Earth's surface and, as blue humanities scholars have noted, the immensity of this hydrosphere challenges us to re-evaluate our assumptions about the liveability of our world. Dan Brayton asks: 'Are we truly at home on this blue globe? Do we even know what the nature of *here* really is? The very concept of place, rooted in culture, agriculture, the hearth, and the social order, belongs to the land.'[31] 'Ocean defines our inhospitable home,' writes Steve Mentz, 'but even that oxymoron doesn't quite capture the tension and urgency, dependence and fear, in the human–sea relationship.'[32] For Eric Chaline, we are 'terrestrial refugees on an aquatic world'.[33] Our bodies immersed in salt water, we can only be temporary guests, unable to dwell, build shelter or even breathe for long. The troubling realisation that we are out of our element on so much of this blue planet and, through our dependence on *terra firma*, experience something of the refugee condition is explored in *Pericles*. By the end of the first scene, Pericles has fled Antioch and returned home to Tyre, yet he still does not feel safe. Worried that Antiochus will seek to silence him somehow, he is advised by a counsellor to 'go travel for a while' (1.2.104). By luring danger away from Tyre, the sea voyage offers an irresistible dream of safety. In a cosy image, he pictures how 'in our orbs we'll live so round and safe' (1.2.120). In reality, Pericles merely exchanges one hostile environment for another, escaping the treacherous intrigues of the court for the turbulent global ocean. Already forcibly displaced by the threat of persecution, environmental circumstances compound the experience of geographical displacement when Pericles loses nearly everything in a shipwreck. In this section, I examine what it means for hospitality in *Pericles* to be a refugee body adrift in a vast expanse of saltwater.

Geographers Kimberley Peters and Philip Steinberg categorise the ocean as a place of drifting and churning.[34] For modern-day asylum seekers crowded together into unseaworthy vessels, choppy waves and swells can induce stomach-churning motion sickness.[35] And yet, it is not only the risk and physical discomfort of the sea voyage, coupled with the at times unwelcoming attitude of the people on shore, which produces for refugees in boats an inhospitable environment. On account of their immersion in salt water, refugees can find their legal status altered, routinely leaving them with a reduced set of citizenship rights or complicating future asylum claims. In *Blue Legalities: The Life and Laws of the Sea*, Elizabeth Johnson and Irus Braverman note that '[i]mmigration and asylum policies and legal regimes also formalize and solidify traumatic ocean routes. Following boats that carry migrants across the Mediterranean and elsewhere, one finds dehumanizing legislation being forged in Europe, in the United States, and in Australia.'[36] One particularly striking example of the ways in which water impacts immigration status is the 'wet foot, dry foot' policy introduced by the Clinton administration in 1994, which allowed Cubans who reached American soil (dry feet people) to remain in the country, but would either deport home or to a third country any Cubans who were apprehended by the authorities while in the water (wet feet people). Discussing this controversial legislation, Suvendrini Perera draws attention to the plight of the 'wet-foot subjects of the oceanic borderlands', arguing that we should attend to 'stories of the movements and blockages of gendered and raced bodies, the making and unmaking of wet feet, "wetback" peoples, caught in the variable, treacherous border spaces between categories and systems'.[37] To give a recent example of the right to residency becoming diluted through ocean waters: at the time of writing, the British home secretary Priti Patel is proposing a reform of the asylum system. Under the planned measures, the mode of transport used to enter the country will be a determining factor in future asylum decisions, with citizenship requests expected to be denied to those who arrive in Britain illegally in small boats or shipping containers.[38] Blue legalities scholarship confirms that migrant bodies in international waters are exposed to other hostile environments beyond that of the wind and the waves.

In *Pericles*, the protagonist's identity is transformed through immersion in the ocean. Following a storm and shipwreck, in Act 2, Pericles washes ashore on the Pentapolis coastline. Standing on the beach, still wet from the sea, he describes himself as '[a] man thronged up with cold' (2.1.71). Hypothermic and driven by an instinctive or animal need for warmth and shelter, Pericles becomes something other than human. The unusual word choice 'thronged', recalls his earlier point that the soil is 'thronged' by the 'blind mole' and 'poor worm' (1.1.101–3) and further emphasises the creaturely resemblance. 'Wet representations', Mentz points out, 'emphasize the shock of immersion and its threat to human understanding and survival.'[39] Or, as Pericles explains when imploring the fishermen for help: 'What I have been I have forgot to know / But what I am want teaches me to think on' (2.1.69–70). Being submerged in cold water has temporarily blotted out Pericles' memories and sense of aristocratic heritage. This is intensified by the loss of his armour, inherited from his father and, as Ann Rosalind Jones and Peter Stallybrass note, an important 'material mnemonic'.[40]

But if the sea is hostile to human life, *Pericles* depicts humankind's inhospitality to the global ocean as well. Capitalist systems of waste and economic expenditure have long since led to the ocean being used as a place to throw unwanted rubbish. In the play, numerous people and objects accidentally end up in the sea, including the drowned bodies of the crew and passengers, not to mention most of Pericles' possessions. On the other hand, when the sailors deliberately toss overboard the chest containing Thaisa (presumed dead), the play evokes a longstanding tradition of humankind using the ocean as a refuse site for discarded waste. Kimberley C. Patton has shown how this trend belongs to a far older belief system based on ideas of water and religious purification:

> The mortal vision of the sea as an immortal means of catharsis predates the era of environmental crisis, manifesting itself in a deeper and older level of religious thinking. For the same reasons that human societies now pollute it, ocean water – and the ocean itself – were believed in many ancient religious traditions to have cathartic powers.[41]

That so much rubbish ends up in the water in this play is clear from the imagery representing the sea as a greedy feeder. Once Pericles lands on the beach, the ocean is likened to a 'drunken knave' (2.1.56), vomiting him up. Later, when the chest washes ashore at Ephesus, Cerimon says:

> If the sea's stomach be o'ercharged with gold,
> 'Tis a good constraint of fortune
> It belches upon us.
> (3.2.56–8)

The sea's 'stomach' is said to be 'o'ercharged' or bloated because it has been overfed with 'gold'. These metaphors imply that, when the ocean's generosity is abused and it is filled with too much junk, it becomes emissive, vomiting back up what it does not want. The personification of the sea as a disgusting eater is redolent of the bad dietary habits in Antioch, inviting us to compare oceanic and land-based examples of inhospitality.

In *Women and English Piracy, 1540–1720: Partners and Victims of Crime*, John Appleby imagines what life at sea was like for women:

> This environment held out little opportunity or appeal for women. They were out of place at sea, straying into a shifting frontier which was also a heavily gendered zone of labour, travel and trade, war and depredation. Neither an extension nor a mirror of the land, the seafaring world developed its own culture which denied or precluded a female presence, except under controlled conditions.[42]

For most women, boats were exclusionary zones that did not seek to welcome them, a fact which coincides with the gendered politics of maritime culture in *Pericles*. After his pregnant wife Thaisa gives birth at sea in Act 3, Pericles reflects that:

> A terrible childbed hast thou had, my dear,
> No light, no fire. Th'unfriendly elements
> Forgot thee utterly
> (3.1.56–8)

By anthropomorphising the *weather* as 'unfriendly', Pericles displaces onto the storm the inhospitality of the ship towards its female passengers. The sailors' unwillingness to accommodate women guests culminates when Thaisa is thought to have died in childbirth and they insist on throwing her overboard:

> Master   Sir, your queen must overboard. The sea works high, the wind is loud and will not lie till the ship be cleared of the dead.
> Pericles   That's your superstition.
> (3.1.47–50)

The superstitious mariners consider the corpse a pollutant of which the boat must be purified before the storm will subside. Thaisa's postpartum condition exacerbates their disquiet because, as Paige Martin Reynolds argues, childbirth in the sixteenth and seventeenth centuries struggled to rid itself of a 'rhetoric of sin and purification', with 'many religious writers unable to separate childbirth from the notion of contamination'.[43]

In contrast, ocean life welcomes men, and boats are an ideal locale for male camaraderie and homosociality. Marina learns how her father was eagerly received into the labouring community of the ship:

> My father, as nurse says, did never fear,
> But cried 'Good seamen!' to the sailors,
> Galling his kingly hands with haling ropes,
> And clasping to the mast endured a sea
> That almost burst the deck.
>   (4.1.51–5)

Phillip Zapkin notes that 'Pericles is not afraid to work like a common sailor when storms at sea call for his action, which makes him a better ruler as he acknowledges the toil of his subjects by toiling himself'.[44] Seafaring cuts across class lines. Marina remembers, too, that a mariner was swept into the water during the storm:

> Never was wind nor waves more violent,
> And from the ladder tackle washes off
> A canvas-climber.
>   (4.1.58–60)

Metonymy identifies the unnamed sailor or 'canvas-climber' solely through the raw materials of the shipping trade. We might view this as an instance of cyborgisation, whereby the sailor's body is fused together with the technology of the ship. 'The cyborg identity of mariners', Mentz argues, 'may depart from some elements of Haraway's late-twentieth-century political theory, but it matches her calls for "couplings between organism and machine" and the formation of a "technological polis." Sailors love boats and rigging, and the culture of maritime labour embraces a powerful romance between humans and technology.'[45] In *Pericles*, the sailor's cyborgisation likewise extends beyond the parameters of the boat. Even after he is washed overboard by the waves, the 'canvas-climber' holds onto his affiliation with the maritime community.

Comparing these examples enables us to see how the text discriminates against those bodies who seemingly *don't* belong at sea. Whereas the cyborg 'canvas-climber' retains his oneness with the boat even while in the water, Thaisa is already exoticised before she is dropped overboard. She is packaged into a chest with 'full bags of spices' and a 'passport' (3.2.64–5). Spices were exotic commodities throughout early modern Europe, associated in the cultural imagination with India and the East.[46] Like the passport, they both speak to the global reach of the play, yet prompt unease about who moves freely through the water. 'Questions of the mobility and blockage of bodies, of who moves, and how, or who cannot, or does not are', for Perera, 'questions of power, naturalised, made invisible.'[47] Furthermore, she reminds us that – alongside the heroic, male bodies of western seafaring literature – there 'are other shadowy, dark bodies: fellow seafarers willing and unwilling, fettered and free'.[48] *Pericles* attests to the uncomfortable truth that we do not all encounter the ocean in the same way and that to be a non-white, non-male body is to experience a far more inhospitable sea altogether.

'To foster is not ever to preserve'

In an influential essay published in 2017, Glenn Albrecht argues that 'ecosystem health and ethical goodness can be seen as mutually supportive and such living together can be the foundation of ideas of good health and the ethically good'.[49] A year later, in 2018, the publication of a volume of essays titled *Eco-Deconstruction: Derrida and Environmental Philosophy* extended Albrecht's thinking in new directions. Several of the contributors apply a vocabulary of hospitality to an ethics of environmental care. Philippe Lynes poses the question: 'doesn't sharing the earth more justly with its other living beings precisely require some proper housekeeping, maintaining the law of the *oikos*, the (h)earth?'[50] Kelly Oliver notes that 'struggles over home and hospitality are at the heart of our relationship to others, particularly when considering the earth as home and our relationship to nonhuman beings for whom this planet is also their one and only "home," whatever that may mean within the limitations of their worlds'.[51] Building on the argument made in the preceding section concerning humankind's inhospitality towards the global ocean, this section examines the famine in Act 1 of *Pericles*. Crop failure is only one of the many forms of ecological instability that can arise from not sharing the Earth and its reserves properly with our neighbours. In the pages which follow, I read the natural disaster in Tarsus as a failure of environmental ethics which, in turn, indicates a broader lack of hospitality.

Ruled over by the governor Cleon and his wife, Dionyza, at the start of the play, the city of Tarsus is in the grip of a disastrous famine. On account of the citizens' overconsumption of the surrounding natural resources, something has gone wrong in the food supply chain. Cleon muses on the population's stark change in appetites:

> These mouths who but of late earth, sea and air
> Were all too little to content and please,
> Although they gave their creatures in abundance,
> As houses are defiled for want of use,
> They are now starved for want of exercise.
> Those palates who, not yet two summers younger,
> Must have inventions to delight the taste
> Would now be glad of bread and beg for it.
> Those mothers, who to nuzzle up their babes
> Thought naught too curious, are ready now
> To eat those little darlings whom they loved.
> (1.4.34–44)

Famine in the early modern period, as Matt Williamson has shown, was regarded as divine retribution for wrongs committed.[52] Despite the liberality with which 'earth, sea and air' all gave 'their creatures in abundance' to satisfy the Tarsan palate, it was nevertheless not enough to 'content and please' the citizens' sophisticated tastes. Luxurious foodstuffs were formerly a status symbol. Cleon also reminisces on how '[t]heir tables were stored full to glad the sight / And not so much to feed on as delight' (1.4.28–9). Seen from an ethical standpoint, it is the citizens' conspicuous consumption which is to blame for their precariously depleted food reserves. Hospitality is, I suggest, a useful theoretical lens through which to interpret the famine in *Pericles*, helping us to better appreciate how the residents of Tarsus have been behaving like bad guests upon the Earth by taking more than their fair share.

Notified by a messenger that a fleet of unknown ships has landed on the coast, the unhappy Cleon presumes that his city is under attack from some neighbouring country who has decided to take advantage of their weakened state. Resigned to their fate, he says: 'Welcome is peace, if he on peace consist / If wars, we are unable to resist' (1.4.81–2). However, as soon as Pericles and his attendants enter the stage (at this point in the play, fresh from leaving Tyre to go travelling and not yet shipwrecked), he quickly moves to reassure his host that this is not the case:

> We have heard your miseries as far as Tyre
> And seen the desolation of your streets;
> Nor come we to add sorrow to your hearts,
> But to relieve them of their heavy load;
> And these our ships, you happily may think
> Are like the Trojan horse was stuffed within
> With bloody veins expecting overthrow,
> Are stored with corn to make your needy bread
> And give them life whom hunger starved half dead.
>   (1.4.86–94)

Reinterpreting the Trojan Horse as a symbol of hope, the newcomers from Tyre have brought in the wooden hold of their ships 'corn to make your needy bread'. Pericles appears a humanitarian relief-worker, visiting a disaster zone to charitably feed its citizens 'whom hunger starved half dead'. Even so, the gift of corn is not as freely given as we may suppose. Pericles' request to Cleon a few lines later for an immediate return on his economic investment in the form of 'harbourage for ourselves, our ships and men' (1.4.98) problematises the precise nature of the relationship between humanitarian aid and exploitation. Gifts have long been used to expedite political negotiations. Discussing how food functions across late medieval networks of gift exchange, C. M. Woolgar argues that 'the gift might be tainted and imply corruption. The word *bribe* in Anglo-Norman French had the primary meaning of a crust or piece of bread.'[53] Distributing bread is a gesture of generosity as old as time. On the other hand, as the etymology of 'bribe' implies, gifts of wheat and corn have another, parallel genealogy as a cynical means of diplomatic manoeuvring. Thus, the bribery implicit in the gift of bread recurs later, in the aftermath of the shipwreck in Act 3, when Pericles asks Cleon and Dionyza to become adoptive parents to Marina. Cleon assures Pericles:

> Fear not, my lord, but think
> Your grace that fed my country with your corn –
> For which the people's prayers still fall upon you –
> Must in your child be thought on.
>   (3.3.18–21)

Cleon's response makes clear that he and Dionyza, as well as the citizens of Tarsus, who have all been saved from famine, remain in the visitor's debt.

In 'A Defence of Environmental Stewardship', Jennifer Welchman reminds us that the concept of stewardship has its origins in the management of the private household. 'The English word', she writes, 'is derived from "*stigweard*"; the old English term for a servant who looks after a hall, manor or landed estate.'⁵⁴ *An Anglo-Saxon Dictionary Online* also defines a *stig-weard* as 'a steward', or, more specifically, 'one who has the superintendence of household affairs; especially matters connected with the table'.⁵⁵ These etymological resemblances between environmental stewardship and the home are underscored in *Pericles* when Cleon and Dionyza become foster parents to Marina. Foster parents and political deputies are familiar figures in Shakespeare's romances.⁵⁶ But if surrogacy is a recognised theme in the present scholarship, what has been neglected is *environmental* stewardship. We have a moral obligation to conserve the Earth for future generations of inhabitants, meaning that this is one of the most important forms of caretaking work that we will ever carry out. Tarsus is associated with famine, environmental degradation and the wider ecosystem distress caused by resource depletion. The citizens' negligent caretaking of the globe and disregard of their ethical responsibilities, particularly as they relate to questions of dwelling, inform the subsequent scenes of Marina's adoption. After taking care of her in their home for fourteen years, Dionyza secretly plans her foster daughter's murder. This act of inhospitality echoes and reinforces the lack of intergenerational care characteristic of Tarsan anti-environmentalism. In the same way that the murder of Marina would obliterate Pericles' ancestral line, the irresponsible environmental stewardship in Tarsus hinges on a sense of intergenerational unfairness by compromising the liveability of the Earth for future generations.

Chivalry and Nostalgia

Now sleep y-slacked hath the rouse,
No din but snores about the house,
Made louder by the o'erfed breast
Of this most pompous marriage feast.

> The cat with eyne of burning coal
> Now couches from the mouse's hole,
> And crickets sing at the oven's mouth
> Are the blither for their drouth.
> (3.0.1–8)

In his quaint, medieval style, Gower describes Pentapolis after the wedding celebrations of Pericles and Thaisa. All is peaceful in this vignette of domestic bliss, with the only sound being 'snores about the house' from the 'o'erfed' wedding party. By including the cat, mouse and crickets, Gower conjectures that the creaturely life of the household is equally well fed and contented. I want to suggest that, by couching the wedding feast and its aftermath in archaic language, Shakespeare and Wilkins associate the Pentapolis celebrations with an older form of hospitality intimately connected to the medieval past.[57] As *Pericles* opens, Gower is also concerned with festivities, telling the audience that he has come to 'sing a song' that 'hath been sung at festivals / On ember eves and holy ales' (1.0.1–6). Jonathan Baldo notes how this line 'operates as a kind of shorthand for the seasonal calendar of festivity and worship of a rural, agrarian society, a calendar that was subject to reform and that became increasingly civic and national during the reigns of Elizabeth and James'.[58] Similarly, Brian Walsh argues that these are 'merry-sounding occasions that belong to an emerging sense of the past as a place of now faded rural folk tradition and exuberant religious celebration'.[59] Gower's song is part of the early festival calendar and arouses feelings of nostalgia for an archaic mode of hospitality that has been lost to us.

Hospitality's capacity to elicit nostalgia for an idealised but irrecoverable past when society was more welcoming than it is today is characteristic of many world cultures past and present. 'In Jordan, Balgawi Bedouin have challenged my ethnographic prejudices', anthropologist Andrew Shryock recalls, 'by insisting that I "find" *karam* not in the abundant generosity they show me as their guest, here and now, but in the past (when people were genuinely hospitable) or in areas far away (in the eastern desert, perhaps, where Bedouin are still generous).'[60] For the Bedouin, authentic hospitality is always to be found elsewhere, either geographically or historically remote from the present moment. Felicity Heal demonstrates that the same was true of early modern England, which deployed a myth of 'the golden age' of hospitality 'as a means of criticizing contemporary failings'.[61] In this section, I focus on the remarkably hospitable residents of Pentapolis with the aim of showing how nostalgia for what Bart van Es calls 'the Indian summer of English chivalry' influences the play's staging of hospitality.[62] Put simply, the Pentapolis scenes' engagement with a chivalrous past offers an idealised version of the hospitality relationship, counteracting some of the nightmarish scenarios which we have seen so far.

As mentioned in passing earlier, the sea transports a hypothermic Pericles to the beach at Pentapolis. Seeing some fishermen working nearby, Pericles pleads that he will die without immediate assistance. In reply, the first fisherman says:

> Die, quotha? Now gods forbid't, an I have a gown here! Come, put it on, keep thee warm. Now, afore me, a handsome fellow! Come, thou shalt go home, and we'll have flesh for holidays, fish for fasting-days, and moreo'er puddings and flapjacks, and thou shalt be welcome.
> (2.1.76–81)

In an extraordinary moment of hospitality offered to the man from the sea, the fisherman charitably offers to feed, clothe, and give shelter to the sea-soaked visitor. Pericles' encounter with this piscatorial Good Samaritan not only romanticises hospitality, but implicitly associates it with the medieval, chivalric past because – as with Gower's commentary on the Pentapolis wedding banquet – the fisherman-host's gastronomic plans for his guest conform to the Elizabethan religious calendar which mandated strict dietary rules about 'flesh for holidays, fish for fasting-days'. Another key aspect of this shoreline hospitality scene is when Pericles, still cold from being in the water, is handed a 'gown' to keep himself warm. Anticipating the chivalric code of Simonides' court, the fisherman's gift emulates the hospitality of noble households in medieval romance where the guest was given something more comfortable to wear indoors. In an interesting reading of hospitality in Arthurian romance, Christoph Siegfried comments on this tradition:

> Clearly, a knight errant would not likely have had a change of clothes, especially expensive and delicate ones, tucked behind his saddle. The option after a cleansing bath would therefore have been limited, both for guest and host: either put a freshly bathed knight at table in his grimy, sweaty traveling clothes, or have something clean at hand.[63]

Julie Kerr, in an article on hospitality in twelfth-century England, notes that there was a symbolic as well as practical advantage to the ritual gift of fresh garments since – in exchanging 'warrior's clothing for domestic attire' – both knight and householder conveyed their 'mutual trust' in one another.[64] Cultural similarities between Pentapolis hospitality and the vanished world of medieval romance acquire more force when we learn from the fishermen that the next day there will be a jousting tournament in honour of Simonides' daughter, Thaisa. As the action now moves inland, from the coast to the court, the play recasts Pericles' global travels in a positive light, distancing him from the refugee experience, instead associating him with the knight errant of chivalric romance.[65]

Following Arnold van Gennep, the anthropologist Julian Pitt-Rivers notes that 'a desire to measure oneself against the stranger' is 'reminiscent of the age of chivalry when knights on meeting found it necessary to test the "valor" or "value" of their new acquaintance'.[66] Pitt-Rivers adds that this impulse to subject the newcomer to a test or ordeal of some kind 'springs from something fundamental in the nature of relations with strangers, such as a necessity to evaluate them in some way or other against the standards of the community'.[67] Based on how they perform during the competition, the outsider will be integrated into the host community or else rejected by it. In Shakespeare and Wilkins' rendering of the contest, it is the 'stranger knight' (2.3.65) who wins the jousting tourney. Afterwards, when Thaisa crowns Pericles with a 'wreath of victory' (2.3.9) and names him 'king of this day's happiness' (2.3.10), the monarchical symbolism attests to the fact that his incorporation into Pentapolis society is complete. The jousting contest in *Pericles* thus serves as an initiation rite that soon gives way to scenes of feasting and community spirit. Simonides is an extremely generous and attentive host. So enamoured is he with the guest of honour that Pericles begins to seem another delicacy at the banquet table:

Simonides	[*aside*] By Jove I wonder, that is king of thoughts,
	These cates resist me, he but thought upon.
Thaisa	[*aside*] By Juno that is queen of marriage,
	All viands that I eat do seem unsavoury,
	Wishing him my meat.
	(2.3.27–31)

In contrast to the nascent cannibalism of the starving Tarsan mothers, who are so hungry for something to eat that they are 'ready now / To eat those little darlings whom they loved' (1.4.43–4), the imagery of anthropophagy at the Pentapolis banquet mirrors a healthy longing to integrate this honourable knight into the social body.

The chivalric code of conduct which we find throughout medieval literature and at the court in Pentapolis has implications for hospitality because it means giving strangers the benefit of the doubt. Before the jousting begins, the knights take it in turns to pass individually over the stage, each presenting his shield with heraldic emblem to Thaisa. Dressed in visibly rusted armour reclaimed from the sea, Pericles carries a 'withered branch that's only green at top' (2.2.42). His eccentric appearance draws amused commentary from some of those present:

> 2 Lord   He may well be a stranger, for he comes
>   To an honoured triumph strangely furnished.
> 3 Lord   And on set purpose let his armour rust
>   Until this day to scour it in the dust.
>   (2.2.50–3)

Simonides, though, notices the 'graceful courtesy' (2.2.40) with which Pericles hands the branch to Thaisa. Simonides' confidence in his guest's nobility is part of a courtly belief system that, as Siegfried demonstrates, governs the reception of strangers within the chivalric universe:

> Even if the guest does not come with the warrant of knightly accoutrements, a courtly context dictates that presumption must err on the side of worthiness. The risk for the host of overvaluing a guest's worthiness is far less significant than the risk of undervaluing a guest, since such undervaluation risks insult to the guest and the brand of incivility for the host. While the assumption of guest worthiness is not always justified, the presumed universality of chivalry remains reflected in the peripatetic aspect of knighthood.[68]

Citing as an example the knight Parzival, who arrives at another court wearing ludicrous clothing, Siegfried notes how 'the assumption underlying hospitality, particularly in its chivalric context, dictates an appropriate explanation'.⁶⁹ In medieval literature, then, the innate gentility of the Fair Unknown knight shows through their poor dress. (In Parzival's case, his outlandish clothes can be blamed on his well-intentioned mother.) Simonides' openminded response to his guest's unconventional appearance is based on the same presumption that there must be a logical explanation as to why one of the knights is wearing rusted armour and carrying a branch instead of a shield. Consistent with the genre of medieval romance, Simonides' belief in the knightly honour system is justified later when he learns of his guest's misfortunes at sea. Revealed to be a victim of natural disaster and shipwreck, any irregularities in Pericles' conduct are retrospectively cancelled out. Simonides puts his faith in strangers and is rewarded when his daughter, Thaisa, marries this noble knight. At the court in Pentapolis, hospitality thus takes place in an idealised cosmos, where strangers (however eccentric) are welcomed as trusted members of a shared chivalric code.

Contrary to Tarsus where the murderous intrigues of the court are allied to environmental devastation, Pentapolis is both hospitable *and* in tune with nature. The second fisherman volunteers to cut up his 'best gown' (2.1.159) and put his needlework skills to use sewing Pericles 'a pair of braces' (2.1.157) for the tournament. If this generous offer raises questions about the ethics of exploiting the local labour force, the fisherman's commitment to the repurposing of materials is admirable. By dressing in rusty armour and second-hand garments, Pericles can be compared to an eco-warrior trying to prevent ecological depletion. Further indication of the environmentalist values of Pentapolis comes in the form of the salvaged branch. Pericles' chivalric motto is *In hac spe vivo* (2.2.43), which translates as 'In this hope I live'. Simonides compliments his guest's creativity and resourcefulness in using the green shoots to illustrate expectancy:

> A pretty moral.
> From the dejected state wherein he is
> He hopes by you his fortunes yet may flourish.
> (2.2.43–5)

In keeping with environmentally friendly Pentapolis, Pericles' emblem signifies regrowth. The medieval world of *Pericles* also emphasises the benefit of recycling old stories. Responding to Ben Jonson's criticism of the play as a stale and mouldy tale, Kurt Schreyer suggests that mould is 'a sign of flourishing as well as deterioration' and that, in *Pericles*, 'the fruitfulness of mouldy poetic soil allows Shakespeare to rework the scandalous theme of incest from Gower's tale'.[70] The correlation which Schreyer hints at here between intertextuality and ecological flourishing is borne out by the play itself. On first introducing himself to the audience, Gower explains his resurrection from 'ashes ancient' (1.0.2). The allusion to ash and biodegradability indicates an organic composting followed by renewal. Gower later refers to 'our fast-growing scene' (4.0.6), again encouraging us to think in terms of cycles of natural growth and repair. Gower's choruses and, by extension, the text's reworking of its medieval sources, are framed in language which evokes the conservation of the Earth and its resources. Recycling in *Pericles* takes different forms, yet is always hospitable to the globe and its reserves. It advocates thrift, goes against the capitalist ethos of waste, and preserves the rich storytelling traditions of the past.

Healing Hospitality

As noted earlier, secrets have a disruptive impact on the early part of *Pericles*, problematising social, political and familial relations, and even putting the time out of joint. But the play does not leave things there. As with Shakespeare's other romances, *Pericles* is at heart a drama of redemption, which values forgiveness and second chances and which ultimately presents us with the joyful reunion of long-separated loved ones. In this section of the chapter, I examine the healing properties of the secret as it relates to hospitality. My analysis focuses on the secret's essential vitality and its promise to be socially transformative. Above all, I am interested in the secret's unique role in health and community building. By offering us positive recuperations of this most enigmatic trope, the play's later scenes reclaim the secret as a life-restoring force for social and political good.

With Cerimon, amateur apothecary and Good Samaritan, the play begins to recuperate the secretive host motif. After the chest containing Thaisa is thrown from the ship, it washes ashore on the beach at Ephesus where it is discovered and opened by Cerimon and his attendants. The audience soon learns that this wealthy lord of Ephesus has an interest in the natural sciences and it is his care and medical expertise which will awaken Thaisa from her deep slumber. In a prelude to this miraculous resurrection scene, Cerimon gives a concise history of his largely self-taught education:

>   'Tis known I ever
> Have studied physic, through which secret art,
> By turning o'er authorities, I have,
> Together with my practice made familiar
> To me and to my aid the blest infusions
> That dwells in vegetives, in metals, stones
>   (3.2.31–6)

Cerimon's expertise in making infusions, together with his knowledge of the many different healing properties contained within plants, metals, stones and other organic matter, is collectively referred to as his 'secret art'. In *Secrets and Knowledge in Medicine and Science, 1500–1800*, Alisha Rankin and Elaine Leong note that:

> For countless individuals, secrets held the key to unlocking the mysteries of nature, curing disease, maintaining good health, making practical everyday substances, and even creating wondrous tricks. Hunting for secrets was one of the main avenues through which early modern men and women attempted to satisfy their desire to understand the natural world around them.[71]

Pericles' unfortunate stay in Antioch attests to the fact that a host with secrets can be cause for terror. Yet whereas Antiochus used secrecy to advance his taboo sexual fantasies, Cerimon's secret art is different. As a result of his curiosity about the natural sciences, and willingness to care for his guests and neighbours in Ephesus, Cerimon rewrites and recovers the figure of the secretive host, transmuting it into a vision of healing hospitality. In Cerimon's welcoming household, secrets serve only therapeutic purposes and are used primarily for the benefit of any strangers who come to the door.

Cerimon not only restores our trust in hospitality, but in the architecture of secrecy as well. Secrets at Antioch were contained within other secrets, creating an intricate trap. Once the action of the play moves to Ephesus, Shakespeare and Wilkins return to the concept of nested secrets, although this time our attention is directed towards boxes, storage chests and other material containers. Thaisa reaches the Ephesian shore within a large watertight container which is variously described by the bystanders on the beach as a 'chest' (3.2.50) and a 'coffin' (3.2.52). Accurately surmising that the 'corpse' (3.2.62) placed inside the box is merely asleep and not dead, Cerimon says to one of his servants:

> They were too rough
> That threw her in the sea. Make a fire within;
> Fetch hither all my boxes in my closet.
> (3.2.78–80)

In her insightful 2021 monograph, *Boxes and Books in Early Modern England: Materiality, Metaphor, Containment*, Lucy Razzall traces the analogy of the apothecary with boxes and well-stocked store cupboards, further identifying

> a visual tradition in which the apothecary is associated with the inscrutability of a shop filled with many boxes, each containing potentially dangerous substances. The attraction of the apothecary's box is that no-one except the apothecary properly understands its contents, but the promise of powerful, exotic drugs is very seductive. The art of the apothecary is extremely specialised, and a layperson's misreading of such boxes could have very dangerous consequences.[72]

Conforming to this cultural stereotype of the powerful apothecary surrounded by boxes, after he opens the box which contains Thaisa, Cerimon sends an attendant to fetch 'all my boxes in my closet', the double possessive implying a proprietorial attitude towards his secret art. *Pericles* again creates an impression of architecturally nested secrets, since the boxes containing Cerimon's drugs are given an additional layer of privacy by being stored inside his personal closet which, as Melissa Auclair reminds us, was 'the most private interior space available in a Renaissance home'.[73] While it is undoubtedly a puzzle of sorts, the unexpected arrival of a lifeless body inside a sea-chest presents no serious difficulty for Cerimon, who combats secrets with secrets, boxes with boxes. As he makes clear, he is well acquainted with nature's mysteries, telling his attendants, 'I heard of an Egyptian / That had nine hours lain dead, who was / By good appliance recovered' (3.2.83–5). Even so, when Cerimon succeeds in reviving Thaisa from her swoon, those present remark on the astonishing efficacy of his healing techniques. The first gentleman says, '[t]he heavens / Through you increase our wonder, and sets up / Your fame for ever' (3.2.94–6). Thaisa's recovery is also called 'strange' and 'rare' (3.2.105). By combining in Cerimon the figures of apothecary and host, *Pericles* offers a welcome corrective to Antiochus' murderous pursuit of secrecy at home, converting the earlier trope of poison into a cure.

In Ephesus, then, secrets are life-restoring and wondrous. Nevertheless, it is worth remembering that – alongside this spectacular display of Cerimon's secret art – the secret also performs a far more mundane but no less important role in the local community. Complimenting Cerimon's philanthropy, the second gentleman says:

> Your honour has
> Through Ephesus poured forth your charity,
> And hundreds call themselves your creatures, who
> By you have been restored.
> (3.2.42–5)

Despite being less visually extraordinary than the resurrection of a stranger corpse, Cerimon's apothecary boxes have enabled essential community building work, restoring the ill or injured to health, at the same time strengthening bonds of fellow feeling between 'hundreds' of local Ephesian residents. The secret is now a force for social good. As opposed to the sick environment of Antiochus' court, here, the host's secrets are healthy and promote soundness of body and mind.

With his secret knowledge of natural remedies, and philanthropy towards his guests and Ephesian neighbours, Cerimon recuperates the secretive host theme. Featuring incest, riddles, and a hired assassin, the court in Antioch was every guest's worst nightmare. In contrast, Cerimon's 'secret art' is used for healing purposes, to the benefit of any newcomers.

'God Neptune's annual feast'

It is surely no coincidence that Cerimon and Marina, the play's two most miraculously effectual hosts, are equally sensitive to the myriad of plant and creaturely life forms that share our planetary home. When Marina restores to health the stranger whom she meets below deck on the boat in Mytilene, the scene can be read as the culmination of a holistic philosophy which advocates neighbourliness and ethical cohabitation with others, including other species.[74] From her first appearance in the play as an adult, Marina is associated with nature. She appears strewing the burial place of her old nursemaid with flowers, a motif which is replicated in her mimetic embroidery:

> with her nee'le composes
> Nature's own shape of bud, bird, branch or berry,
> That even her art sisters the natural roses.
> (5.0.5–7)

Even after entering the brothel, Marina continues to be allied with the natural environment. The brothel employees repeatedly use imagery of gardening and agriculture to convey how they plan to educate this novice in their profession. Marina is 'a young foolish sapling and must be bowed' (4.2.79–80). She is compared to 'a rose' that 'grows to the stalk; never plucked yet' (4.5.42–8), and, as Bolt says, 'if she were a thornier piece of ground than she is, she shall be ploughed' (4.5.148–9). In an ecofeminist reading of the play, Miriam Kammer argues that '[a]t the brothel, the exploitation of women is closely associated with environmental exploitation, as Pander, Bawd, and Bolt tend to use plant and animal imagery when discussing the prostitutes, reinforcing the identification of a dangerous, commodified female body with aspects of the natural world.'[75]

Throughout the play, Marina is a vocal campaigner for interspecies co-operation and environmentally sustainable modes of dwelling. She persuades Bolt to leave the brothel and move into a more ecologically friendly career:

> Do anything but this thou dost. Empty
> Old receptacles or common shores of filth,
> Serve by indenture to the common hangman,
> Any of these ways are yet better than this.
> For what thou professes a baboon, could he speak,
> Would own a name too dear.
> (4.5.177–82)

Whereas several of the other characters in the play pollute the ocean with their waste, Marina urges Bolt to find employment emptying sewage containers or cleaning rubbish from beaches. An exemplar for interspecies thinking, she admonishes him that even a baboon (an animal synonymous with lust in the seventeenth century) would scorn Bolt's current occupation 'could he speak'. Earlier in Act 4, not understanding why her adoptive mother, Dionyza, has conspired to have her killed, Marina gives her would-be murderer a glimpse into her approach to animal welfare:

> Why would she have me killed now?
> As I can remember, by my troth,
> I never did her hurt in all my life.
> I never spake bad word, nor did ill turn
> To any living creature. Believe me, la,
> I never killed a mouse nor hurt a fly.
> I trod upon a worm against my will,
> But I wept for't.
> (4.1.69–76)

Marina subscribes to a branch of environmental ethics that rejects anthropocentrism. Rather than considering humankind the most important organism, her speech collapses the conventional hierarchies implicit in the great chain of being. Indeed, when Marina describes her caring attitude towards nature, it is the humblest animal which seems to move her the most, since she weeps over a squashed worm.

Environmental awareness and hospitality are, in *Pericles*, values which are found to be mutually reinforcing and life-affirming. Marina's ecological thinking, coupled with her empathy and identification with all living creatures, is an extension of her hospitality, culminating when she brings Pericles, a guest in Mytilene, back to life. Conversely, her foster mother's inhospitality (her conspiracy to murder a guest in her home) reflects a broader lack of kinship towards creaturely life forms. Cross-species collaboration is, to Dionyza, something to be jeered at like a joke. Scornfully mocking her husband Cleon for worrying that Marina's murder will be discovered, Dionyza says:

Be one of those that thinks
The petty wrens of Tarsus will fly hence
And open this to Pericles. I do shame
To think of what a noble strain you are
And of how coward a spirit.
    (4.3.21–5)

In her Arden edition, Gossett notes that 'Dionyza alludes to folk tales in which murders are revealed by birds', noticing a similarity to Macbeth's ornithophobia and fear that 'magot-pies, and choughs, and rooks' have in the past been known to expose murderers.[76] Revealing of Dionyza's anthropocentric worldview, the prospect of birds helping humankind is an old tale that, as Lady Macbeth puts it, 'would well become / A woman's story at a winter's fire'.[77] Their contemptuous ridicule of avian assistance echoes the inhospitality which Lady Macbeth and Dionyza display towards their house guests.

Marina, however, embraces folk wisdom when she says that, rather than stay in the brothel, she would prefer to be changed to 'the meanest bird / That flies i'th' purer air!' (4.5.101–6).

Pericles does not shy away from the dangers surrounding hospitality, yet it also shows us that anything is possible, interweaving the wonder of the romance genre with the guest and host relationship. Echoing the theme of recycling old stories, the latter part of the play reworks the tragic material of the opening scenes, translating the nightmares into redemptive visions of healing and forgiveness. As the play concludes, the citizens of Mytilene are celebrating 'God Neptune's annual feast' (5.0.17). Contrary to the destructive eating habits of the early part of the action, including the unchecked resource extraction at Tarsus, Mytilene is offering religious obeisance to the sea god. Fish is presumably the *plat du jour* at Neptune's feast, but the people of Mytilene do not just take unthinkingly and incessantly from the sea; instead, they celebrate it and give back to it. The ending thus presents us with a sustainable form of nutrition which involves eating from and *with* the ocean.[78] In a play filled with festivities, this concluding celebration of the ocean allows us to imagine new modes of hospitality which prioritise intergenerational and interspecies care, as well as the nurturing of friends, guests, strangers and, above all, the Earth.

Notes

1. Verna A. Foster, *The Name and Nature of Tragicomedy* (London and New York: Routledge, 2004), p. 53.
2. Lawrence Danson, 'The Shakespeare Remix: Romance, Tragicomedy, and Shakespeare's "distinct kind"', in *Shakespeare and Genre: From Early Modern Inheritances to Postmodern Legacies*, ed. Anthony R. Guneratne (New York: Palgrave, 2011), pp. 101–18, p. 103.
3. Randall Martin, *Shakespeare and Ecology* (Oxford: Oxford University Press, 2015), p. 3.

4. William Shakespeare and George Wilkins, *Pericles*, ed. Suzanne Gossett (London: Bloomsbury, 2004), 1.0.19. Further references are to this edition and given parenthetically in the text.
5. Katelijne Schiltz, *Music and Riddle Culture in the Renaissance* (Cambridge: Cambridge University Press, 2015), p. 16.
6. Gaston Bachelard, *The Poetics of Space*, trans. Maria Jolas (Boston, MA: Beacon Press, 1994), p. 81.
7. Bachelard, *The Poetics of Space*, p. 82.
8. *Pericles*, 1.1.65–6n. For a detailed consideration of food in the play, see Anthony J. Lewis, '"I Feed on Mother's Flesh": Incest and Eating in *Pericles*', *Essays in Literature*, 15:2 (1988), 147–63.
9. Elizabeth Archibald, *Incest and the Medieval Imagination* (Oxford: Clarendon Press, 2001), p. 6.
10. James Petty, 'The London Spikes Controversy: Homelessness, Urban Securitisation and the Question of "Hostile Architecture"', *International Journal for Crime, Justice and Social Democracy*, 5:1 (2016), 67–81, p. 76. Alongside metal spikes on floors and window ledges, other examples of the turn towards exclusionary mechanisms in modern urban design planning include armrests on park benches to prevent the homeless from sleeping comfortably and UV lighting in restrooms making it difficult for heroin addicts to locate veins. The rationale behind these environmental obstructions is always the same – either to deter people from visiting an area, or from making themselves at home there.
11. Tiffany Stern, *Making Shakespeare: From Stage to Page* (London: Routledge, 2004), p. 9.
12. Katharine Eisaman Maus, *Inwardness and Theatre in the English Renaissance* (Chicago: University of Chicago Press, 1995), p. 195.
13. William W. E. Slights, 'Secret Places in Renaissance Drama', *University of Toronto Quarterly*, 59:3 (1990), 363–81; Shannon Miller, 'Constructing the Female Self: Architectural Structures in Mary Wroth's *Urania*', in *Renaissance Culture and the Everyday*, ed. Patricia Fumerton and Simon

Hunt (Philadelphia: University of Pennsylvania Press, 1999), pp. 139–61; Lena Orlin, *Locating Privacy in Tudor London* (Oxford: Oxford University Press, 2007); Henry Dietrich Fernández, 'A Secret Space for a Secret Keeper: Cardinal Bibbiena at the Vatican Palace', in *Visual Cultures of Secrecy in Early Modern Europe*, ed. Timothy McCall, Sean Roberts and Giancarlo Fiorenza (Pennsylvania: Penn State University Press, 2013), pp. 149–61.
14. Georg Simmel, 'The Sociology of Secrecy and of Secret Societies', *American Journal of Sociology*, 11:4 (1906), 441–98, p. 484.
15. Simmel, 'Secret Societies', pp. 466–87.
16. Anne Dufourmantelle, *In Defense of Secrets*, trans. Lindsay Turner (New York: Fordham University Press, 2021), p. 81.
17. Jacques Derrida, *The Gift of Death & Literature in Secret*, trans. David Wills (Chicago: University of Chicago Press, 2008), p. 92.
18. Simmel, 'Secret Societies', p. 477.
19. Dufourmantelle, *In Defense of Secrets*, p. 81.
20. Simmel, 'Secret Societies', p. 465.
21. Dufourmantelle, *In Defense of Secrets*, pp. 35–43.
22. Michael Taussig, *Defacement: Public Secrecy and the Labour of the Negative* (Stanford: Stanford University Press, 1999), p. 157.
23. Taussig, *Defacement*, p. 160.
24. *Pericles*, 1.1.117n.
25. Corinne Squire, 'Partial Secrets', *Current Anthropology*, 56:12 (2015), 201–10, p. 201.
26. Steven Mullaney, '"All That Monarchs Do": The Obscured Stages of Authority in *Pericles*', in *Pericles: Critical Essays*, ed. David Skeele (New York and London: Taylor & Francis, 2000), pp. 168–83, p. 170.
27. Dufourmantelle, *In Defense of Secrets*, p. 16.
28. Charles Barbour, *Derrida's Secret: Perjury, Testimony, Oath* (Edinburgh: Edinburgh University Press, 2018), p. 8.
29. Barbour, *Derrida's Secret*, p. 39.
30. Barbour, *Derrida's Secret*, p. 38.

31. Dan Brayton, *Shakespeare's Ocean: An Ecocritical Exploration* (Charlottesville and London: University of Virginia Press, 2009), p. 166.
32. Steve Mentz, *Ocean* (London: Bloomsbury, 2020), p. 3. Mentz revisits the concept of the inhospitable ocean elsewhere; see: 'Toward a Blue Cultural Studies: The Sea, Maritime Culture, and Early Modern English Literature', *Literature Compass*, 6:5 (2009), 997–1013; *Shipwreck Modernity: Ecologies of Globalization, 1550–1719* (Minnesota: University of Minnesota Press, 2015).
33. Eric Chaline, *Strokes of Genius: A History of Swimming* (London: Reaktion Books, 2017), p. 17.
34. Kimberley Peters, 'Drifting: Towards Mobilities at Sea', *Transactions of the Institute of British Geographers*, 40:2 (2015), 262–72; Philip Steinberg and Kimberley Peters, 'Wet Ontologies, Fluid Spaces: Giving Depth to Volume through Oceanic Thinking', *Environment and Planning*, 33 (2015), 247–64.
35. In a chapter on 'Settler Colonial Territorial Imaginaries: Maritime Mobilities and the "Tow-Backs" of Asylum Seekers', Kate Coddington argues that criticism should attend to the body of the asylum seeker, considering the lived experiences of those in boats; see: *Territory Beyond Terra*, ed. Kimberley Peters, Philip Steinberg and Elaine Stratford (London and New York: Rowman & Littlefield International, 2018), pp. 185–202.
36. Irus Braverman and Elizabeth R. Johnson, 'Introduction: Blue Legalities Governing More-Than-Human Oceans', in *Blue Legalities: The Life and Laws of the Sea* (Durham, NC, and London: Duke University Press, 2020), pp. 1–24, pp. 10–11.
37. Suvendrini Perera, 'Oceanic Corpo-graphies, Refugee Bodies and the Making and Unmaking of Waters', *Feminist Review*, 103 (2013), 58–79, pp. 63–78.
38. https://www.theguardian.com/uk-news/2021/mar/24/how-is-priti-patel-planning-to-change-the-uks-asylum-system [accessed May 2022].
39. Mentz, *Shipwreck Modernity*, p. 1.

40. Ann Rosalind Jones and Peter Stallybrass, *Renaissance Clothing and the Materials of Memory* (Cambridge: Cambridge University Press, 2001), p. 258. Lowell Duckert notes that Pericles undergoes 'oceanic erasure', 'Pericles's Deep Ecology', *Studies in English Literature, 1500–1900*, 59:2 (2019), 367–81, p. 376.
41. Kimberley C. Patton, *The Sea Can Wash Away All Evils: Modern Marine Pollution and the Ancient Cathartic Ocean* (New York: Columbia University Press, 2007), p. 27.
42. John C. Appleby, *Women and English Piracy, 1540–1720: Partners and Victims of Crime* (Woodbridge: Boydell & Brewer, 2013), p. 191. Appleby adds that '[f]or most women, especially those who were poor and dependent, the experience of the sea was more likely to be an ordeal. Living in cramped, unhygienic spaces, lacking privacy and suffering sickness, such women could face routine bullying and intimidation. They were, moreover, acutely vulnerable to physical and sexual abuse' (p. 196).
43. Paige Martin Reynolds, 'Sin, Sacredness, and Childbirth in Early Modern Drama', *Medieval & Renaissance Drama in England*, 28 (2015), 30–48, pp. 35–6.
44. Phillip Zapkin, 'Salt Fish: Fishing and the Creation of Empires in *Pericles* and Contemporary Oceans', *South Atlantic Review*, 82:2 (2017), 78–96, p. 81.
45. Mentz, *Ocean*, p. 56.
46. Paul Freedman, *Out of the East: Spices and the Medieval Imagination* (New Haven and London: Yale University Press, 2008).
47. Perera, 'Oceanic Corpo-graphies', p. 60.
48. Perera, 'Oceanic Corpo-graphies', p. 60.
49. Glenn Albrecht, 'Solastalgia and the New Mourning', in *Mourning Nature: Hope at the Heart of Ecological Loss and Grief*, ed. Ashlee Cunsolo and Karen Landman (Montreal: McGill-Queen's University Press, 2017), pp. 292–315, p. 303.
50. Philippe Lynes, 'The Posthuman Promise of the Earth', in *Eco-Deconstruction Derrida and Environmental Philosophy*,

ed. Matthias Fritsch, Philippe Lynes and David Wood (New York: Fordham University Press, 2018), pp. 101–20, p. 102.
51. Kelly Oliver, 'Earth: Love It or Leave It?', in *Eco-Deconstruction*, ed. Fritsch, Lynes and Wood, pp. 339–54, p. 345.
52. Matt Williamson, 'Imperial Appetites: Cannibalism and Early Modern Theatre', in *To Feast on Us as Their Prey: Cannibalism and the Early Modern Atlantic*, ed. Rachel B. Herrmann (Fayetteville: University of Arkansas Press, 2019), pp. 115–34.
53. C. M. Woolgar, 'Gifts of Food in Late Medieval England', *Journal of Medieval History*, 37:1 (2011), 6–18, p. 17.
54. Jennifer Welchman, 'A Defence of Environmental Stewardship', *Environmental Values*, 21:3 (2012), 297–316, p. 299.
55. Joseph Bosworth, 'stig-weard', in *An Anglo-Saxon Dictionary Online*, ed. Thomas Northcote Toller, Christ Sean and Ondřej Tichy (Prague: Faculty of Arts, Charles University, 2014).
56. On political surrogates, a good starting point is Stuart M. Kurland, '"The care . . . of subjects' good": *Pericles*, James I, and the Neglect of Government', *Comparative Drama*, 30:2 (1996), 220–44. On foster parenting in *Pericles*, see Joseph Campana, *Childhood, Education and the Stage in Early Modern England* (Cambridge: Cambridge University Press, 2017), and Marianne Novy, 'Multiple Parenting in *Pericles*', in *Pericles: Critical Essays*, ed. Skeele, pp. 238–48. The textual history of *Pericles* lends itself to imagery of dubious parentage. As Stephen Dickey puts it, '[p]artially deprived of Shakespeare's authorship, disowned by the First Folio, its quarto bad, the bastard *Pericles* has provoked numerous speculations about its parentage of collaboration, adaptation, or revision', 'Language and Role in *Pericles*', *English Literary Renaissance*, 16:3 (1986), 550–66 (p. 550).
57. For further reading on Gower, see: F. David Hoeniger, 'Gower and Shakespeare in *Pericles*', *Shakespeare Quarterly*, 33:4 (1982), 461–79; Steele Nowlin, *Chaucer, Gower, and the Affect of Invention* (Columbus: Ohio State University Press, 2016); Bart van Es, 'Late Shakespeare and the Middle Ages', in *Medieval Shakespeare: Pasts and Presents*, ed. Ruth Morse,

Helen Cooper and Peter Holland (Cambridge: Cambridge University Press, 2013), pp. 37–51.
58. Jonathan Baldo, 'Recovering Medieval Memory in Shakespeare's *Pericles*', *South Atlantic Review*, 79:3–4 (2014), 171–89, p. 179.
59. Brian Walsh, '"A Priestly Farewell": Gower's Tomb and Religious Change', *Religion & Literature*, 45:3 (2013), 81–113, p. 94. For more on the early festival calendar, see Ronald Hutton, *The Stations of the Sun: A History of the Ritual Year in Britain* (Oxford: Oxford University Press, 1996).
60. Andrew Shryock, 'Hospitality Lessons: Learning the Shared Language of Derrida and the Balga Bedouin', *Paragraph*, 32:1 (2009), 32–50, pp. 35–6.
61. Felicity Heal, 'Hospitality and Honor in Early Modern England', *Food and Foodways*, 1:4 (1987), 321–50, p. 335.
62. Van Es, 'Late Shakespeare and the Middle Ages', p. 46.
63. Siegfried Christoph, 'Hospitality and Status: Social Intercourse in Middle High German Arthurian Romance and Courtly Narrative', *Arthuriana*, 20:3 (2010), 45–64, p. 56.
64. Julie Kerr, '"Welcome the coming and speed the parting guest": Hospitality in Twelfth-Century England', *Journal of Medieval History*, 33:2 (2007), 130–46, p. 134.
65. Michelle M. Dowd makes a related point in *The Dynamics of Inheritance on the Shakespearean Stage* (Cambridge: Cambridge University Press, 2015): 'Thus the risks (both financial and physical) of long-distance travel are dramatically transformed into noble sacrifice and redemption via the tropes of chivalric adventure; male heroism and bravery are retooled for a proto-capitalist culture invested in both commercial enterprise and the preservation of patrilineal economies' (p. 194).
66. Julian Pitt-Rivers, 'The Law of Hospitality', in *From Hospitality to Grace: A Julian Pitt-Rivers Omnibus*, ed. Giovanni da Col and Andrew Shryock (Chicago: HAU Books, 2017), pp. 163–85, pp. 164–5.
67. Pitt-Rivers, 'The Law of Hospitality', p. 165.
68. Christoph, 'Hospitality and Status', p. 48.
69. Christoph, 'Hospitality and Status', p. 49.

70. Kurt A. Schreyer, 'Moldy *Pericles*', *Exemplaria: A Journal of Theory in Medieval and Renaissance Studies*, 29:3 (2017), 210–33, pp. 226–7.
71. Elaine Leong and Alisha Rankin, 'Introduction: Secrets and Knowledge', in *Secrets and Knowledge in Medicine and Science, 1500–1800*, ed. Elaine Leong and Alisha Rankin (London: Routledge, 2016), pp. 1–20, p. 3.
72. Lucy Razzall, *Boxes and Books in Early Modern England: Materiality, Metaphor, Containment* (Cambridge: Cambridge University Press, 2021), p. 96.
73. Melissa Auclair, 'Coming into the Closet: Spatial Practices and Representations of Interior Space', *Shakespeare*, 13:2 (2017), 147–54, p. 147.
74. Julia Reinhard Lupton calls this her 'environmental connectedness', also noting Marina's 'world-building and soul-healing capacities'; *Shakespeare Dwelling: Designs for the Theatre of Life* (Chicago: University of Chicago Press, 2018), pp. 144 and 118.
75. Miriam Kammer, 'Shakespeare as Ecodrama: Ecofeminism and Nonduality in *Pericles, Prince of Tyre*', *Journal of Dramatic Theory and Criticism*, 32:1 (2017), 29–48, p. 43.
76. *Pericles*, 4.3.22–3n; William Shakespeare, *Macbeth*, ed. Kenneth Muir (London: Thomson Learning, 2006), 3.4.124.
77. *Macbeth*, 3.4.63–4.
78. Elspeth Probyn, *Eating the Ocean* (Durham, NC, and London: Duke University Press, 2016).

AFTERWORD

Being on the threshold, in every sense of that phrase, is about the risks and benefits of openness. Acts of hospitality open us to others in ways that can highlight the vulnerability of permeable bodies, physical environments and social worlds. My analysis of Shakespeare's plays has often stressed the dangers of hospitality because there is no encounter without the risk of things going wrong, of relationships being poisoned, of outsiders being marginalised, stigmatised and excluded. Thresholds can be means of warding off others at the moment of offering welcome. But I have also tried to show how thresholds are positive and transformational. The possibility of hope is thus core to the ethics of hospitality. In Shakespeare's drama, encounters with the stranger, the guest or the outsider suggest new opportunities, new modes of care and compassion.

The concept of hospitality that has emerged from this book is nuanced, ambiguous and often elusive. I have sought out instances of hospitality in some unlikely places, often focusing on the individual or even microscopic levels of sensation, emotion and bodily affect, arguing that there is a poetics of hospitality interwoven into the plays that calls attention to the embodied sensuality of the guest and host relationship. At the same time, I have shown how hospitality relates to broader collective issues. The close readings of the plays' language have been conducted with a view to social and political concerns surrounding the treatment of migrants, the mechanics of government bureaucracy, and the role of economics and the legal system. In this fashion, I have attempted to demonstrate how Shakespeare's drama invites us to reconsider the nature of hospitality as well as its significance to far-reaching problems of ethical, philosophical and political importance. Indeed, even the language of the plays fashions a kind of threshold between text and reader that performs the very modes of hospitality being described. Shakespeare is not simply bearing witness to the lively, sometimes unpredictable exchanges between guest and host in the theatre space, but offering us new ways of encountering this subject.

One of the central questions that has animated this research is what prevents hospitality from being given unconditionally. What leads our gestures of openness and welcome, in our own lives and in our societies, to become provisional and qualified? We live in a time when governments across the globe are building walls and closing their borders to refugees, migrants and asylum seekers. Racial and xenophobic hatred of the stranger is, sadly, one of the defining features of international politics today. Contemporary authoritarianism, too, thrives on closing off the world-making potential inherent in hospitality and preventing critical reflection on what it means to be a welcoming person, place or nation. My hope is that this book will have some resonance beyond the literary study of the early modern period while affirming the continuing relevance of Shakespeare's drama. It may be naive, of course, to believe that literature or literary study can do very much to make the world a better place. But I subscribe to the sentiment so powerfully expressed by Seamus Heaney: 'in one sense the efficacy of poetry is nil – no lyric has ever stopped a tank. In another sense, it is unlimited.'[1] Shakespeare's poetics of hospitality offers us a means of holding on to the promise of this unlimited power.

Note

1. Seamus Heaney, *Finders Keepers: Selected Prose 1971–2001* (New York: Farrar, Straus and Giroux, 2002), p. 207.

BIBLIOGRAPHY

Adelman, Janet, '"Anger's my meat": Feeding, Dependency, and Aggression in *Coriolanus*', in *Shakespearean Tragedy*, ed. John Drakakis (London and New York: Longman, 1992), pp. 353–73

Agamben, Giorgio, *Homo Sacer: Sovereign Power and Bare Life*, trans. Daniel Heller-Roazen (Stanford: Stanford University Press, 1998)

Agier, Michel, *Managing the Undesirables: Refugee Camps and Humanitarian Government* (Cambridge: Polity Press, 2011)

Ahmed, Sara, 'Affective Economies', *Social Text*, 22:2 (2004), 117–39

Akhimie, Patricia, *Shakespeare and the Cultivation of Difference: Race and Conduct in the Early Modern World* (New York: Routledge, 2018)

Albrecht, Glenn, 'Solastalgia and the New Mourning', in *Mourning Nature: Hope at the Heart of Ecological Loss and Grief*, ed. Ashlee Cunsolo and Karen Landman (Montreal: McGill-Queen's University Press, 2017), pp. 292–315

Appleby, John C., *Women and English Piracy, 1540–1720: Partners and Victims of Crime* (Woodbridge: Boydell & Brewer, 2013)

Archibald, Elizabeth, *Incest and the Medieval Imagination* (Oxford: Clarendon Press, 2001)

Ariès, Philippe, *Western Attitudes toward Death from the Middle Ages to the Present*, trans. Patricia M. Ranum (London: Marion Boyars, 1974)

Auclair, Melissa, 'Coming into the Closet: Spatial Practices and Representations of Interior Space', *Shakespeare*, 13:2 (2017), 147–54

Bachelard, Gaston, *The Poetics of Space*, trans. Maria Jolas (Boston, MA: Beacon Press, 1994)

Bakhtin, Mikhail, *Rabelais and his World*, trans. Hélène Iswolsky (Bloomington: Indiana University Press, 1984)

Baldo, Jonathan, 'Recovering Medieval Memory in Shakespeare's *Pericles*', *South Atlantic Review*, 79:3–4 (2014), 171–89

Balibar, Étienne, *We, the People of Europe? Reflections on Transnational Citizenship*, trans. James Swenson (Princeton and London: Princeton University Press, 2004)

Barbour, Charles, *Derrida's Secret: Perjury, Testimony, Oath* (Edinburgh: Edinburgh University Press, 2018)

Barthes, Roland, *Mourning Diary: October 26, 1977–September 15, 1979*, trans. Richard Howard (New York: Hill & Wang, 2010)

——, *The Responsibility of Forms: Critical Essays on Music, Art and Representation*, trans. Richard Howard (Berkeley: University of California Press, 1991)

Bauman, Zygmunt, *Strangers at Our Door* (Cambridge: Polity Press, 2016)

Bayley, John, 'Time and the Trojans', *Essays in Criticism*, 25:1 (1975), 55–73

Benhabib, Seyla, *The Rights of Others: Aliens, Residents, and Citizens* (Cambridge: Cambridge University Press, 2012)

Benveniste, Émile, *Dictionary of Indo-European Concepts and Society*, trans. Elizabeth Palmer (Chicago: HAU Books, 2016)

Berry, Edward, 'Laughing at "Others"', in *The Cambridge Companion to Shakespearean Comedy*, ed. Alexander Leggatt (Cambridge: Cambridge University Press, 2002), pp. 123–38

Bhabha, Homi, 'The World and the Home', *Social Text*, 31/32 (1992), 141–53

Bloom, Gina, *Voice in Motion: Staging Gender, Shaping Sound in Early Modern England* (Pennsylvania: University of Pennsylvania Press, 2007)

Bonfil, Michel, *Jewish Life in Renaissance Italy*, trans. Anthony Oldcorn (Berkeley: University of California Press, 1994)

Bours, Patrick, and Adrian Evensen, 'The Shakespeare Experiment: Preliminary Results for the Recognition of a Person

Based on the Sound of Walking', 2017 *International Carnahan Conference on Security Technology* (2017), 1–6

Braverman, Irus, and Elizabeth R. Johnson, 'Introduction: Blue Legalities Governing More-Than-Human Oceans', in *Blue Legalities: The Life and Laws of the Sea* (Durham, NC, and London: Duke University Press, 2020), 1–24

Brayton, Dan, *Shakespeare's Ocean: An Ecocritical Exploration* (Charlottesville and London: University of Virginia Press, 2009)

Brogan, Boyd, 'His Belly, Her Seed: Gender and Medicine in Early Modern Demonic Possession', *Representations*, 147 (2019), 1–25

Bruster, Douglas, *Drama and the Market in the Age of Shakespeare* (Cambridge: Cambridge University Press, 1992)

Burton, Robert, *The Anatomy of Melancholy*, vol. 1, ed. Thomas C. Faulkner, Nicholas K. Kiessling and Rhonda L. Blair (Oxford: Oxford University Press, 2012)

Butler, Judith, *Precarious Life: The Powers of Mourning and Violence* (London and New York: Verso, 2004)

Caciola, Nancy, *Discerning Spirits: Divine and Demonic Possession in the Middle Ages* (Ithaca and London: Cornell University Press, 2003)

Campana, Joseph, *Childhood, Education and the Stage in Early Modern England* (Cambridge: Cambridge University Press, 2017)

Candido, Joseph, 'Dining out in Ephesus: Food in *The Comedy of Errors*', *Studies in English Literature, 1500–1900*, 30:2 (1990), 217–41

Cartwright, Kent, 'Language, Magic, the Dromios, and *The Comedy of Errors*', *Studies in English Literature, 1500–1900*, 47:2 (2007), 331–54

Chaline, Eric, *Strokes of Genius: A History of Swimming* (London: Reaktion Books, 2017)

Christoph, Siegfried, 'Hospitality and Status: Social Intercourse in Middle High German Arthurian Romance and Courtly Narrative', *Arthuriana*, 20:3 (2010), 45–64

Clark, Stuart, *Thinking with Demons: The Idea of Witchcraft in Early Modern Europe* (Oxford: Oxford University Press, 2005)

Clement, Jennifer, 'Bowels, Emotion, and Metaphor in Early Modern English Sermons', *The Seventeenth Century*, 35:4 (2020), 435–51

Cobham Brewer, Ebenezer, *Dictionary of Phrase and Fable* (Cambridge: Cambridge University Press, 2014)

Coddington, Kate, 'Settler Colonial Territorial Imaginaries: Maritime Mobilities and the "Tow-Backs" of Asylum Seekers', in *Territory Beyond Terra*, ed. Kimberley Peters, Philip Steinberg and Elaine Stratford (London and New York: Rowman & Littlefield International, 2018), pp. 185–202

Cosgrove, Thomas, 'The Commodity of Errors: Shakespeare and the Magic of the Value-Form', *Shakespeare*, 14:2 (2018), 149–56

Cotta, John, *The Major Works of John Cotta: The Short Discovery (1612) and The Trial of Witchcraft (1616)*, ed. Todd H. J. Pettigrew, Stephanie M. Pettigrew and Jacques A. Bailly (Leiden: Brill, 2018)

Cowen Orlin, Lena, *Locating Privacy in Tudor London* (Oxford: Oxford University Press, 2007)

Crooke, Helkiah, *Microcosmographia* (London, 1616)

Curran, Kevin, 'Hospitable Justice: Law and Selfhood in Shakespeare's Sonnets', *Law, Culture and the Humanities*, 9:2 (2013), 295–310

——, *Shakespeare's Legal Ecologies: Law and Distributed Selfhood* (Evanston: Northwestern University Press, 2017)

Daniel, Drew, 'Syllogisms and Tears in *Timon of Athens*', *English Studies*, 94:7 (2013), 799–820

Danson, Lawrence, 'The Shakespeare Remix: Romance, Tragicomedy, and Shakespeare's "distinct kind"', in *Shakespeare and Genre: From Early Modern Inheritances to Postmodern Legacies*, ed. Anthony R. Guneratne (New York: Palgrave, 2011), pp. 101–18

Darwin, Charles, *The Expression of the Emotions in Man and Animals*, ed. Francis Darwin (Cambridge: Cambridge University Press, 2010)

Davids, Karel, 'Craft Secrecy in Europe in the Early Modern Period: A Comparative View', *Early Science and Medicine*, 10:3 (2005), 341–8

de Grazia, Margreta, 'Imprints: Shakespeare, Gutenburg and Descartes', in *Alternative Shakespeares*, vol. 2, ed. Terence Hawkes (London: Routledge, 1996), pp. 63–95 de Sousa, Geraldo U., 'Home and Abroad: Crossing the Mediterranean in Shakespeare's *The Comedy of Errors*', *Mediterranean Studies*, 26:2 (2018), 145–58

——, '"My hopes abroad": The Global/Local Nexus in *The Merchant of Venice*', in *Shakespeare and Immigration*, ed. Ruben Espinosa and David Ruiter (Farnham: Ashgate, 2014), pp. 37–59

——, *Shakespeare's Cross-cultural Encounters* (Basingstoke: Macmillan, 1999)

Derrida, Jacques, *Adieu to Emmanuel Levinas*, trans. Pascale-Anne Brault and Michael Naas (Stanford: Stanford University Press, 1999)

——, *The Death Penalty*, vol. 1, ed. Geoffrey Bennington, Marc Crépon and Thomas Dutoit, trans. Peggy Kamuf (Chicago and London: University of Chicago Press, 2014)

——, *The Death Penalty*, vol. 2, ed. Geoffrey Bennington, and Marc Crépon, trans. Elizabeth Rottenberg (Chicago and London: University of Chicago Press, 2017)

——, *Deconstruction Engaged: The Sydney Seminars*, ed. Paul Patton and Terry Smith (Sydney: Power, 2001)

——, 'Derelictions of the Right to Justice', in *Negotiations: Interventions and Interviews, 1971–2001*, ed. and trans. Elizabeth Rottenberg (Stanford: Stanford University Press, 2002), pp. 133–46

——, 'Economimesis', trans. Richard Klein, *Diacritics*, 11:2 (1981), 3–25

——, *The Gift of Death & Literature in Secret*, trans. David Wills (Chicago: University of Chicago Press, 2008)

——, *Given Time: I. Counterfeit Money*, trans. Peggy Kamuf (Chicago: University of Chicago Press, 1992)

——, 'Hostipitality', in *Acts of Religion*, ed. Gil Anidjar (London and New York: Routledge, 2002), pp. 356–421

——, 'Hostipitality', *Angelaki*, 5:3 (2000), 3–18

——, 'Hospitality, Justice and Responsibility: A Dialogue with Jacques Derrida', in *Questioning Ethics: Contemporary Debates in Philosophy*, ed. Richard Kearney and Mark Dooley (London: Routledge, 1999), pp. 65–83

——, *Of Hospitality: Anne Dufourmantelle Invites Jacques Derrida to Respond*, trans. Rachel Bowlby (Stanford: Stanford University Press, 2000)
——, *On Cosmopolitanism and Forgiveness*, trans. Mark Dooley and Michael Hughes (London: Routledge, 2001)
——, *On Touching – Jean-Luc Nancy*, trans. Christine Irizarry (Stanford: Stanford University Press, 2005)
——, 'The Principle of Hospitality', *Parallax*, 11:1 (2005), 6–9
——, *Specters of Marx: The State of Debt, the Work of Mourning and the New International*, trans. Peggy Kamuf (New York: Routledge, 1994)
——, 'Ulysses Gramophone: Hear Say Yes in Joyce', in *A Derrida Reader: Between the Blinds*, ed. Peggy Kamuf (New York: Columbia University Press, 1991), pp. 569–601
——, 'What is a "Relevant" Translation?', trans. Lawrence Venuti, *Critical Inquiry*, 27:2 (2001), 174–200
——, *The Work of Mourning*, ed. and trans. Pascale-Anne Brault and Michael Naas (Chicago: University of Chicago Press, 2001)
Dickey, Stephen, 'Language and Role in *Pericles*', *English Literary Renaissance*, 16:3 (1986), 550–66
Dolan, Frances, *Dangerous Familiars: Representations of Domestic Crime in England, 1550–1700* (Ithaca: Cornell University Press, 1994)
Douglas, Mary, *Purity and Danger: An Analysis of Concepts of Pollution and Taboo* (London: Routledge, 2002)
Dowd, Michelle M., *The Dynamics of Inheritance on the Shakespearean Stage* (Cambridge: Cambridge University Press, 2015)
Duckert, Lowell, 'Pericles's Deep Ecology', *Studies in English Literature, 1500–1900*, 59:2 (2019), 367–81
Duffy, Eamon, *The Stripping of the Altars: Traditional Religion in England, 1400–1580* (New Haven and London: Yale University Press, 1992)
Dufourmantelle, Anne, 'Hospitality – Under Compassion and Violence', in *The Conditions of Hospitality: Ethics, Politics, and Aesthetics on the Threshold of the Possible*, ed. Thomas Claviez (New York: Fordham University Press, 2013), pp. 13–23

——, *In Defense of Secrets*, trans. Lindsay Turner (New York: Fordham University Press, 2021)

Eisaman Maus, Katharine, *Inwardness and Theatre in the English Renaissance* (Chicago: University of Chicago Press, 1995)

Elliott, G. R., 'Weirdness in *The Comedy of Errors*', *University of Toronto Quarterly*, 9:1 (1939), 95–106

Engle, Lars, *Shakespearean Pragmatism: Market of his Time* (Chicago: Chicago University Press, 1993)

Escolme, Bridget, *Emotional Excess on the Shakespearean Stage: Passion's Slaves* (London and New York: Bloomsbury, 2014)

Eustachi, Bartolomeo, *An Epistle on the Organs of Hearing: An Annotated Translation*, trans. C. D. O'Malley, *Clio Medica*, 6 (1971), 49–62

Farrier, David, *Postcolonial Asylum: Seeking Sanctuary Before the Law* (Liverpool: Liverpool University Press, 2011)

Fernández, Henry Dietrich, 'A Secret Space for a Secret Keeper: Cardinal Bibbiena at the Vatican Palace', in *Visual Cultures of Secrecy in Early Modern Europe*, ed. Timothy McCall, Sean Roberts and Giancarlo Fiorenza (Pennsylvania: Penn State University Press, 2013), pp. 149–61

Fernie, Ewan, *Shame in Shakespeare* (London and New York: Routledge, 2002)

Fielder, Leslie, *The Stranger in Shakespeare* (New York: Stein and Day, 1972)

Fitzpatrick, Joan, *Food in Shakespeare: Early Modern Dietaries and the Plays* (Aldershot: Ashgate, 2007)

Folkerth, Wes, *The Sound of Shakespeare* (London: Routledge, 2002)

Ford, John R., 'Following Hapless Egeon: Casting the Wanderers in *The Comedy of Errors*', *POMPA: Publications of the Mississippi Philological Association* (2006), 19–23

Foster, Verna A., *The Name and Nature of Tragicomedy* (London and New York: Routledge, 2004)

Freedman, Barbara, 'Egeon's Debt: Self-Division and Self-Redemption in *The Comedy of Errors*', *English Literary Renaissance*, 10:3 (1980), 360–83

——, 'Reading Errantly: Misrecognition and the Uncanny in *The Comedy of Errors*', in *The Comedy of Errors: Critical*

Essays, ed. Robert S. Miola (London: Routledge, 2012), pp. 261–97

Freud, Sigmund, *The Origins of Religion: Totem and Taboo, Moses and Monotheism and Other Works*, trans. James Strachey (London: Penguin, 1990)

——, 'Repression', in *The Standard Edition of the Complete Psychological Works of Sigmund Freud*, vol. 14, trans. James Strachey (London: The Hogarth Press, 1981), pp. 141–58

——, 'The Uncanny', in *The Standard Edition of the Complete Psychological Works of Sigmund Freud*, vol. 17, trans. James Strachey (London: The Hogarth Press, 1981), pp. 217–56

Fusch, Daniel, 'Wonder and Ceremonies of Waking in Shakespeare's Late Plays', *Mediterranean Studies*, 14 (2005), 125–47

Garber, Marjorie, *Coming of Age in Shakespeare* (London and New York: Routledge, 1981)

Garrett, Julia M., 'Witchcraft and Sexual Knowledge in Early Modern England', *The Journal for Early Modern Cultural Studies*, 13:1 (2013), 32–72

Gil Harris, Jonathan, *Sick Economies: Drama, Mercantilism, and Disease in Shakespeare's England* (Philadelphia: University of Pennsylvania Press, 2004)

Girard, René, *Violence and the Sacred*, trans. Patrick Gregory (London and Baltimore: Johns Hopkins University Press, 1977)

Goldstein, David, *Eating and Ethics in Shakespeare's England* (Cambridge: Cambridge University Press, 2013)

Gordon, Avery F., *Ghostly Matters: Haunting and the Sociological Imagination* (Minneapolis: University of Minnesota Press, 2008)

Gordon, Colby, 'Two Doors: Personhood and Housebreaking in *Semayne's Case* and *The Comedy of Errors*', in *Renaissance Personhood: Materiality, Taxonomy, Process*, ed. Kevin Curran (Edinburgh: Edinburgh University Press, 2020), pp. 62–84

Gordon, Colette, 'Crediting Errors: Credit, Liquidity, Performance and *The Comedy of Errors*', *Shakespeare*, 6:2 (2010), 165–84

Gorfain, Phyllis, 'Puzzle and Artifice: The Riddle as Metapoetry in *Pericles*', *Shakespeare Survey*, 29 (1976), 11–20

Grady, Hugh, *Shakespeare's Universal Wolf: Studies in Early Modern Reification* (Oxford: Oxford University Press, 1996)

Greenblatt, Stephen, *Learning to Curse: Essays in Early Modern Culture* (New York and London: Routledge, 1990)

Greenfield, Matthew A., 'Fragments of Nationalism in *Troilus and Cressida*', *Shakespeare Quarterly*, 51:2 (2000), 181–200

Gullestad, Anders M., 'Literature and the Parasite', *Deleuze Studies*, 5:3 (2011), 301–23

Habib, Imtiaz, 'The Black Alien in *Othello*: Beyond the European Immigrant', in *Shakespeare and Immigration*, ed. Ruben Espinosa and David Ruiter (Farnham: Ashgate, 2014), pp. 135–58

Hall, Kim F., 'Guess Who's Coming to Dinner? Colonisation and Miscegenation in *The Merchant of Venice*', *Renaissance Drama*, 23 (1992), 87–111

Heal, Felicity, 'Hospitality and Honor in Early Modern England', *Food and Foodways*, 1:4 (1987), 321–50

——, *Hospitality in Early Modern England* (Oxford: Oxford University Press, 1990)

Heaney, Seamus, *Finders Keepers: Selected Prose 1971–2001* (New York: Farrar, Straus and Giroux, 2002)

Heffernan, James A. W., *Hospitality and Treachery in Western Literature* (New Haven and London: Yale University Press, 2014)

Heinze, Eric, '"Were it not against our laws": Oppression and Resistance in Shakespeare's *Comedy of Errors*', *Legal Studies*, 29:2 (2009), 230–63

Hillis Miller, J., 'The Critic as Host', *Critical Inquiry*, 3:3 (1977), 439–47

Hillman, David, *Shakespeare's Entrails: Belief, Scepticism and the Interior of the Body* (Basingstoke and New York: Palgrave Macmillan, 2007)

Hocart, A. M., *The Life-giving Myth and Other Essays*, ed. Lord Raglan (London: Methuen, 1952)

Hoeniger, F. David, 'Gower and Shakespeare in *Pericles*', *Shakespeare Quarterly*, 33:4 (1982), 461–79

Homem, Rui Carvalho, 'Offshore Desires: Mobility, Liquidity and History in Shakespeare's Mediterranean', *Critical Survey*, 30:3 (2018), 36–56

Homer, *The Odyssey*, trans. Walter Shewring (Oxford: Oxford University Pres, 2008)

Hughes, Krista E., 'Cultivating Listening as a Civic Discipline', in *Ecological Solidarities: Mobilizing Faith and Justice for an Entangled World*, ed. Krista E. Hughes, Dhawn B. Martin and Elaine Padilla (Pennsylvania: Pennsylvania State University Press, 2019), pp. 201–7

Hunt, Arnold, *The Art of Hearing: English Preachers and their Audiences, 1590–1640* (Cambridge: Cambridge University Press, 2010)

Hunt, Maurice, 'Qualifying the Good Steward of Shakespeare's *Timon of Athens*', *English Studies*, 82:6 (2001), 507–20

Hutton, Ronald, *The Stations of the Sun: A History of the Ritual Year in Britain* (Oxford: Oxford University Press, 1996)

James I, *Daemonologie*, in *King James VI and I: Selected Writings*, ed. Neil Rhodes, Jennifer Richards and Joseph Marshall (London and New York: Routledge, 2016)

James, Heather, *Shakespeare's Troy: Drama, Politics, and the Translation of Empire* (Cambridge: Cambridge University Press, 1997)

Jelloun, Ben, *French Hospitality: Racism and North African Immigrants* (Columbia: Columbia University Press, 1999)

Jones, Ann Rosalind, and Peter Stallybrass, *Renaissance Clothing and the Materials of Memory* (Cambridge: Cambridge University Press, 2001)

Jonson, Ben, *Volpone, or The Fox*, in *Ben Jonson, Vol. 5: Volpone; Epicoene; The Alchemist; Catiline*, ed. C. H. Herford and Percy Simpson (Oxford: Oxford University Press, 2012)

Jütte, Daniel, 'Sleeping in Church: Preaching, Boredom, and the Struggle for Attention in Medieval and Early Modern Europe', *American Historical Review*, 125:4 (2020), 1146–74

——, 'They Shall Not Keep Their Doors and Windows Open: Urban Space and the Dynamics of Conflict and Contact in Premodern Jewish–Christian Relations', *European History Quarterly*, 46:2 (2016), 209–37

Kahn, Coppélia, '"Magic of Bounty": *Timon of Athens*, Jacobean Patronage, and Maternal Power', *Shakespeare Quarterly*, 38 (1987), 34–57

Kallendorf, Hilaire, *Exorcism and Its Texts: Subjectivity in Early Modern Literature of England and Spain* (Toronto: University of Toronto Press, 2003)

Kammer, Miriam, 'Shakespeare as Ecodrama: Ecofeminism and Nonduality in *Pericles, Prince of Tyre*', *Journal of Dramatic Theory and Criticism*, 32:1 (2017), 29–48

Kant, Immanuel, 'Toward Perpetual Peace: A Philosophical Sketch', in *Toward Perpetual Peace and Other Writings on Politics, Peace, and History*, ed. Pauline Kleingeld, trans. David L. Colclasure (Binghamton: Yale University Press, 2006), pp. 67–109

Katajala-Peltomaa, Sari, *Demonic Possession and Lived Religion in Later Medieval Europe* (Oxford: Oxford University Press, 2020)

Kern Paster, Gail, *The Body Embarrassed: Drama and the Disciplines of Shame in Early Modern England* (Ithaca: Cornell University Press, 1993)

——, *The City in the Age of Shakespeare* (Athens, GA: University of Georgia Press, 1985)

Kerr, Julie, '"Welcome the coming and speed the parting guest": Hospitality in Twelfth-Century England', *Journal of Medieval History*, 33:2 (2007), 130–46

Kilgour, Maggie, *From Communion to Cannibalism: An Anatomy of Metaphors of Incorporation* (Princeton: Princeton University Press, 1990)

Kottman, Paul, 'Hospitality in the Interval: *Macbeth*'s Door', *Oxford Literary Review*, 18:1 (1996), 87–115

Kristeva, Julia, *Strangers to Ourselves*, trans. Leon S. Roudiez (New York: Columbia University Press, 1991)

Kurland, Stuart M., '"The care … of subjects' good": *Pericles*, James I, and the Neglect of Government', *Comparative Drama*, 30:2 (1996), 220–44

Ladwig, Patrice, 'Visitors From Hell: Transformative Hospitality to Ghosts in a Lao Buddhist Festival', *Journal of the Royal Anthropological Institute*, 18 (2012), 90–102

Lange, Marjory E., *Telling Tears in the English Renaissance* (Leiden: Brill, 1996)

Leggatt, Alexander, *Shakespeare's Tragedies: Violation and Identity* (Cambridge and New York: Cambridge University Press, 2005)

Leong, Elaine, and Alisha Rankin, 'Introduction: Secrets and Knowledge', in *Secrets and Knowledge in Medicine and Science, 1500–1800*, ed. Elaine Leong and Alisha Rankin (London: Routledge, 2016), pp. 1–20

Levack, Brian P., *The Devil Within: Possession & Exorcism in the Christian West* (London and New Haven: Yale University Press, 2013)

Levinas, Emmanuel, 'No Identity', in *Collected Philosophical Papers*, trans. Alphonso Lingus (Dordrecht and London: Kluwer Academic, 1993), pp. 141–53

Lévi-Strauss, Claude, *The Origin of Table Manners: Introduction to a Science of Mythology*, vol. 3, trans. J. and D. Weightman (London: Cape, 1978)

———, *The Raw and the Cooked: Introduction to a Science of Mythology*, trans. J. and D. Weightman (London: Pimlico, 1994)

Lewis, Anthony J., '"I Feed on Mother's Flesh": Incest and Eating in *Pericles*', *Essays in Literature*, 15:2 (1988), 147–63

Linhart Wood, Jennifer, *Sounding Otherness in Early Modern Drama and Travel: Uncanny Vibrations in the English Archive* (Palgrave, 2019)

Lipari, Lisbeth, 'Listening Otherwise: The Voice of Ethics', *International Journal of Listening*, 23:1 (2009), 44–59

———, 'Rhetoric's Other: Levinas, Listening, and the Ethical Response', *Philosophy & Rhetoric*, 45:3 (2012), 227–45

Lupton, Deborah, *The Emotional Self: A Sociocultural Exploration* (London: SAGE, 1998)

Lupton, Julia, 'Making Room, Affording Hospitality: Environments of Entertainment in *Romeo and Juliet*', *Journal of Medieval and Early Modern Studies*, 43:1 (2013), 145–72

———, *Thinking with Shakespeare: Essays on Politics and Life* (Chicago: University of Chicago Press, 2011)

Lynes, Philippe, 'The Posthuman Promise of the Earth', in *Eco-Deconstruction Derrida and Environmental Philosophy*, ed.

Matthias Fritsch, Philippe Lynes and David Wood (New York: Fordham University Press, 2018), pp. 101–20
Maitra, Ellorasrhee, 'Toward an Ethical Polity: Service and the Tragic Community in *Timon of Athens*', *Renaissance Drama*, 41 (2013), 173–98
Martin Reynolds, Paige, 'Sin, Sacredness, and Childbirth in Early Modern Drama', *Medieval & Renaissance Drama in England*, 28 (2015), 30–48
Martin, Randall, *Shakespeare and Ecology* (Oxford: Oxford University Press, 2015)
Marx, Steven, 'Shakespeare's Pacifism', *Renaissance Quarterly*, 45:1 (1992), 49–95
Mauss, Marcel, 'Gift, Gift', in *The Logic of the Gift: Toward an Ethic of Generosity*, ed. Alan D. Schrift (London and New York: Routledge, 1997), pp. 28–33
Mazzio, Carla, *The Inarticulate Renaissance: Language Trouble in an Age of Eloquence* (Pennsylvania: University of Pennsylvania Press, 2009)
McNulty, Tracy, *The Hostess: Hospitality, Femininity, and the Expropriation of Identity* (Minneapolis: University of Minnesota Press, 2007)
Meads, Chris, *Banquets Set Forth: Banqueting in English Renaissance Drama* (Manchester: Manchester University Press, 2001)
Mentz, Steve, *Ocean* (London: Bloomsbury, 2020)
——, *Shipwreck Modernity: Ecologies of Globalization, 1550–1719* (Minnesota: University of Minnesota Press, 2015)
——, 'Toward a Blue Cultural Studies: The Sea, Maritime Culture, and Early Modern English Literature', *Literature Compass*, 6:5 (2009), 997–1013
Milesi, Laurent, 'Believing in Deconstruction', in *Credo Credit Crisis: Speculations on Faith and Money*, ed. Laurent Milesi, Christopher John Müller and Aidan Tynan (London and New York: Rowman & Littlefield International, 2017), pp. 271–99
Millar, Charlotte-Rose, 'Diabolical Men: Reintegrating Male Witches into English Witchcraft', *The Seventeenth Century* (2020), 1–21

Millbank, Jenni, '"The Ring of Truth": A Case Study of Credibility Assessment in Particular Social Group Refugee Determinations', *International Journal of Refugee Law*, 21:1 (2009), 1–33

Miller, Shannon, 'Constructing the Female Self: Architectural Structures in Mary Wroth's Urania', in *Renaissance Culture and the Everyday*, ed. Patricia Fumerton and Simon Hunt (Philadelphia: University of Pennsylvania Press, 1999), 139–61

Mullaney, Steven, '"All That Monarchs Do": The Obscured Stages of Authority in *Pericles*', in *Pericles: Critical Essays*, ed. David Skeele (New York and London: Taylor & Francis, 2000), pp. 168–83

Munday, Anthony, Henry Chettle, Thomas Dekker, Thomas Heywood and William Shakespeare, *Sir Thomas More*, ed. John Jowett (London: Bloomsbury, 2011)

Murray, Amy Jo, and Kevin Durrheim, 'Introduction: A Turn to Silence', in *Qualitative Studies of Silence: The Unsaid as Social Action*, ed. Amy Jo Murray and Kevin Durrheim (Cambridge: Cambridge University Press, 2019), pp. 1–20

Nancy, Jean-Luc, *Corpus*, trans. Richard A. Rand (New York: Fordham University Press, 2008)

Neill, Michael, *Issues of Death: Mortality and Identity in English Renaissance Tragedy* (Oxford: Oxford University Press, 1997)

Noschka, Michael, 'Thinking Hospitably with *Timon of Athens*: Toward an Ethics of Stewardship', in *Shakespeare and Hospitality: Ethics, Politics, and Exchange*, ed. David Goldstein and Julia Lupton (London and New York: Routledge, 2016), pp. 242–64

Novy, Marianne, 'Multiple Parenting in *Pericles*', in *Pericles: Critical Essays*, ed. David Skeele (New York and London: Taylor & Francis, 2000), pp. 238–48

——, *Shakespeare and Outsiders* (Oxford: Oxford University Press, 2013)

Nowlin, Steele, *Chaucer, Gower, and the Affect of Invention* (Columbus: Ohio State University Press, 2016)

Nuttall, A. D., *Shakespeare the Thinker* (New Haven and London: Yale University Press, 2007)

Oliver, Kelly, 'Earth: Love It or Leave It?', in *Eco-Deconstruction Derrida and Environmental Philosophy*, ed. Matthias Fritsch,

Philippe Lynes and David Wood (New York: Fordham University Press, 2018), pp. 339–54

Ovid, *Metamorphoses*, trans. A. D. Melville (Oxford: Oxford University Press, 2008)

Palmer, Daryl, *Hospitable Performances: Dramatic Genre and Cultural Practices in Early Modern England* (West Lafayette: Purdue University Press, 1992)

Parker, Patricia, *Shakespeare from the Margins: Language, Culture, Context* (Chicago: University of Chicago Press, 1996)

Patton, Kimberley C., *The Sea Can Wash Away All Evils: Modern Marine Pollution and the Ancient Cathartic Ocean* (New York: Columbia University Press, 2007)

Perera, Suvendrini, 'Oceanic Corpo-graphies, Refugee Bodies and the Making and Unmaking of Waters', *Feminist Review*, 103 (2013), 58–79

Perkins, William, *A Discourse of the Damned Art of Witchcraft* (London, 1610)

Perry, Curtis, 'Commerce, Community, and Nostalgia in *The Comedy of Errors*', in *Money in the Age of Shakespeare: Essays in New Economic Criticism*, ed. Linda Woodbridge (Basingstoke and New York: Palgrave, 2003), pp. 39–51

Peters, Kimberley, 'Drifting: Towards Mobilities at Sea', *Transactions of the Institute of British Geographers*, 40:2 (2015), 262–72

Petty, James, 'The London Spikes Controversy: Homelessness, Urban Securitisation and the Question of "Hostile Architecture"', *International Journal for Crime, Justice and Social Democracy*, 5:1 (2016), 67–81

Pitt-Rivers, Julian, 'The Law of Hospitality', in *From Hospitality to Grace: A Julian Pitt-Rivers Omnibus*, ed. Giovanni da Col and Andrew Shryock (Chicago: HAU Books, 2017), pp. 163–84

Pollard, Tanya, *Drugs and Theatre in Early Modern England* (Oxford: Oxford University Press, 2005)

Probyn, Elspeth, *Blush: Faces of Shame* (Minneapolis and London: University of Minnesota Press, 2005)

——, *Eating the Ocean* (Durham, NC, and London: Duke University Press, 2016)

Raber, Karen, *Animal Bodies, Renaissance Culture* (Pennsylvania: University of Pennsylvania Press, 2014)

Rae McDermott, Jennifer, '"The Melodie of Heaven": Sermonizing the Open Ear in Early Modern England', in *Religion and the Senses in Early Modern Europe*, ed. Wietse de Boer and Christine Göttler (Leiden: Brill, 2012), pp. 177–97

Raman, Shankar, 'Marking Time: Memory and Market in *The Comedy of Errors*', *Shakespeare Quarterly*, 56:2 (2005), 176–205

Razzall, Lucy, *Boxes and Books in Early Modern England: Materiality, Metaphor, Containment* (Cambridge: Cambridge University Press, 2021)

Reinhard Lupton, Julia, *Citizen-Saints: Shakespeare and Political Theology* (Chicago: University of Chicago Press, 2005)

——, *Shakespeare Dwelling: Designs for the Theatre of Life* (Chicago: Chicago University Press, 2018)

Roper, Lyndal, *Witch Craze: Terror and Fantasy in Baroque Germany* (New Haven: Yale University Press, 2004)

Rosello, Mireille, *Postcolonial Hospitality: The Immigrant as Guest* (Stanford: Stanford University Press, 2001)

Ruiter, David, 'Shakespeare and Hospitality: Opening *The Winter's Tale*', *Mediterranean Studies*, 16 (2007), 157–77

Sahlins, Marshall, 'The Stranger-King or, Elementary Forms of the Politics of Life', *Indonesia and the Malay World*, 36:105 (2009), 177–99

Sawday, Jonathan, *The Body Emblazoned: Dissection and the Human Body in Renaissance Culture* (London and New York: Routledge, 1995)

Schiltz, Katelijne, *Music and Riddle Culture in the Renaissance* (Cambridge: Cambridge University Press, 2015)

Schreyer, Kurt A., 'Moldy *Pericles*', *Exemplaria: A Journal of Theory in Medieval and Renaissance Studies*, 29:3 (2017), 210–33

Scot, Reginald, *The Discoverie of Witchcraft* (London, 1584)

Serres, Michel, *The Five Senses: A Philosophy of Mingled Bodies*, trans. Margaret Sankey and Peter Cowley (London: Continuum, 2008)

——, *The Parasite*, trans. Lawrence R. Schehr (Minneapolis: University of Minnesota Press, 2007)

Seymour, Laura, 'The Feasting Table as the Gateway to Hell on the Early Modern Stage and Page', *Renaissance Studies*, 34:3 (2020), 392–411

Shakespeare, William, *As You Like It*, ed. Juliet Dusinberre (London: Bloomsbury, 2006)

——, *The Comedy of Errors*, ed. Kent Cartwright (London: Bloomsbury, 2016)

——, *The Comedy of Errors*, ed. T. S. Dorsch (Cambridge: Cambridge University Press, 2004)

——, *Coriolanus*, ed. Peter Holland (London: Bloomsbury, 2013)

——, *Hamlet*, ed. Ann Thompson and Neil Taylor (London: Bloomsbury, 2016)

——, *Julius Caesar*, ed. David Daniell (London: Thomson Learning, 2006)

——, *Love's Labour's Lost*, ed. H. R. Woudhuysen (London: Methuen Drama, 1998)

——, *Macbeth*, ed. Kenneth Muir (London: Thomson Learning, 2006)

——, *Measure for Measure*, ed. J. W. Lever (London: Thomson Learning, 2006)

——, *The Merchant of Venice*, ed. John Drakakis (London: Bloomsbury, 2010)

——, *Much Ado About Nothing*, ed. Claire McEachern (London: Bloomsbury, 2006)

——, *Othello*, ed. E. A. J. Honigmann (London: Bloomsbury, 1997)

——, *Richard II*, ed. Charles R. Forker (London: Bloomsbury, 2002)

——, *Romeo and Juliet*, ed. Brian Gibbons (London: Thomson Learning, 2003)

——, *Shakespeare's Sonnets*, ed. Katherine Duncan-Jones (London: Methuen Drama, 2010)

——, *The Tempest*, ed. Stephen Orgel (Oxford: Oxford University Press, 2008)

——, *Timon of Athens*, ed. Karl Klein (Cambridge: Cambridge University Press, 2001)

——, *Troilus and Cressida*, ed. David Bevington (London: Cengage Learning, 1998)

——, *Twelfth Night*, ed. Keir Elam (London: Bloomsbury, 2008)
——, *The Winter's Tale*, ed. John Pitcher (London: Bloomsbury, 2010)
Shakespeare, William, and Thomas Middleton, *Timon of Athens*, ed. Anthony B. Dawson and Gretchen E. Minton (London: Bloomsbury, 2008)
Shakespeare, William, and George Wilkins, *Pericles*, ed. Suzanne Gossett (London: Bloomsbury, 2004)
Shannon, Laurie, *The Accommodated Animal: Cosmopolity in Shakespearean Locales* (Chicago: University of Chicago Press, 2013)
Sharpe, James, *Instruments of Darkness: Witchcraft in England, 1550–1750* (London: Penguin, 1997)
Shryock, Andrew, 'Hospitality Lessons: Learning the Shared Language of Derrida and the Balga Bedouin', *Paragraph*, 32:1 (2009), 32–50
Simmel, Georg, *The Philosophy of Money*, ed. David Frisby, trans. Tom Bottomore and David Frisby (London and New York: Routledge, 2005)
——, 'The Sociology of Secrecy and of Secret Societies', *American Journal of Sociology*, 11:4 (1906), 441–98
Slights, William, W. E., 'Secret Places in Renaissance Drama', *University of Toronto Quarterly*, 59:3 (1990), 363–81
Smith, Bruce R., *The Acoustic World of Early Modern England: Attending to the O-Factor* (Chicago: University of Chicago Press, 1999)
——, 'The Ethics of Compassion in Early Modern England', in *Compassion in Early Modern Literature and Culture: Feeling and Practice*, ed. Kristine Steenbergh and Katherine Ibbett (Cambridge: Cambridge University Press, 2021), pp. 25–43
——, *Homosexual Desire in Shakespeare's England: A Cultural Poetics* (Chicago: University of Chicago Press, 1991)
Sokol, B. J., *Shakespeare and Tolerance* (Cambridge: Cambridge University Press, 2009)
Sophocles, *Oedipus at Colonus*, in *Sophocles: The Three Theban Plays: Antigone, Oedipus the King, Oedipus at Colonus*, trans. Robert Fagles (London: Penguin, 1982)

Squire, Corinne, 'Partial Secrets', *Current Anthropology*, 56:12 (2015), 201–10

Steenbergh, Kristine, 'Mollified Hearts and Enlarged Bowels: Practising Compassion in Reformation England', in *Compassion in Early Modern Literature and Culture*, ed. Kristine Steenbergh and Katherine Ibbett (Cambridge: Cambridge University Press, 2021), pp. 121–38

Steinberg, Philip, and Kimberley Peters, 'Wet Ontologies, Fluid Spaces: Giving Depth to Volume through Oceanic Thinking', *Environment and Planning*, 33 (2015), 247–64

Still, Judith, *Derrida and Hospitality: Theory and Practice* (Edinburgh: Edinburgh University Press, 2010)

Sugg, Richard, *The Smoke of the Soul: Medicine, Physiology and Religion in Early Modern England* (Basingstoke: Palgrave, 2013)

Sullivan, Ceri, 'The Art of Listening in the Seventeenth Century', *Modern Philology*, 104:1 (2006), 34–71

Tatlock, John, 'The Siege of Troy in Elizabethan Literature, Especially in Shakespeare and Heywood', *PMLA*, 30:4 (1915), 673–770

Taussig, Michael, *Defacement: Public Secrecy and the Labour of the Negative* (Stanford: Stanford University Press, 1999)

Traub, Valerie, 'Jewels, Statues, and Corpses: Containment of Female Erotic Power in Shakespeare's Plays', in *Shakespeare and Gender: A History*, ed. Deborah E. Barker and Ivo Kamps (London and New York: Verso, 1995), pp. 120–42

van Dijkhuizen, Jan Franz, *Devil Theatre: Demonic Possession and Exorcism in English Renaissance Drama, 1558–1642* (Woodbridge: D. S. Brewer, 2007)

van Es, Bart, 'Late Shakespeare and the Middle Ages', in *Medieval Shakespeare: Pasts and Presents*, ed. Ruth Morse, Helen Cooper and Peter Holland (Cambridge: Cambridge University Press, 2013), pp. 37–51

van Gennep, Arnold, *The Rites of Passage*, trans. Monika B. Yizedom and Gabrielle L. Caffee (Chicago: University of Chicago Press, 1960)

Vingerhoets, Ad, *Why Only Humans Weep: Unravelling the Mysteries of Tears* (Oxford: Oxford University Press, 2013)

Virgil, *Aeneid*, trans. Stanley Lombardo (Indianapolis: Hackett Publishing Company, Inc., 2005)

Visser, Margaret, *The Rituals of Dinner: The Origins, Evolution, Eccentricities, and Meaning of Table Manners* (London: Penguin, 1992)

Walsh, Brian, '"A Priestly Farewell": Gower's Tomb and Religious Change', *Religion & Literature*, 45:3 (2013), 81–113

Walsham, Alexandra, *Charitable Hatred: Tolerance and Intolerance in England, 1500–1700* (Manchester: Manchester University Press, 2006)

Waters, Dan, and Tim Ko, 'The Hungry Ghosts Festival in Aberdeen Street, Hong Kong', *Journal of the Royal Asiatic Society Hong Kong Branch*, 44 (2004), 41–55

Welchman, Jennifer, 'A Defence of Environmental Stewardship', *Environmental Values*, 21:3 (2012), 297–316

Wilkinson, Robert, *Sermon of hearing, or, A jewell for the eare* (London, 1643)

Williamson, Matt, 'Imperial Appetites: Cannibalism and Early Modern Theatre', in *To Feast on Us as Their Prey: Cannibalism and the Early Modern Atlantic*, ed. Rachel B. Herrmann (Fayetteville: University of Arkansas Press, 2019), pp. 115–34

Woolgar, C. M., 'Gifts of Food in Late Medieval England', *Journal of Medieval History*, 37:1 (2011), 6–18

Zapkin, Phillip, 'Salt Fish: Fishing and the Creation of Empires in *Pericles* and Contemporary Oceans', *South Atlantic Review*, 82:2 (2017), 78–96

INDEX

adoptive parents *see* foster parents
Ahmed, Sara, 15, 20, 28
Antiochus' riddle *see* riddles
anti-Semitism, 58–9, 78–9, 82
architecture
    boxes as hiding places, 177, 208–10
    doors, 5, 16, 23, 45–9, 61–2, 70–2, 80–4
    and hearing, 67–72
    hostile, 179–82, 215n
    and secrecy, 177–83, 208–9
    windows, 6, 68–9, 82–4
Ariès, Philippe, 167
As You Like It, 4
asylum seekers, 15, 22–3, 25–6, 190–1, 217n

Bachelard, Gaston, 179
    The Poetics of Space, 177–8
banquets
    battle of the centaurs, 39–40
    Hamlet, 85
    'God Neptune's annual feast', 211–14
    Homer, *The Odyssey*, 38–9
    Pentapolis celebrations, 200–6
    Timon of Athens, 134–56, 146–51, 156
    see also eating
Bauman, Zygmunt, *Strangers at Our Door*, 14
Bedouins, 200–1
Benhabib, Seyla, 87–8
Benveniste, Émile, 183
    Dictionary of Indo-European Concepts and Society, 4, 27
Bhabha, Homi, 15
birds, 213–14
birdsong, 93–4
blue legalities, 190–1
blushing, 108–14
bodies, refugees, 188–95
body
    armoured, 109
    and blood, 140–1
    effluvia, 42
    gesture, 117–18
    and intestines, 105–6, 127–8
boiled food, 150–1
boxes as hiding places, 177, 208–10

Bruster, Douglas, 114–15
bureaucracy, 21–4
Burton, Robert, *The Anatomy of Melancholy*, 33
burying the dead, 164–5, 167–9
Butler, Judith, 165

Candido, Joseph, 38
cannibalism, 148, 178
capitalism, 114–21, 191, 220n
    state execution and, 30–1
Cartwright, Kent, 13, 37, 49n, 56n
casket test, 72–4, 77, 95–6, 100–1n
centaurs, 39–40
Christianity
    and Jewish interactions, 77–85
    listeners, 93–4
    and the supernatural, 12
Circe, 38–9
The Comedy of Errors, 12–57
commensality, 29–30, 41–2, 141–2; see also banquets
conditional hospitality, 61, 86–7, 90, 128–9
Coriolanus, 1–2, 5, 71, 152
Cotta, John, *The Trial of Witchcraft*, 37–8
Cowen Orlin, Lena, 80
credibility assessment, 26–7
credit, 26–8
crime of hospitality, 18–19; see also law
Crooke, Helkiah, *Microcosmographia*, 68–70

de Sousa, Geraldo, 73, 100–1n
death
    burying the dead, 164–5, 167–9
    death penalty, 17–32
    mourning rites, 164–5, 167–9
    state execution and capitalism, 30–1
debts, 164–9
demons as trespassers *see* trespassers
Derrida, Jacques, 8, 18–19, 25, 47, 63–4, 76–7, 84, 86–7, 89, 106, 128–9, 139, 142–5, 155, 158, 166–8, 182
    The Death Penalty, 30–1, 48
    Given Time: I. Counterfeit Money, 143–4
    Of Hospitality, 2–3, 4, 90
    The Work of Mourning, 168
Dolan, Frances, 37, 42
Douglas, Mary, 42
Dufourmantelle, Anne, 159–60, 183, 187
    In Defense of Secrets, 181–2
dwellings
    beehive, 33
    brothel, 211–14
    entertaining guests, 86–91
    folklore, 41; see also superstition
    homelessness, 156, 179, 215n
    houses under supernatural attack, 33–6
    Jewish homes under attack, 78–9, 82
    'lock-out' scene, 16, 23, 34
    murder of guests at home, 1–2, 175, 179–80, 184, 210, 213
    privacy at home, 80–1, 209,
    and the uncanny, 44–5, 56n

ears, 67–70
earth, 156–65, 195–9, 206
eating
　boiled food, 150–1
　cannibalism, 148, 178
　Eucharist, 140–1
　famine, 195–9
　Jewish dietary laws, 59
　not eating, 164, 172n
　roasted food, 150–1
　sacrifice and feast, 140–1, 147–8
　spices, 195
　and superstition, 40–1, 55n
　vomiting
　and vulnerability, 171n
　see also banquets
eavesdropping, 72–7, 80–2
Eisaman Maus, Katharine, 113, 180
empathy, 19–20, 126, 139, 213
environment, 211–14
environmental awareness, and hospitality, 211–14
environmental care, ethics of, 195–9, 204–6
Eustachi, Barlolomeo, *An Epistle on the Organs of Hearing*, 67–70, 78
exchange of gifts, 41–2
exorcism, 32–7, 53n, 55n

famine, 195–9
Farrier, David, 25–6
　Postcolonial Asylum: Seeking Sanctuary before the Law, 23
feasts *see* banquets
festivals, 200
　Hungry Ghost Festival, 46–7

Fieldler, Leslie, *The Stranger in Shakespeare*, 8
Folkerth, Wes, 63–4, 71–2, 93
food *see* eating
foster parents, 175–6, 186, 198–9, 212–13
Freud, Sigmund, 44–5, 64–5
　Totem and Taboo, 141

Garber, Marjorie, 164–5
ghosts, 14–16, 43–4, 46–8, 56n; *see also* Hungry Ghost Festival
gifts
　bribes, 198
　counterfeit, 114–21
　and economy, 114–21
　exchange of, 41–2, 198
　of food and drink, 46–7
　poisonous, 137–8
　pourable, 137
　pure, 128–9
　refusal of, 41
　remembering, 142–51
　Trojan horse, 104–6, 197–8
　in the underworld, 46
Girard, René, 147–8
　Violence and the Sacred, 158
'God Neptune's annual feast', 211–14

Hamlet, 14, 25, 46, 72, 85
Heal, Felicity, 6–7, 201
　Hospitality in Early Modern England, 132n
hearing *see* listening
Heffernan, James A. W., 120
　Hospitality and Treachery in Western Literature, 5–6

Homer, *The Odyssey*, 38–9
hospitality, 3–5
  and bureaucracy, 21–4, 31, 223
  and the chivalric tradition, 199–206, 220n
  and the classical tradition, 40, 48
  conditional, 61, 86–7, 90, 128–9
  counterfeit, 106–7, 114–21
  crime of, 17–32
  and economics, 114–21
  environmental awareness and, 211–14
  female hostesses, 38–9, 164
  to ghosts, 14–16, 43–4, 46–8, 56n
  healing, 206–10
  inhospitality, 21, 60, 111–12, 120, 158, 191–3, 196, 199, 213–4
  kinetics of, 66
  and the law, 17–32
  maternal, 159–62
  mercenary, 29–30
  and mourning, 164–5, 167–9
  nostalgia for, 199–206
  obligation and reciprocity, 3, 88, 90, 120, 132n, 165, 169, 199
  secretive, 175–221
  and the senses, 71–2, 81–2
  on the shoreline, 190–2, 202, 207–8
  soundscapes of, 58–103
  and the supernatural, 12–57
  time of, 21–2, 107, 117–19, 124–5, 143–4, 184–5
  and trust, 1, 14–15, 25–7, 66, 90, 108, 129–30, 138, 183–4, 188, 202, 205, 208
  unconditional, 87, 128–9, 139, 223
  unspoken rules, 88–91
  in wartime, 106–7, 124–6
hostage diplomacy, 21
hostile architecture, 179–82, 215n
houses *see* dwellings
human rights, 19–20
Hungry Ghost Festival, 46–7

immigration, 3, 9, 15, 21, 26–8, 104, 154, 190–1, 223
incest, 177–88
inhospitality, 21, 60, 111–12, 120, 158, 191–3, 196, 199, 213–4; *see also* dwellings: murder of guests at home
intruders, 33–6, 38, 43–5, 65, 71, 83, 129; *see also* trespassers

Jabès, Edmond, *Le Livre de l'hospitalité*, 3
Jelloun, Ben, *French Hospitality: Racism and North African Immigrants*, 3, 154–5
Judaism
  and Christian interactions, 77–85
  dietary laws, 59
  ghetto in Venice, 101n
  soundscapes, 77–85, 97–8
Jews, hostility towards, 78–9, 82; *see also* anti-Semitism

Jonson, Ben, 206
  Volpone, 62
Julius Caesar, 62

Kahn, Coppélia, 159, 164
Kant, Immanuel, 18
  'Toward Perpetual Peace: A Philosophical Sketch', 86–7
Kern Paster, Gail, 42, 110
kinetics of hospitality, 66
King Lear, 161

law
  blue legalities, 190–1
  crime of hospitality, 18–19
  death penalty, 17–32
  legal language, 89–91
  state execution and capitalism, 30–1
Levinas, Emmanuel, 128
Lévi-Strauss, Claude, 163
  The Origin of Table Manners, 149–51
  The Raw and the Cooked: Introduction to a Science of Mythology, 148
listening, 58–103
  and architecture, 67–72
  Christian listeners, 93–4
  in church, 69–70, 93–4
  eavesdropping, 72–7, 80–2
  Jewish soundscapes, 77–85, 97–8
  silence, 64, 82–3, 95–8
lukewarm water, 147–9, 156
Lupton, Julia Reinhard, 142
  Shakespeare Dwelling: Designs for the Theatre of Life, 7

Macbeth, 41–2, 117–18, 213
magic, 12–57
Mahood, Molly, 7
Martin, Randall, 176
masques, 83, 154
  masque of the five senses, 141–2
Mauss, Marcel, 137
Measure for Measure, 38, 163–4
Mentz, Steve, 189, 191, 194
mercenary hospitality, 29–30
The Merchant of Venice, 58–103
Minton, Gretchen, 136, 141, 149, 172n
money
  capitalism, 114–21, 191, 220n
  credit, 26–8
  debts, 164–9
  economics and hospitality, 114–21
  reimbursement, 142–51
  state execution and capitalism, 30–1
mourning and hospitality, 164–5, 167–9
Much Ado About Nothing, 163
Mullaney, Steven, 186
Murillo, Bartolomé Esteban, *Two Women at a Window*, 6
music, 59–60, 91–5

Nancy, Jean-Luc, 43, 65
national stereotyping, 74–6
nationalism, 90
nostalgia for hospitality, 199–206
Novy, Marianne, *Shakespeare and Outsiders*, 8

oceans, 82, 188–95
  blue legalities, 190–1
  refugee bodies in the water, 188–95
  shipwreck, 26, 30, 189, 191, 197–8, 205
  shoreline hospitality, 190–2, 202, 207–8
open-house policy, 138–9
Othello, 62, 83–4, 149
Ovid, *Metamorphoses*, 38–40, 46

parasites, 134–174, 172n, 178
Parker, Patricia, 7, 106
Pericles, 175–221
Pitt-Rivers, Julian, 5, 46, 202–3
  'The Law of Hospitality', 13–14
poison, 19, 72, 137–8, 162, 178–9
prayers, 12, 34, 49n, 97
pure gifts, 128–9

questioning of strangers, 24–6;
  see also riddles

The Rape of Lucrece, 4
refugees, 15, 22–3, 48, 50n
  bodies, 188–95
reimbursement, 142–51
Richard II, 152
riddles, 176–88
  Antiochus' riddle, 176–88
  see also stranger contests
right of residence, 87
roasted food, 150–1
Rosello, Mireille, *Postcolonial Hospitality: The Immigrant as Guest*, 3

sacred stranger, 45–9
sacrifice and feast, 140–1, 147–8
salutations, 111–12, 143
'sans-papiers', 18–19
scarcity principle, 28, 118–19
seas *see* oceans
secrecy, 175–221
  and architecture, 177–83, 208–9
  and eroticism, 183–4
  and society, 187–8
sermons, 71
Serres, Michel, 82–3, 96, 158
  The Parasite, 151, 153–4
silence, 64, 82–3, 95–8
Simmel, Georg, 181, 182, 183, 188
  The Philosophy of Money, 27
Sir Thomas More, 29
smells, 162–3
Smith, Bruce R., 63–4, 127, 130
social exclusion, 15, 67, 74–8, 96, 179, 181–2, 193, 215n
Sonnet 73, 156–7
Sophocles, *Oedipus at Colonus*, 24–5, 166–7
soundscapes of hospitality, 58–103
  Jewish, 77–85, 97–8
  see also listening
spices, 195
state execution and capitalism, 30–1
stewardship, 198–9
Still, Judith, 65–6, 129, 140
stranger contests
  casket test, 72–4, 77, 95–6, 100–1n

jousting tournament, 203–4
  questioning of, 24–6
  riddles, 176–88
  testing of, 202–4
supernatural, 43–4
  and hospitality, 12–57
  and houses, 33–6
superstition, and eating, 40–1, 55n
sympathy, 19–20, 81, 108, 126–8

The Tempest, 34–5, 62
testing of strangers, 202–4
thresholds,
  acoustic, 81–2
  architectural, 6
  doors, 5, 16, 23, 45–9, 61–2, 70–2, 80–4
  Murillo, Bartolomé Esteban, *Two Women at a Window*, 6
  windows, 6, 68–9, 82–4
Timon of Athens, 134–74
Titus Andronicus, 28
trespassers, 33–6, 44–5, 177–8
  demons as trespassers, 33–6
Troilus and Cressida, 104–33
Trojan Horse, 104–6, 197–8
Trojan War, 104–33

unconditional hospitality, 87, 128–9, 139, 223
unheimlich, 44–5, 64–5
unveiling, 112

van Gennep, Arnold, 5, 46, 202–3
vegetarianism, 157–8
Virgil, *Aeneid*, 105–6

wartime hospitality, 106–7, 124–6
water
  and duplicity, 148–9
  lukewarm, 147–9, 156
  muddied, 122–3
  and religious purification, 35, 191–2
watery imagery, 136–8, 145
weeping, 138–9, 144–5, 164
witchcraft, 33–4, 37–8, 41–2
women
  Circe, 38–9
  entertaining the Devil, 36–42
  maternal hospitality, 159–62
  and rotten food, 163–4
  and the sea, 192–3, 218n
  see also witchcraft

xenophobia, 2, 29, 74, 94–5, 223

EU representative:
Easy Access System Europe
Mustamäe tee 50, 10621 Tallinn, Estonia
Gpsr.requests@easproject.com